How I Built
MY SIX-SIDED LOG HOME
from scratch

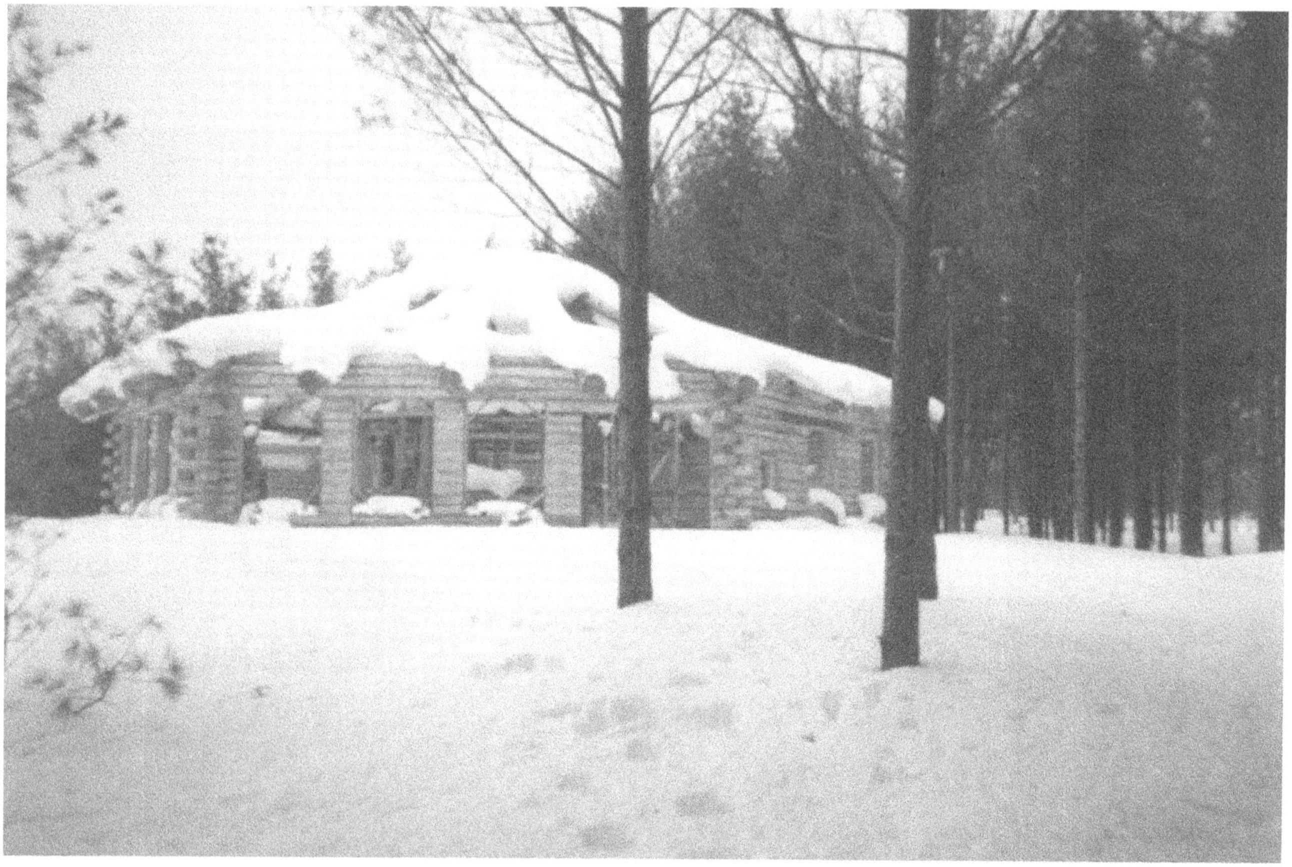

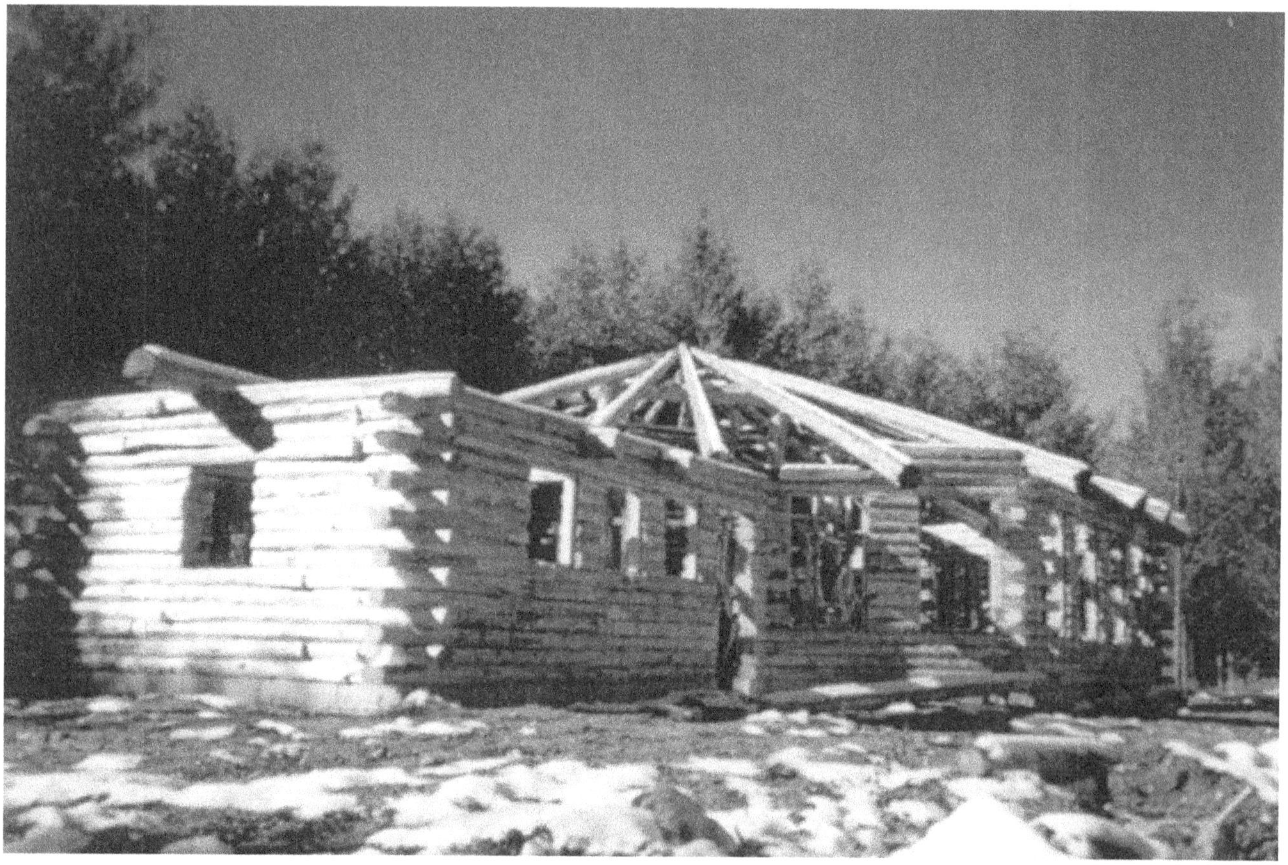

How I Built
MY SIX-SIDED LOG HOME
from scratch

As I was building it... they came!

A step-by-step illustrated guide on how to build your own log home mortgage free!

CONSTANTINE ISSIGHOS

Awaqkuna Books Inc.
Canada

Copyright 2007 © Contantine Issighos. Printed and bound in Canada. All rights reserved. No part of this book may be reproduced or transmitted in any form or by any means, electronic or mechanical, including photocopying, recording, or by an information storage and retrieval system – expect by a reviewer who may quote brief passages in a review to be printed in a magazine, newspaper, or on the web – without permission in writing from the publisher. For information, please contact:

Northwater is an inprint of:
Awaqkuna Books Inc.
www.awaqkunabooks.com

Library and Archives Canada Cataloguing in Publication

Issighos, Constantine, 1945-
   How I built my six-sided log home from scratch : as I was building it -- they came : a step-by-step illustrated guide on how to build your own log home mortgage free! / Constantine Issighos.

Includes bibliographical references and index.
ISBN 0-9782018-0-9

   1. Log cabins--Design and construction. I. Title. II. Title: My six-sided log home.

TH4840.I57 2007   690'.837   C2006-905380-4

This book was designed by the author.

Graphic Design: Stephan Voss
              Concept Art, Owen Sound, Ontario, Canada

   Although the author and publisher have made every effort to ensure the accuracy and completeness of information contained in this book, we assume no responsibility for errors, inaccuracies, omissions, or any inconsistency herein.
   Any slights of people, places, or organizations are unintentional.
   Log home construction, landscaping and logging are inherently dangerous activities, and should be regarded as such.
   Follow your local building codes and asked for advice from your building inspector. Authors are not responsible for personal injury, property damage, or loss of actions inspired by information in this book. Due to the variability of climate and other conditions, material, skills, building site and etc., some advice and suggestions containing in this book may not be appropriate or accurate in your situation. When in doubt the contents of this book, ask for advice and recommendation from equipment manufacturers and with federal, state, provincial and local agencies.
   ATTENTION CORPORATIONS, UNIVERSITIES, COLLEGES, LIBRARIES AND PROFESSIONAL ORGANIZATIONS: Quantity discounts are available on bulk purchases of this book for educational, gift purposes, or as premiums for increasing magazine subscriptions or renewals. Special books or book excerpts can also be created to fit special needs.

DEDICATION

I dedicate this book to all those who have a dream... a sense of adventure... to those who take risks... to those who struggle with their doubts... to those who sit behind a desk wondering what it would feel like... to those who subdue their fears... I say to all of you... just get up and go... just do it... right now... take a chance on yourself... just go for it!!! As I did!!

AND

To those who came ... while I was building it... I will introduce you to my readers ... one by one through these pages...

Constantine Issighos

When a man,
So living, centers on his soul, his thoughts
Tightly restrained - untouched within
By stress of sense - he achieves true discipline, See!
Like an unwavering lamp which burns sheltered from the wind;
Such is the steadiness of the disciplined mind.

The Bhagavad-Gita

ACKNOWLEDGEMENTS

There is a popular saying that nothing much is accomplished alone. This is an overstatement, for I'm the proof of how much an individual by himself can achieve. At the same time, however, when you have others involved with you, the moral support you received is priceless.

First, I would like to thank all the countless people who dropped in just to talk to me about log homes and building methods. They were fascinated when they discovered my lack of means and the improvisations I used to accomplish my task. This, along with the house itself, became part of the story. These good people and come-as-you-are visitors told others about my unique project.

As more came, they brought with them their own ideas, aspirations and encouragement for my work. Such moral support, in turn, helped those who gave it to reflect on their own hopes and aspirations. Of the "Living Angels" who came while I was building my log home, and got involved with my project, they have my eternal gratitude and brotherly love.

To **Raymount Lihou**, who 'came to take a look' and gave me his unfailing support for the rest of the project.

To the **Old-man Frank**, who guided me when I was completely 'green' and confused about what I was doing.

To **Wayne Orr** who constructed my foundation walls in a barter deal.

My heart felt gratitude to **Jim and his wife Alenka** who at times of financial desperation helped me with meeting my mortgage payment.

To **Jon and Cathy**, from Jonsteel: thanks for the breaks.

To **Earl Reid**, who always helped when little things became too much to handle and was there to take the slack.

To my young friend **Joseph Trudell**, who came at the time when I most needed an extra hand, and who stayed with me for the duration of the construction of the log house.

To all those who came-as-you-are I hope you had as much fun looking at the unique log home design as much as I had explaining to you how I came up with the idea of it!

A SPECIAL DEDICATION TO MY CHILDREN:

Anna-Maria
Vittorio
Melissa

And

In memory of my son Robert who is no longer with us. You left a void in our lives.

WHY I WROTE THIS BOOK

I wrote this book to show you how to build your own log home!

I wrote this book to show you how to finance it, mortgage free!

I wrote this book to show you what is attainable!

I wrote this book to encourage you!

I wrote this book to find peace within myself!

I wrote this book to meet with my ghosts!

I wrote this book to make peace with my ghosts!

I wrote this book to make peace with those who are no longer with me.

I wrote this book to show you what is possible through focus, discipline and endurance!

I wrote this book to get out of my nightmares and into my dreams!

I wrote this book because I remembered!

I wrote this book because I wanted to forget!

I wrote this book to get out of my anger and into my passion!

I wrote this book to find my silence!

I wrote this book to put an order into my inconsistencies!

I wrote this book for you!

I wrote this book because I believe in you!

I wrote this book because I know you can do it!

I wrote this book in order to subdue my fears!

I wrote this book so you too can subdue your fears!

I wrote this book out of sheer indulgence!

I wrote this book so you can see the ridiculousness of this list!

Constantine Issighos

CONTENTS

INTRODUCTION 11

CHAPTER ONE:
GETTING STARTED 21
EVENTS AND WISDOM 32

CHAPTER TWO:
PLANNING YOUR PROJECT 39
EVENTS AND WISDOM 52

CHAPTER THREE:
FOUNDATIONS 55
EVENTS AND WISDOM 68

CHAPTER FOUR:
LOG WALL CONSTRUCTION 73
EVENTS AND WISDOM 96

CHAPTER FIVE:
BUILDING YOUR ROOF 103
EVENTS AND WISDOM 118

CHAPTER SIX:
INSIDE CONSTRUCTION 121
EVENTS AND WISDOM 134

CHAPTER SEVEN:
INTERIOR FINISHING 139
EVENTS AND WISDOM 168

CHAPTER EIGHT:
OUTDOOR CONSTRUCTION 171
EVENTS AND WISDOM 191

CHAPTER NINE:
ADDITIONAL OUTDOOR PROJECTS 195

CHAPTER TEN:
GROUND WORK FOR FINANCING
AND FINAL THOUGHTS 223
EPILOGUE 247

REFERENCES 253

GLOSSARY 258

LOG HOME AND CORDWOOD
BUILDING SCHOOLS 266

INDEX 269

PART ONE:
PLANNING

PART TWO:
BUILDING

INTRODUCTION

This book tells a story about an unconventional approach to financing and building your own log home. It is also a narrative about uplifting events and helpful 'Living Angels' – in human form – appearing when I most needed them.

It is also a how-to-book about construction and landscaping. Above all, it is a written guide for those whose budget is limited; and, therefore need to take an unconventional approach to 'finance' their project. This and other pertinent information is imbedded in the story itself.

There are three basic ways to finance the construction of your log home:
1) have a rich relative to give you the money,
2) borrow the money from a lender at high interest,
3) be creative, positive, plan ahead, and prepare to do the hard work, and read this book from cover to cover. When you finish read it over again.

I don't know your current financial situation but I can tell you about mine. At the time I was inspired to build my log house, I was a man with plenty of ideas but virtually no money. I had no credit, no steady job, no rich friends, or relatives. And, coming out of a bankrupt business to boot. What I had going for me was great ideas teamed with passion, energy, audacity, willingness, positive attitude and a work ethic. Later on I had Lady Luck to boot!

It is said that from an aerodynamic standpoint a bumblebee should not be able to fly. Fortunately the scientists forgot to tell the bee. I was like the bumblebee. I was armed with an amateurish passion evidently only in a man who is not aware of all the problems associated with building a log home with no money at the bank. That worked just fine for me! Because had I'd known *that this was not the way things were done*, I would have buckled down by all the 'evidence' presented to me by those experienced in real estate and home building.

It all started with a post card showing a typical Canadian winter and a log cabin surrounded by snow-covered cedar and pine trees. I showed it to Cecilia and my daughter Melissa. We looked at it longingly. Sitting around the kitchen table in our rented apartment, we began daydreaming about country living, flower gardens and fresh vegetables.

It was then that I revealed of my life long dream. "I too will build my own log home." Gently Cecilia reminded me that we only had $1,850 in the bank, no steady income and no prospects to find a good paying job. At this point I decided it was best not to tell her I knew nothing about building a log home.

However, I was determined. I started visiting the local library and began reading all the home building magazines and how-to books it had available. Most of these books on log homes referred to build with log-kits ranging from $200,000 to $500,000 and up. Nevertheless, I learned as much as possible as one can learn from books. I decided very quickly that these log-kits were out of my league.

Think of it for a moment. If I wanted to build my own log home I needed money to pay for labour and building materials. Both were expensive and something I could not afford.

I began to ask myself how the pioneers built their own log homes at a time when most of them didn't have a penny in their pockets. Questions turned in to ideas and soon enough I came to realize that these old pioneers had two things going for them: they had their own labour power and they 'financed' their project by using material from their own property. They didn't need cash or rather not as much!.

The solution seemed simple. I had to find a wood lot to get my material from and I had to put my labour to build my home. Could I do it? My answer was yes - if the pioneers did it I could too.

I started looking at newspapers for wood lots for sale as well as visiting real estate agencies. Most of the prices were out of my reach. Most expensive advertisements were advertising equally expensive properties.

I soon came to realize that I was looking in the wrong place. If I wanted to find a wood lot that I could afford I had to find an owner who could not afford the expensive Toronto real estate advertisements. I figured the real opportunities would come from owners who tried unsuccessfully to sell their properties by putting a simple sign 'for sale' in the front of their land waiting year after year for a buyer to come along. But how could I find such an opportunity?

I decided the answer was to go where the properties were. I contacted real estate agencies within 150 km radius from our apartment and asked them to fax me about wood lots for sale in their areas. This provided me with all sorts of vacant lands for sale.

We spent most weekends driving around the countryside following leads on wood lots. Each week we visited different areas. These trips turned into family excursions complete with stops for an ice cream and snacks. Having our homemade food which Cecilia prepared, our only expense was gas for our van.

During the week I played with different ideas about styles of log homes and methods of stacking logs. I began to sketch various styles with the help of popsicle sticks. These ideas turned into family conversation around the kitchen table with everyone having their own opinions. Out of all this I came to realize that most log homes, with small variations, were rectangular. I decided to build a round log house. Why round, Cecilia asked. Because everyone else had a box-like log home I answered. I wanted a round one.

Following many attempts and far more hours, I finally had 'constructed' two model log homes with popsicle sticks. They looked gorgeous on top of the TV for all to see! All I needed now was to find my wood lot cut down the trees and build my log home!

First things first. I needed to find money for a down payment (assuming that the owner would be willing to hold a mortgage). Second, I needed to find the right building wood lot that would supply me with plenty of trees. I became consumed with the idea of building my very own log home using material from the land.

A few weeks later, Cecilia asked me how large the log home would be and I replied, "Over 2000 square feet". Her question made me think that perhaps she truly believed in me that somehow, I would find the solution to our perpetual shortage of money and come up with a down payment. I suppose she was swept by the excitement of the moment and truly believed that things would turn okay at the end.

After weeks of searching I found it -the perfect vacant lot. A mix of white cedars and pines, a natural pond, and a year-round creek with 45 acres. All I had to do was come up with the sale price of $40,000. How? From where? As I was walking around admiring this fantastic lot, the only thing I was sure of was that this land was my land! I staked my claim by taking a vigorous piss and by shouting "You are mine!"

You see, at that moment, I truly had no idea how I would turn things around. Did I feel helpless? No way! I was determined to find a solution; the kind of solution that does not come from bank credit (which I had none) or from steady income (which I had little).

Returning to our apartment, I contacted the land owner. Talking to him over the telephone, I found out that he was an absentee landlord (first opportunity) who had been trying to sell his property for the last twelve years (second opportunity), that he had no use for it and hardly ever visited his property (third opportunity).

Over the phone we agreed to begin negotiations after the real estate listing expired, which was in about thirty days.

I now had 30 days to figure things out. First, I had to come up with a 'respectable' down payment, although the owner wanted payment in full. How much was I willing to pay for the land? How was I going to approach the negotiations?

First I asked, what did I know about the landlord and his relationship with his property? So far, I knew that he had been trying to sell his property for twelve years. He was paying property taxes and didn't care much about his property because he hardly ever visited his land. The big question was whether the owner viewed his property as a 'white elephant'. If this property was in fact an economic burden to him, then I had a good chance to purchase that land at a good price.

Keeping in touch with the landlord, periodically, I learned what I wanted to learn: that he was tired of paying taxes year in and year out, he was looking for someone to take this property out of his hands, pay the full price and with no mortgage held. Of course, since he did not ask me if I had $40,000 available, I did not volunteer the information.

Cecilia thought that it was irresponsible of me to negotiate with the owner while I still had no money to buy the land. It was then that I gave her my best smile and asked her if she still had faith in me. Somewhat lukewarmly, she said "yes".

I decided a yes, no matter how uncertain, was still a yes and that was good enough for me.

This was an opportunity of a lifetime. I simply had to capture the moment, for without money at least for a down payment, there was no chance that I would make anything out of this opportunity.

Initial model constructed with square and round dowels. These models made it easier for the architect to see what I had in mind for the style of the log house.

I reviewed my options. Sometime ago, Cecilia and I had imported various hand-knitted items with the idea of establishing a craft store. The business was unsuccessful and we had it closed down. But most of the stock was now sitting in a rented storage space. What if I sold these items for a large discount? I hated to lose money on them, but they were just sitting there costing us money. In the balance of things, losing money on these items would actually be a gain in a form of a down payment.

The plan was to find a buyer, offer the handcrafts at a big discount for cash and take it from there. A few phone calls later I had an appointment with a large discount store to show my wares. Next day, I packed my van with approximately $14,000 of goods. After an hour of negotiations, I walked out the discount store with a $7,000 cheque. I returned home with a chocolate cake and my daughter's favourite video to celebrate the good news.

It was now time to overcome another hurdle; to have the owner of the land accept my small down payment rather than an outright full purchase. Also, somehow I had to recover the loss of $7,000 from the wholesaler.

A week later I met with Jim, the property owner, for the first time. After a short lunch and a lecture by me on the "poor state of the economy" we began negotiations. Reluctantly he agreed to drop the price to $34,000 from original asking price of $40,000.

It was now time to tell him about the down payment, but instead I decided to return to him within a week or two. We departed friends and we both looked forward to closing the deal.

Two weeks later I called Jim to "apologize." The deal could not go through because the "bank" had refused my loan. Could he instead accept a down payment of $5,000? By now he was making his own plans, glad that he had the 'white elephant' off his back. I sensed that in his mind he had already sold his property. His final agreement came via fax. We were the new owners of the land. My gamble had paid off!

But this was not the end. By the time we paid the down payment and all the legal costs, we had only a few dollars left in the bank. We could not maintain a monthly mortgage payment plus continue renting our apartment. We had to move. The question was, to where? Moving to another place close to our property would have been the ideal solution, except we needed money for moving out: for security deposit, and first and last month in advance. In total, I needed $1,800 - an amount that I simply did not have. Remembering Jim's comment about an abandoned cabin in our property, I decided to take a look and check the condition of the cabin. To my disappointment, the cabin was a ruin and not fit for occupancy.

As I walked back to my van in front of my property, I noticed a couple walking towards me, waving hello. They introduced themselves as Jim and Alenka Bingeman. They have always come to pick wild apples and take long walks in the park-like setting of the property. I gave them permission to pick as many apples they wanted. As we chatted, I told them I came from Toronto to investigate the condition of the cabin, but I had to look for an alternative. Alenka suggested we move a trailer onto my property, as they did when they were building their own home. I agreed the idea was good but I had no money to buy one at the moment.

"Oh! That's not a problem," Jim said. "We have one that we no longer use." If I was willing to move it myself, I could have it for free. Being suspicious by nature, I found it hard to believe they would offer something of value for free. I wanted to look at the trailer.

It was better than I expected! Thirty feet long, with a fridge, propane stove and a shower. It was the best solution, under the circumstances. In turn I offered them a crocheted bedspread as barter. They gladly accepted.

Isn't it something, I said to myself. How these good people came out of nowhere and offered to help me at the time I needed help the most? Just like 'Living Angels.' What luck.

We quickly moved into the trailer with no electricity, no phone and no running water. The future looked good!

What I learned – and I hope you will too – is that there is and always will be all kinds of opportunities out there if you are willing to capture the moment. Don't accept the usual answers. If you really want something that seems out of reach, try some unconventional thinking. Then, just go for it!

This is my story. This is how I did it. And this is how you too can capture the moment. And if you are willing to take a risk, I truly believe the 'Living Angels' will come for you too!

Chapter One

GETTING STARTED

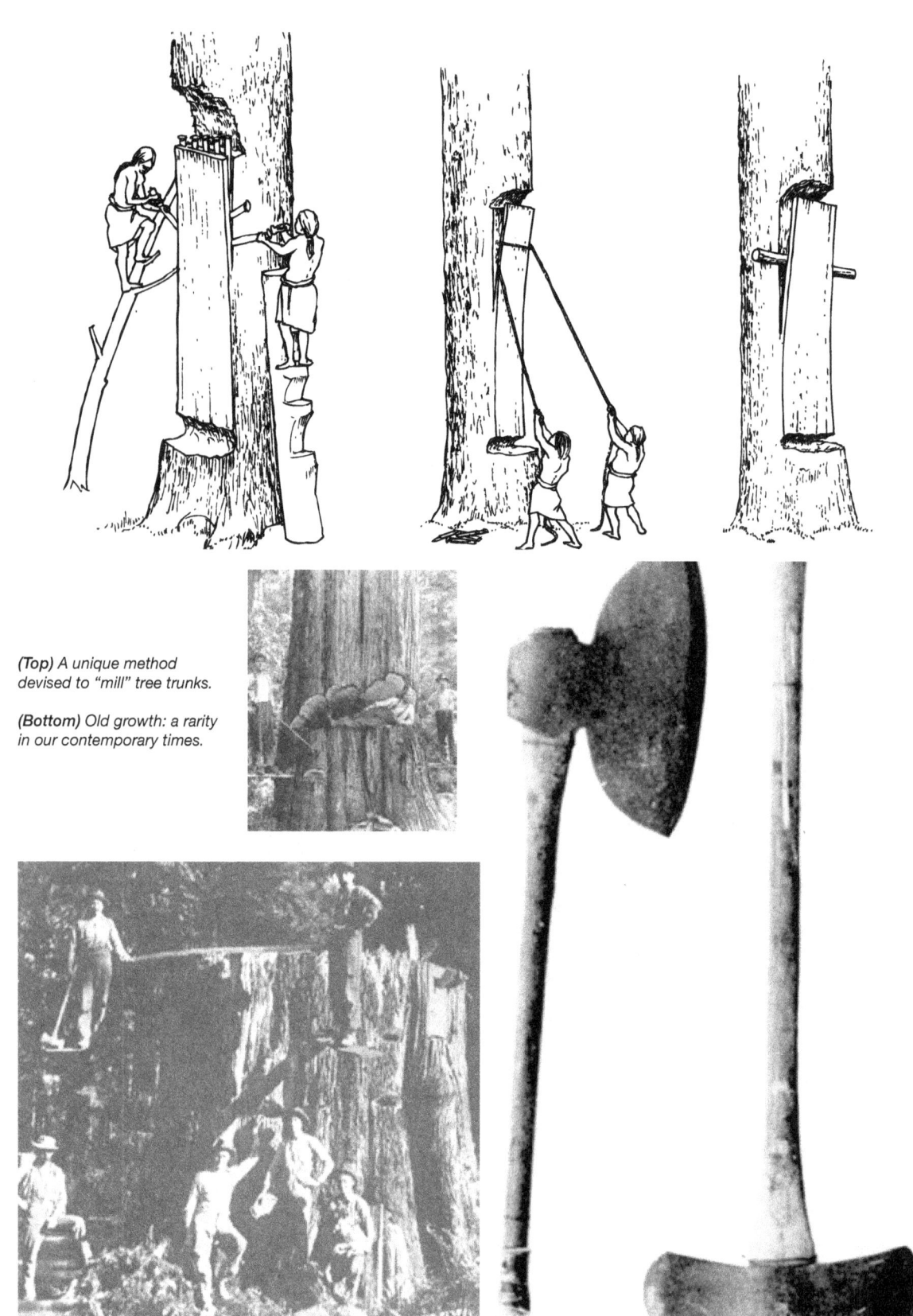

(Top) A unique method devised to "mill" tree trunks.

(Bottom) Old growth: a rarity in our contemporary times.

22　**PART ONE:** PLANNING

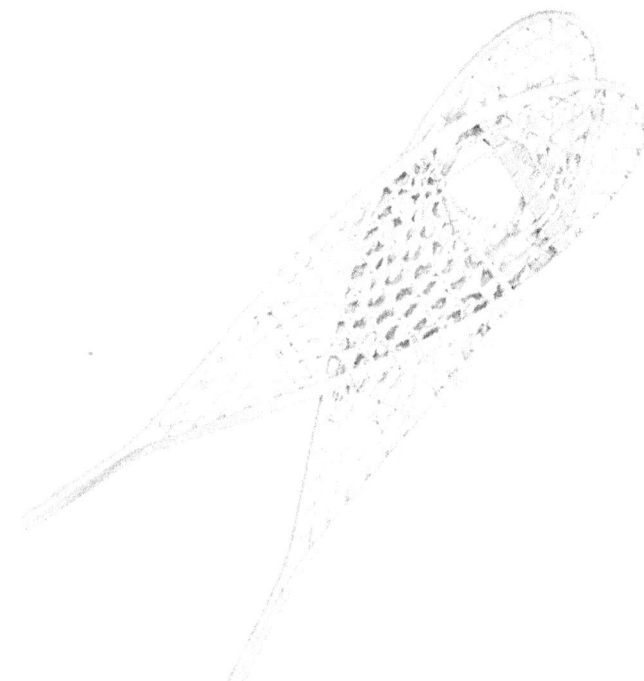

LOG HOME KITS

Since this is not just the story of how I built my log home, but a how-to guide for others, I can't avoid discussing log home kits. But be warned. I'm going to do my best to dissuade you from using one. While it is easier to pull out your chequebook or go into hock at the bank to get a ready-to-assemble log home, it won't truly be yours. When you have used your own sweat and muscle to cut down trees, and your own imagination to figure out where each log should go, you build a relationship with the house. There is something special about pointing to a flaw in the wall

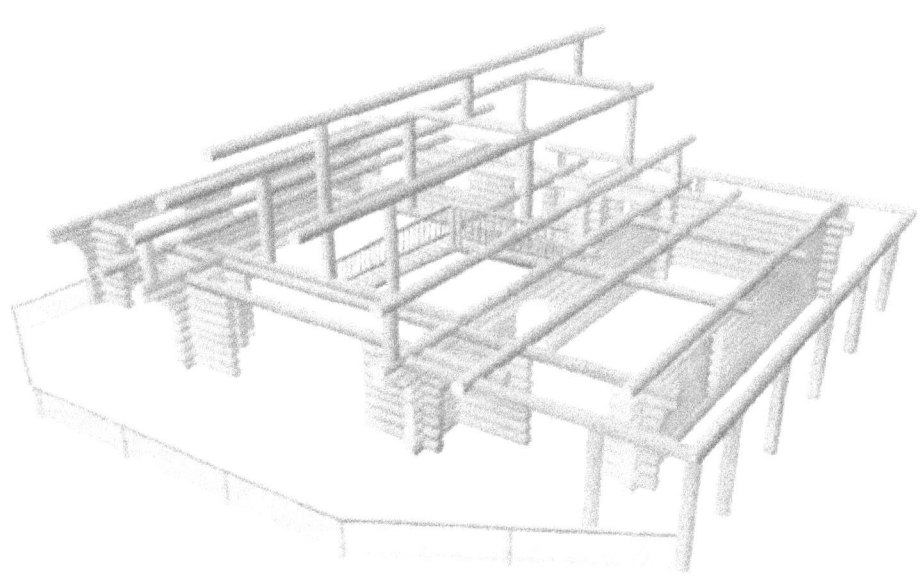

A basic log house kit shell delivered and set up at your building lot. Kits come in all sizes.

CHAPTER ONE: Getting Started 23

and saying, "Let me tell you how that happened."

There are a number of reputable manufacturers in the U.S., Canada and Europe who will sell you a log home in a kit form. A log kit structure consists of the outside walls with a number of openings for doors and windows. A kit log structure or "shell" ranges from $35,000 to $40,000 for a small cabin to exclusive, complete luxury log home structures worth many times more. These log structures are delivered to your building lot at no extra charge.

If you are willing to pay someone to assemble the log structure, then your cost will be considerably higher. If you plan to build some of it yourself then you can save quite a bit. The price estimates presented here are for discussion only. Prices will vary from country to country and from one geographical area to another.

A backbreaking method for piling up logs.

Remember that a log kit is a log-shell only and does not include extras unless you specify them in your contract with the manufacturer. A two side, flat sawn log-kit 34' x 42' (15.5m X 19m) would cost you sixty thousand dollars to have it delivered to your lot but not assembled. Add $20,000 for assembly and your log shell has cost you $80,000 and up.

For $80,000 you get a shell structure. To get an enclosed structure with conventional rafters, sub-floor, joists, plywood and a full-length porch 8'x42' (19m x3.6m), roof sheeting and shingles, would cost you extra. All assembled for you, you now have an enclosed log kit home structure.

If you had to pay for a complete conventionally finished interior, a log home of 1428 sq. ft (132.7m^2), ready to move in, add a mark-up of 3½ times the cost of the log shell. This would total $280,000 plus the cost of landscaping.

Let's assume that you want to order a kit log structure. If you are willing to do the construction yourself, you can save a considerable amount of money: by roofing it over, you can finish the inside later on a part time basis. If you choose this approach, the end result can be rewarding both economically and in the terms of your self esteem. If you decide to do the interior work, you may save 25% for your effort: your cost will be $210,000 or a savings of $70,000.

A break-down of construction cost can be done by a conventional construction company, by a log-home manufacturer or search the internet for cost-construction sites. When taking a construction estimate to your local banker, don't forget to add the interest payments, for a partial loan, over the next several years. Remember, a mortgage that is amortized over 25 years will cost you two to three dollars for every one dollar you borrow.

A standard way of comparing construction cost of different sized homes is by using the cost per square foot. The cost per square foot for a 1428 square foot log home would be as follows: $280,000 ÷ 1428 = $196.08 per square foot. For comparison, my log home of 2200 square foot cost me $34.77 per square foot. This is because most of the material came from the land itself.

A NON-CONVENTIONAL METHOD OF FINANCING YOUR LOG HOME

Starting From Scratch

Before I put some numbers on paper, allow me to explain. My log home is a large one by residential averages. Without a basement, it is still 2200 square feet (205 m^2) including the mezzanine. There are 2 full bathrooms, custom-made kitchen cabinetry and bathroom vanities, all made from solid red cherry wood (from my property). There are nine custom-made, solid, 2" white cedar doors, 2 double-doors for 2 walk-in closets, 2" white pine floor, a full cathedral cedar 2x6" planking ceiling, 24' full log length rafters 21 feet long, a steel spiral stairs, flagstone floor, in the rotunta and more. (see pictures for details)

Other than plywood, drywall, light, plumbing fixtures and general hardware, my log home was built entirely by material supplied to me by nature and through my labour. **So, of everything you see in the pictures — material wise — 90% was "financed" by my land and 85% by my labour.**

The term financing takes a different meaning when you start building your own log home from material growing on your own property rather than using cash to buy them. Lets put aside a sentimental notion of building your log home because you want to "go back to nature." Instead, let us look at the notion of "financing" your log home construction with an accountant's logic.

There are two sources of dollar value or equity in your log home: the construction derived from your labour and the material you accumulate through a mix of labour and material (lumber/logs). As you cut down trees and turn some of them into logs and others into lumber, you save money and accumulate value or equity. Your direct profit, if you turn material into cash by selling them, comes from your labour. Your equity is the material you set aside for your log home. In other words, the more labour you put, the more material you accumulate, the more equity you have. This is a reality, not merely a point of view or some mental exercise. What we are talking about is "cold hard dollar value." If everyone thought this way it would bring a banker to chills from the thought of losing so much mortgage business.

Lets look at this more closely: the cost of my log shell is

$5,500 in real labour time. The materials came for free. Think about it for a moment. A 203 foot long log shell for a mere $5,500 compared to a kit-log shell of 132 long log-shell for $60,000 and you can see the reality of it. This labour induced equity is an unconventional method of financing your own log home. Wait! There is more! The equity increases 20 times or more when you turn your trees into lumber material – before you even begin building - for your stud walls, roof, doors, door frames, windows, floors and cabinetry.

How do you self-finance your own log home? By accumulating logs and lumber before you begin your construction. Remember, when you cut down a tree and separate your logs for your log shell, there is an equity that has cost you little or no dollars at all. You have just financed your log-shell of your dream house. Most important, if you choose hard work over convenience, labour induced equity over borrowing money, then *you* are master of your own destiny and not the banker. This may sound radical but it's not. It is an old fashioned idea – one the pioneers used to great success. And it still works today.

PURCHASE YOUR OWN LOGS

When it comes to building and financing your log home, it is convenient to have your own wood lot. You can harvest as many trees as you need for both your log home and for sale to others. If you have just a building lot however, with little or no trees to use, you may need to purchase logs. You can get them from loggers in your area or directly from a land owner if you plan to cut down the trees yourself.

When purchasing logs or whole trees it is best, and most economical, to go directly to the source. Approach a logger before he delivers his logs to the sawmill. Once the logs arrive to the sawmill, logs are sold by adding on the middleman's profit. Most sawmills give priority to turning logs to lumber rather than selling logs to the public.

Small-scale loggers advertise their services in local newspapers. Ask your neighbours or local contractors and businessmen to recommend someone who is reliable. Ask questions and get to know the going price. Above all, sound like you know what you are doing. Then make a deal. Purchased as many full-length trees as you can and have them delivered to your building lot. Consider buying whole trees rather than logs. You may find it much cheaper. The following may give you some ideas about using the whole tree. Prices may vary from one area to another.

(Top) Human habitation at its most natural form.

Let's look at the economics of a single 30' tree. Unless you choose otherwise, a cedar tree on the ground is cut into 8' sections. An average tree in my area would give 3 sections of 8' and one of 6' long. The bottom end (butt-end) 8' section is used to produce lumber for decks and stud walls. On average a 10" diameter (on top end) would produce 5 plain planks of 1½" x 8" decking. At $12 to $15 each, that's $60 to $75.

The second section is normally used for fence posts, which may bring you $8 to $10 each. The third section is also used as fence posts and can be sold for $6 each. The last 6' section may bring $1.50 each. This last section – the grape stick- is normally used by grape growers to keep their grape plants off the ground. A tree, therefore, could bring you a $75.50 to $92.50 retail.

You may wish to keep or sell some of your planks or logs to recover part of your cost or to break even. If you do this, the remaining material will cost you little or nothing at all.

If you are willing to work hard - long before you start with your project - and are willing to be inventive, you too can use an unconventional method for financing your project.

Lastly, by hiring your local portable sawmill operator you can "pay" his cost in exchange for lumber.

PART ONE: PLANNING

(Top) Portable sawmill squaring my logs and milling for much needed planks.

(Bottom) Cordwood construction of my tool shed.

BUILDING MY FIRST STRUCTURE: STACKING CORDWOOD

My first priority was to build a small storage shed to keep our tools safe – both from the elements and from thieves. I began to experiment with cord-wood, which I had plenty of on our property.

Because of a land slope, I decided to build my floor joists on cedar posts. At this point in the construction, my daughter Melissa (Bebe) had most of the fun. This was the first time she had an open space for running and playing. I bought her a small hammer and she even tried a little carpentry! The storage shed served us for many years and secured our tools and equipment. Constructing with cordwood was an experience in itself.

CHAPTER ONE: Getting Started

Time to work and play. Cedar posts were used to form the foundation with floor joists resting on top of them.

Cordwood construction is an environmental use of leftovers from logging. Pieces of 16" logs are the most common size of cordwood. For Melissa it was time to practice a little carpentry?

EVENTS AND WISDOM

The Beginning of a Long Journey

Spring was in the air! We had been living on our land for about a month. I was looking forward to the experience of working on my log home project and the skills that this project would demand of me. I was also aware of some short-comings. Regardless of my best efforts, it was impossible to begin this project without the necessary tools and equipment.

An impressive size of tree trunk

For the time being, I had my mini-chain saw to continue cutting down cedar trees. Soon, however, I would need a tractor, chains and hooks to skid the trees and logs out of the bush and into the open and clear space to sort out the lengths and sizes of logs. There is no denying that things can get desperate, for without safety boots and gear how could I continue? Logging is dangerous work.

I remember my father saying, "When things get tough and you think you are drowning, reach down inside you and bring yourself up." That is what I was trying to do. A number of friends who visited me told me that I was stubborn, impulsive and did not know when to stop. Whatever the reasons for taking on such project, I knew that I was the right kind of person to successfully complete the job.

As spring turned into summer and the days got hotter, I continued to go back into the bush cutting down cedar trees near the walking path. This way I could use Cecilia's little Toyota Corolla to skid out short logs and posts that I needed to sell. I needed $1,600 to buy an old Newfield 460 tractor. At every opportunity I would put Cecilia's Corolla to "work", especially when she was in the library and couldn't see me abusing her car.

Skidding out logs is heavy work and the Corolla was not built to take the beating I was giving it. Eventually the back fender was torn off. I repaired it as best I could with wire and duct tape. Not surprisingly, one day Cecilia returned from shopping complaining that the fender had fallen off the car. I quickly blamed this on the previous owner for doing such a poor job with the fender.

Even with the damaged car I soon had enough posts and logs to sell. When they sold I took the money and became the proud owner of an old Newfield 460. I still remember the feeling. It was one of the best days of my life. I could now pull, lift and go over things. I felt like superman. Cecilia told me I looked very proud when I was driving my tractor. I just knew I was well on the way.

Old-man Frank, my neighbour and an experienced logger, kept visiting me in the bush to be sure I was okay. He became my trusted advisor, giving me tips about safety and getting better logging results. When my two short 12' chains were not enough to skid out logs that were further in the bush his expertise came to the rescue. He told me to hook one end of the chain onto one end of a long (but thin) cedar and the second chain onto the other end. This way I gained extra length to use to reach further. I increased the total length by 12 to 16 feet and was able to skid out a number of cedar posts.

In a few weeks, I became an "expert" in small-scale logging. I continued to separate my 12' logs for my future log walls while still cutting posts to sell to various farmers. Still, I had no proper safety gear for such a dangerous job. I was still using my runners instead of proper logging boots.

And then disaster. With the first October snow I slipped and fell while stepping on a snow-covered log. My foot became wedged between two logs. I painfully pried my foot out. When it was finally free, my foot looked messy but I thought it was nothing to be too concerned about. I returned to the trailer and had Cecilia clean and bandage it.

I continued to work. The pain and swelling increased each day. Every morning I would shovel the snow out of the driveway and keep cutting down trees. Soon I was supporting myself with a walking stick, still refusing to see the doctor. It must be something with a guy's brain to refuse medical attention. For the next 8 days, I continued to work until both girls insisted that I visit the doctor or else. But being a guy, it still took another 6 days before I would go to the doctor. It was then that I found I had broken the fibula in two places.

Like most guys, I was not a good patient. I spent the next six weeks in bed wearing a foot cast. In general I behaved like a spoiled child, complaining about everything while being an idiot.

I knew winter was coming fast and I wanted to cut down more trees and put aside more logs for my house. By the time I recovered and my cast was removed, the winter season was already upon us. Drifting snow had made the paths inaccessible. I went crazy doing very little for days at a time. I worked on the design of the house but itched to get back into the bush. Cecilia and my daughter found me unbearable and spent most of their time in school or in the local library.

Have you ever spent a Canadian winter in a small trailer? It wasn't fun. With two propane heaters working steadily, and the moisture created by cooking and breathing, the inside walls of our trailer were coated with a thin layer of ice. When the heat melted the ice, it fell on our bedding and our cloths which absorbed the moisture completely. Life became hard and very uncomfortable, especially for the girls. I was very proud of them, but at the same time very concerned about their health. They complained very little, at least while I was with them. Once or twice when the temperature dropped to 35 or 40 below zero, I took them to a nearby motel for a few days.

A hard day's work.

At times I wanted very much to apologize to them for following me and my crazy ideas; for my willingness to put up with anything; for my obsession to build my log home. To this day I have not apologized for being too proud to accept friends' invitations to take shelter in their warm house for the duration of the winter. In fact, I never told my family about the invitations at all.

Winter came and left, and April returned once again

along with my extended avian family: the Canada geese, ducks, wild turkeys and a variety of migrating birds. With the promise of better weather in the air and only a few snow-banks remaining, my passion returned. Once again I cranked on my old tractor and off I went back to work. This time however, I was conscious about my accident and was concerned about working alone in the bush. Not wanting to alarm my family, I told them nothing about my concerns; instead I asked them to visit me in the bush from time to time, just to keep me company and bring me some coffee.

A number of well-meaning friends and acquaintances continued to question my attempted project; in fact, the whole project. How could I make them understand that they weren't going to find logical answers by asking me? I honestly couldn't tell them what was my driving force.

Looking back now, the winter months were not a total waste of time. I had completed the final design of the log home and the blueprints were ready. I still owed $800 for my blueprints, and I was determined to pay off such a debt as soon as possible. It also became a daily ritual for me to explain to my family how close we were to starting with the construction of the foundation of our log home.

I was determined to keep their spirits high and their hopes intact. I suspected that, at times, they had their own doubts about the whole adventure. I remember a movie I once saw with Harrison Ford, called **The Mosquito Coast**. In this movie, Ford plays a brilliant inventor who becomes disillusioned with his life in the United States. He moves his family to the rain forest of Central America to create a new life but gradually his obsession threatens to destroy his family. I began wondering if I was becoming the character of that movie.

Still, there was hard work to be done and plenty of it. The paths had to be cleared of toppled trees from the winter storms for which this area was famous.

I looked around me and visualized preparing the building site. While the Canada geese in the pond, along with the beavers, were doing what they normally do, I felt that I was on the right track. With a few more days of back breaking work, I was sure my body would refuse to allow my mind to indulge in esoteric thoughts.

A good method of keeping floodwater out of your house. Such elevation styles are common around the world.

By the end of May, I had made good progress collecting logs for my home. I had collected 380 12-foot logs, which had been drying since April of last year, all waiting to be milled. I had made a few sales of cedar posts and had managed to pay all my debts while saving $2,000 in the bank.

One day I decided to give my family a psychological lift by purchasing the concrete blocks for the foundation. This would get us one step closer to building the foundation of our house. I visited a nearby concrete block plant. The usual price was $2.50 per block. Since I needed 1,000 blocks, I would need $2,500 plus tax and delivery. Once again, good luck came my way. The plant had overproduced some blocks from another order and had 1,000 blocks they just wanted to get rid of. I was able to purchase these blocks for $0.25 each. I also had a free delivery as the plant simply wanted to get them out of the way to allow for more space. The total cost to me: $300 and a case of beer for the driver.

CHAPTER ONE: Getting Started

Chapter Two
Planning Your Project

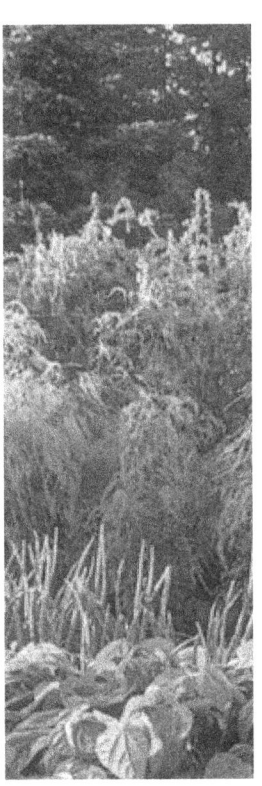

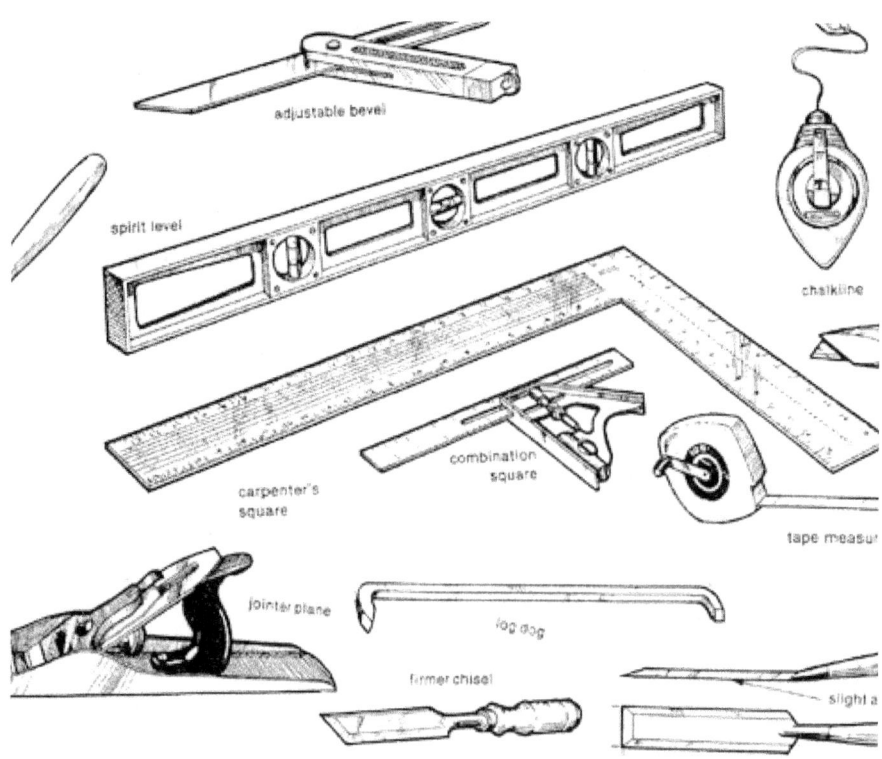

40   PART ONE: PLANNING

CEDAR LOGS: THE RIGHT BUILDING MATERIAL

This book is written to inspire suburbanites to review their clustered lifestyle and embrace harmony with nature. It is also addressed to people who admire natural-log construction. Natural logs are the strongest and most long-lasting building forms throughout the world. Of course, one must take the necessary steps to protect natural-log construction from the harsh elements of nature – rain and snow soaking – log building will rival any other natural material.

Are there unnatural logs? Of course there are. When a healthy and beautiful cedar tree is processed through stripping, chipping, cooking, chemical treatment and compression, it is transformed into a manufactured product of industrial technology. What's wrong with that? A natural-log house awakes your senses with the smell of the sweet incense of sap and resin and by the acoustic quality that

A well-preserved log cabin with its stone fireplace.

makes sound richer. There is a deep sense of harmony, living in a log home that is made of natural trees. A manufactured log-product has no resemblance with a once living tree; it has been stripped of all it natural dignity, beauty and life.

Building with logs does require hard work. At the same time it is healthy and pleasing; and it is not at all beyond the strength of an average person. Starting from scratch enables you to be creative. In exchange for your labour and ingenuity, rather than mortgage indebtedness, you too can be proud of your accomplishment. I truly believe that you can accomplish a great deal by being innovative, bartering with others and being a good neighbour. If you do these things the 'Living Angels' will come!

Storing and air-drying rafters and logs. Leaving a driving space between piles of logs makes their removal easier.

So, let's begin my narrative of how to build your own log home and ensure your home will turn into a work of art.

Let's begin with a close look at the tree as it stands in nature and its physical properties. The body of a cedar tree (or any other tree) is made of hollow cells packed closely together. It resembles a honeycomb where vital fluids and nutrients are stored. In the summer this honeycomb is full of fluids providing nutrients for healthy growth. In the winter, these honeycomb cells have their fluids considerably reduced to prevent frost expansion which can destroy the body of the tree. It is in the winter months – when these fluids are in their lowest level - that is the best time to cut down a tree. With less fluid in the body of the tree, the natural drying process will be quicker.

When a cedar tree is cut down and all the fluids have dried, the honeycomb cells become tiny air pockets. Space and air are the perfect insulated building material. This explains why natural-log homes are cool in summer and warm during winter. Therefore, a cedar tree as it exists naturally is the most perfect building material. A coat or two of linseed oil will sufficiently water proof the interior to resist house vapour. One must also remember that a tree is a product of nature, shaped by time and proven successful by millions of years of tree trial. It is, therefore, up to you and I to give the cedar tree the dignity and respect it so much deserves.

LOGGING

Begin by selecting which trees you'll cut and mark them with spray paint. Ensure all markings are facing the same direction. Make sure the tree you choose to cut down will have an opening to fall to the ground in the direction the tree is leaning. If not it will dangerously 'hang' on the other trees.

If you happen to have a 'hung' tree avoid walking under it, for a simple shift of wind could cause the tree to fall on its own. This is called 'widow-maker'.

  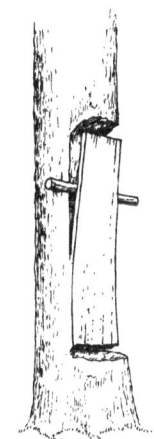

Cedar trees are best cut in winter when moisture in the trunk is less. The next best season is late fall – when the trees begin to reduce their intake of fluids. Spring and summer cutting is not advisable because trees contain much more sap and fluids. On the other hand, spring cut logs tend to peel much easier.

If you are planning to log in spring or summer, leave the trees with the strongest limbs on. Those will keep the whole tree off the wet ground, speeding up the drying process. Leave the bark on, so the trunk can be protected from direct sun and heat. Trim the rest of the limbs to allow air flow. Remember, direct sun-heat on the green log without bark tends to cause deep cracks. Slow drying has it merits.

To a small degree, it is possible to determine if a tree is healthy or touched by disease. Look for hardy shoots, uniform leaves and smooth bark visible beneath the outer bark; all are signs of a healthy growth.

To determine the quality of timber or lumber, peel a small portion of bark on the south side. Striking the 'peel-off' spot on a healthy tree gives a clear ring. On fallen trees this test involves striking the 'butt-end'. A dull sound or no sound at the opposite end indicates an unhealthy tree. These tips come directly from Old-man Frank who at the tender age of 87 still can teach us a thing or two about preservation of trees and logs.

STORING YOUR LOGS

Stack and store your logs by providing air spaces between them and let nature take its course. A well-dried trunk is free of starch, shows no wind shake and is resistant to insects and fungi.

Ideally, logs should be allowed to dry for a whole year. But, if you cut your logs the previous fall, by springtime cedar logs are ready to be stacked for walls. By the time you clear the building site, hire a back hoe for digging your footing and build your foundation wall, your logs will be quite dry. If you plan to have two-side square logs, mill them as soon as the weather permits. The flat surface will permit the acceleration of moisture evaporation.

If you will have full-length rafters, position these to dry straight. You want to avoid sagging in the centre section of the rafter. In natural sagging place 'hump' the reverse.

SELECTING YOUR BUILDING SITE

Most log home owners are the kind of people who associate the idea of a log home with nature and peacefulness, away from noise, crowded and busy malls, to seek a simple retreat. I wanted the same. Soon after we moved into our property, I began to look for the right spot where one day I would build my log home. Going from site to site, after while all spots looked good to me! I simply had no idea what the 'right' building site must look like. One thing for sure, I wanted to stay away from the noise of the high traffic road in front of my property.

Clearing the building site beginning with logging and removing stumps, branches and top soil.

It was during one of those moments that Old-man Frank came to rescue me; he probably guessed from the look on my face that something was troubling me. "I'm looking for the right building site", I said.

Frank, in his grandfatherly voice, told me that this geographical area was a "snow-belt". In winter high winds often resulted in snow drifts. It was wise, therefore, to choose a building site that was protected by trees against high winds and snow-drifts.

Ground drainage capacity was another important factor, especially for the septic bed. A building site located on high ground would be preferable. Regardless of your choice, you may have to compromise on some aspects.

Had I chosen the front part of the property, I could have eliminated long snow plowing of the driveway and general area of the entrance. It would have cost much less to bring in electrical power and would have eliminated the need to

CHAPTER TWO: Planning Your Project

install three electrical posts. This side also had the benefit of a wind breaker of wall of cedar trees which would protect the house from the harsh weather. The only problem was the high traffic and constant noise would have been our permanent companion.

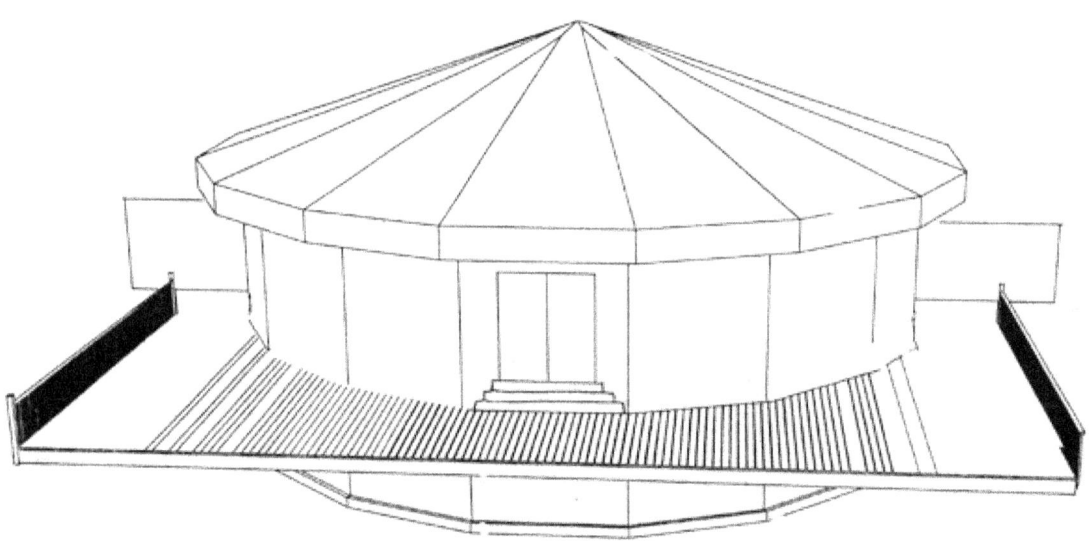

Frontal Site

Back Site

The second option to finding the right building site was the present one! We had to clear the building site by clear-cutting a 300 x 400 foot area to accommodate the log home, lawn, driveway and septic system.

The selected building site was situated on high ground and protected by high trees against winds and snowdrifts which tended to concentrate around the pond. Sunny, with a mixture of sand and clay, the ground was not subject to floods. Located approximately 450 feet from the front road, traffic noise was hardly noticeable.

There were, of course, shortcomings. We had to install hydro posts and construct a 620 foot long driveway to serve the home and the septic bed.

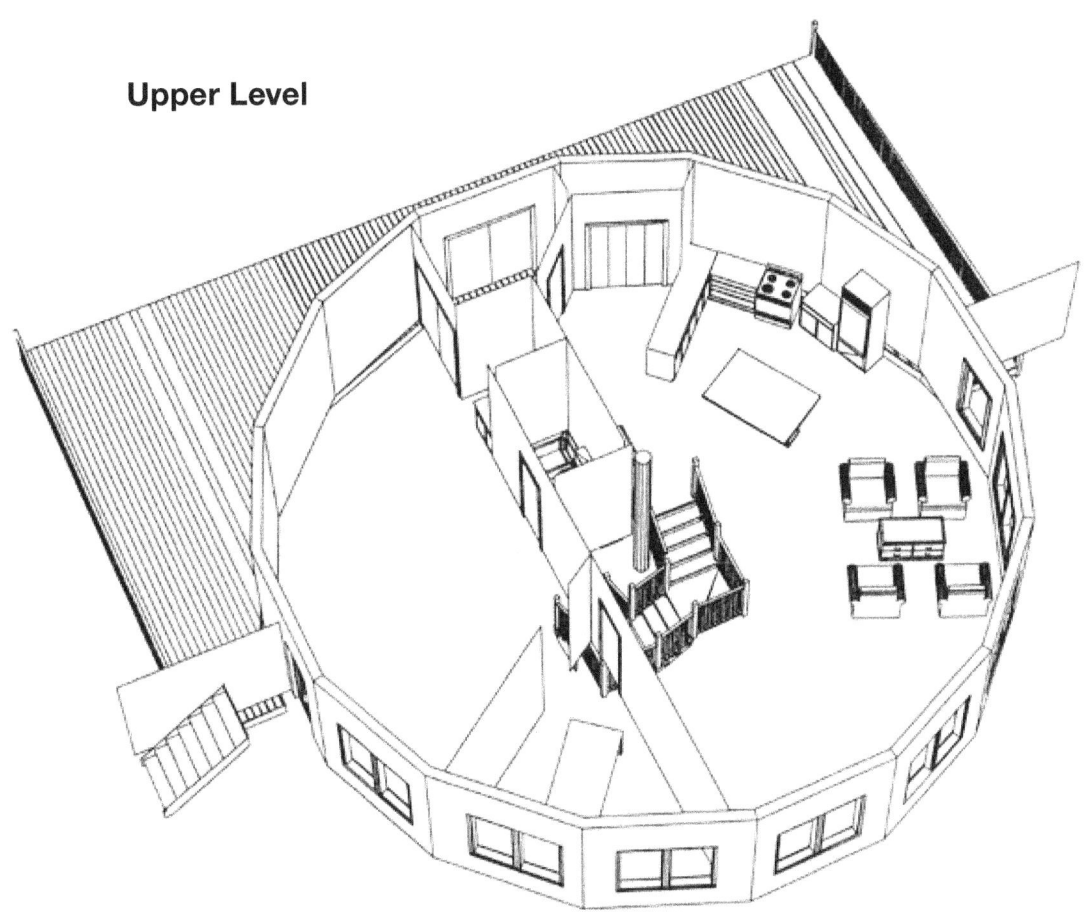

An over-ambitious planning of a two story, 60' diameter, round log house. It is however, a unique construction. This plan was revised in favour of the new design.

Upper Level

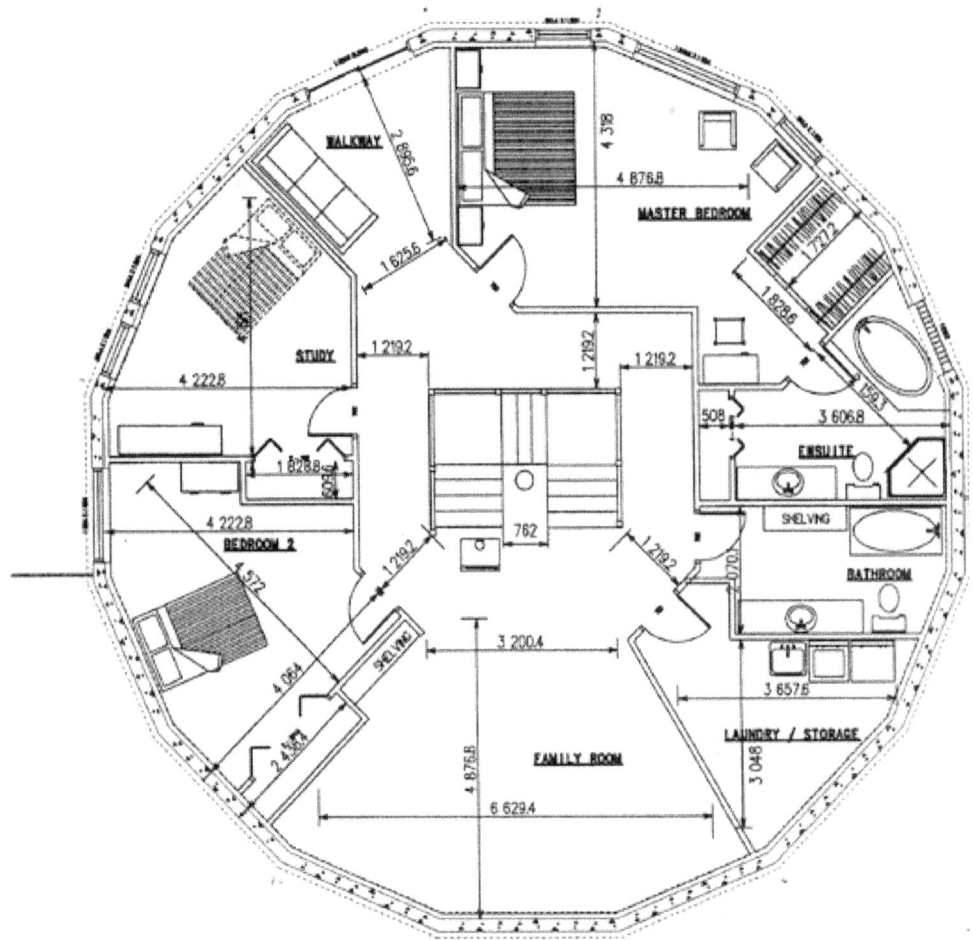

Lower Level

Those were the factors we had to deal with in order to choose the right building site. On choosing the right building site, one must not restrict and cramp the size and shape of the log house, nor restrict its location or narrow down its surroundings and retard the family's lifestyle. Choosing the right building site should meet the personal needs of the occupants, for their convenience, as well as the building code requirements.

DESIGNING YOUR LOG HOME

A log home design should be a personal matter, one that reflects something about you. Try to be in harmony with your surroundings, with the natural colouring and contours of the landscape. Avoid 'transplanting' a suburban monstrosity that so many professional 'planners' consciously aim to do in the cities. Blending your log house design with nature will always have a head-start over a suburban clone house.

I deplore having houses lined up in rows, all looking and behaving alike. Their sterile essence lies with its so-called resale value. Discover your personal concept of style with pleasing space for all the members of your family. Make designing space of your log home a family affair. This will result in function and purpose of a happy home.

Further on I have included log home plans with fully detailed partitions. You may wish to alternate and prepare new blueprints.

Lower Level

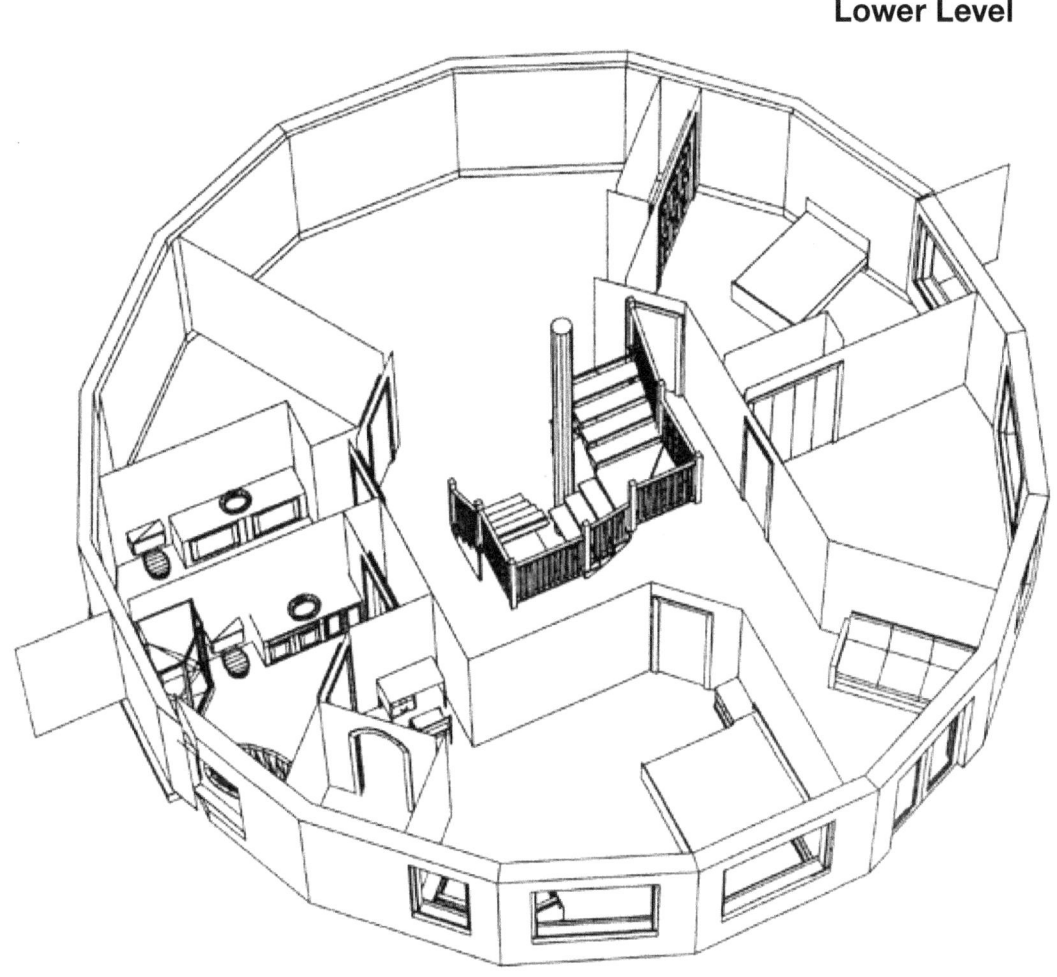

CHAPTER TWO: Planning Your Project   49

TOOLS AND EQUIPMENT
LOGGING

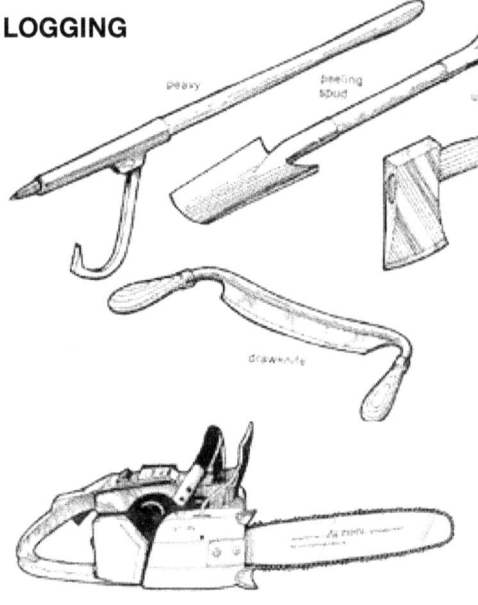

Utility Axe: an inexpensive wood handle axe for general use.

Drawknife: used to remove the inner cambium bark. It is also used for shaping and touching up damaged surfaces of logs.

Spokeshave: useful tool for cleaning up knots.

Pealing Spud: useful tool for removing the heavy bark from logs.

Peavy: very useful tool for moving logs around. A pair of them will often be a great help and can save your back.

Chainsaw: a must-have tool for log-wall construction and logging.

CONSTRUCTION

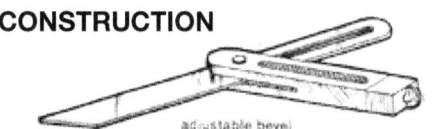

Mortal tools: shovel, wheelbarrow, trowel, jointer & hoe.

Adjustable Bevel: for copying and transferring angles and bevels.

Chalkline: a case containing blue chalk line. When it is unwound, pulled tight and snapped against surfaces, it leaves a straight guide-line along the stretched position.

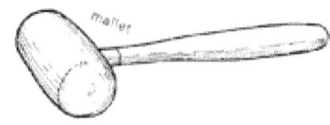

Chisels: a chisel and mallet are all you need.

Hand Plane: handy to reduce the size of a tight fitting tenon.

Log Dogs: used to hold down and in positions logs, and to prevent logs from moving while you are working on them.

LIFTING EQUIPMENT

Instead of using brute force, choose mechanical devices to lift heavy objects. In order to save your back, I'll recommend one or more of these mechanical devices.

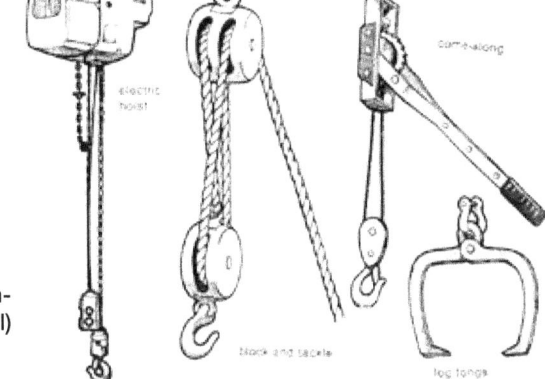

BUILDING TOOLS

Split Level: a 24" and a 48" are recommended. Used to indicate plumb (vertical) and level (horizontal) planes.

Carpenter's Square: a basic necessity.

Combination Square: used for 90° and 45° layouts.

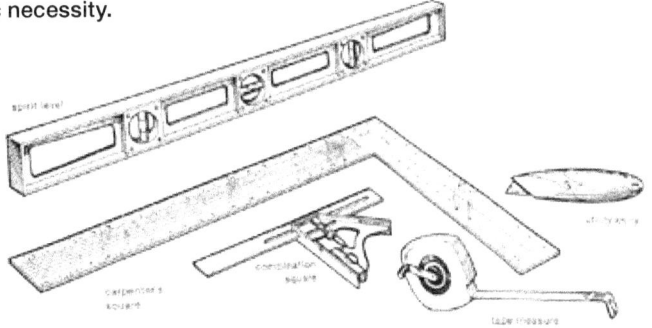

Tape measure: a common 25' (8m) for general building purposes.

ELECTRICAL TOOLS

Electrical Tools:

Circular Saw: for cutting lumber and frame work.

Electric Drill: preferably ½" (12mm) reversing drill.

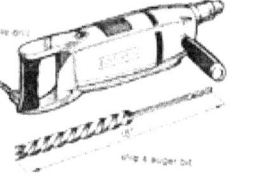

RENTAL TOOLS

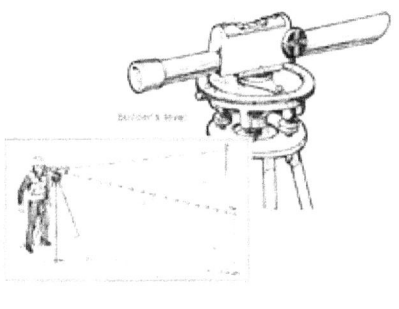

EVENTS AND WISDOM

To thank Old-man Frank for helping me select the right building site, I took him to the local watering hole for a cold one. When I returned to my trailer, Cecilia's first question was, "Where will we find the money to do all the things you are planning?" I told her not to worry - something will come up. Next day, I overheard her telling a friend that I must be from another planet because nothing seems to worry me. Little did she know, I was not only worried, in fact, I was terrified.

After making arrangements with the local excavator, we began to clear the building site. I had to cut down about 50 pine trees, making sure that I would cut 24" above ground. This will allow the bulldozer to use its blade to push out all the tree stumps. All the pine trees were put away for possible future use. At that moment I didn't know what for.

Now we had to test the soil to determine its absorption capacity. We dug a five foot deep hole from which we extracted a soil sample to be sent to the local geology lab to test its drainage time.

When you test soil conditions for absorption capacity you do so to find out the most economical method to dispose household sewage and 'brown matter'. Explore the soil of the intended building and septic site and carefully do a visual inspection of the virgin soil for rocks. The existence of heavy clay soil and stones along with sand would be determined the best location for your septic bed. So, a site of the best esthetic location for building your log home, give the site selection careful thought and planning.

I know a guy who had to 'import' material for the bottom of the septic tile. It cost him over $20,000 to do the job. In order to avoid future problems, before you start clearing your building site, get someone with a backhoe to dig a test hole sample. The cost of $200 for testing and digging is far less that $20,000 you may have to pay later to fix any problems.

By now, I learned to view my land in more than my once limited ways. Where once I could not see the economic value of my land, I now developed a broader view of the economic potential that was before me. **Trees** could become logs, decking lumber, 8" and 6" posts, 3"x12' braid support-post and wine sticks. **Large stones**, which time and weathered had scarred, are in demand for landscape décor.

Field stones become a prime product for building stone walls for both gardens and retaining walls, and could bring a few dollars when sold to masonry builders. **Small cedar and maple trees**, no more than 4 feet high, could bring extra income when sold to commercial greenhouses and landscapers. **Black topsoil** could be sold to local landscapers for few dollars per truck-load. A cleared section of land next to a driveway can be turned into **open storage** for boats and trailers and rented per season. You could also charge few dollars to **day campers** to camp or to pitch a tent for $10 per day.

By planning ahead and use your land's potential, you can go a long way to being financially self sufficient.

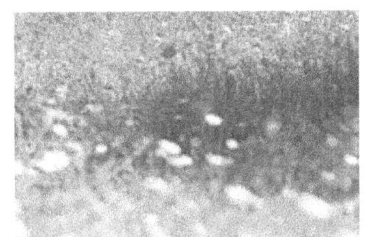

Chapter Three
Foundations

FOUNDATIONS

By brief definition a foundation is a supportive structure which serves to keep the house above ground, at the same time distribute equally the weight of the building to the ground. The installation of a foundation involves the basic procedures; soil testing, foundation layout, grate levels and excavation and foundation construction.

A good building site should have a slight slope to allow for good drainage away from the foundation. A word of advice, stay away from low-lands with wet clay soil and a high water table.

To see if the site you've selected is suitable, dig a 5' deep test hole in the centre of your building site and leave it overnight to see if it fills with water. Local building codes may require a drainage test of a soil sample to determine its drainage ability, and may recommend the installation of perimeter drainage tile around the foundation footing.

In geographical areas where winter frost is a natural occurrence you must also consider the frost level, which is the depth

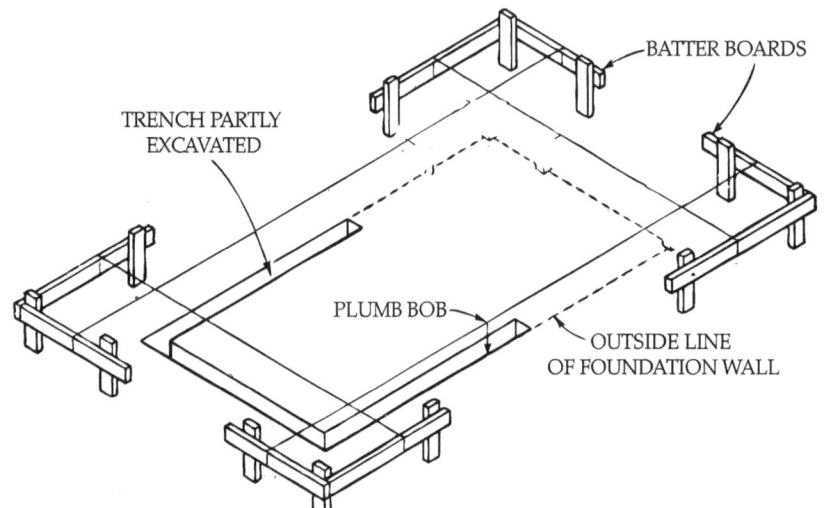

Rectangular foundation layout: ditch must be 12" wider than required to provide ample working space.

that the winter frost penetrates into the ground. The foundation footings must be below frost level to prevent frost damage to the foundation, which in turn, will throw the building off level.

CONCRETE FOUNDATION: LAYOUT

When a house is rectangular or square, the layout procedure does not require a surveying instrument. Construct batter-boards 8' away from the outside line of the proposed house wall. Batter-boards are horizontal boards attached level to stakes and are used to mark out the perimeter of the building. By fastening base lines (stretched strings) to the batter-boards you can indicate the outlines of foundation walls or perimeter of the building. To fix your base line, mark one end or side of the proposed house. Spray paint on the ground just below the base line. Allow time for the operator to study the layout. Remove the base line just before excavating begins. Once the excavation is completed, place base line back in position and begin the layout of the footing by using a plumb bob.

Elaborated Layout:

For more elaborate foundations - layouts such as my hexagon - you can take your time or hire a professional to establish the house perimeters. Even though a six-sided foundation layout is somewhat more challenging than a square or rectangular shape, the basics are the same. I was determined to take on the challenge on my own. I thought perhaps a home-made tool (instead of a professional with a builder's transit) would do the job as well.

Each side of the hexagon was equal, at 25', with a house diameter of 42'. The rectangle shape of the added kitchen would require the above basic layout.

First thing I had to do was decide where the center of the house would be located. Once I made my decision, I drove a 24" steel rod into the ground, leaving 8" above ground. I now had the center of the house marked.

By joining two lengths of 2" x 2", I made a 25' long measuring stick, representing a single side of the house. Next, I measured and marked the exact center of the measuring stick, at 12' 6". Now that I had the exact center I proceeded to mark the base line from the center-rod to the center of the measuring stick. The radius (the length from the center rod to the center of the measuring stick) of the house was 21'.

Next I established the desired position of the first side and hooked longitudinal lines from the ends of the measuring stick to the center rod. Both longitudinal lines were of equal length, at 24'5". One end of each line was tied to a metal ring. This ring fit loosely over the center rod for easier movement. Once the first side was in place, a steel rod was driven into the ground on each end of the 'measuring stick'. This marked the position of the first side of the hexagon.

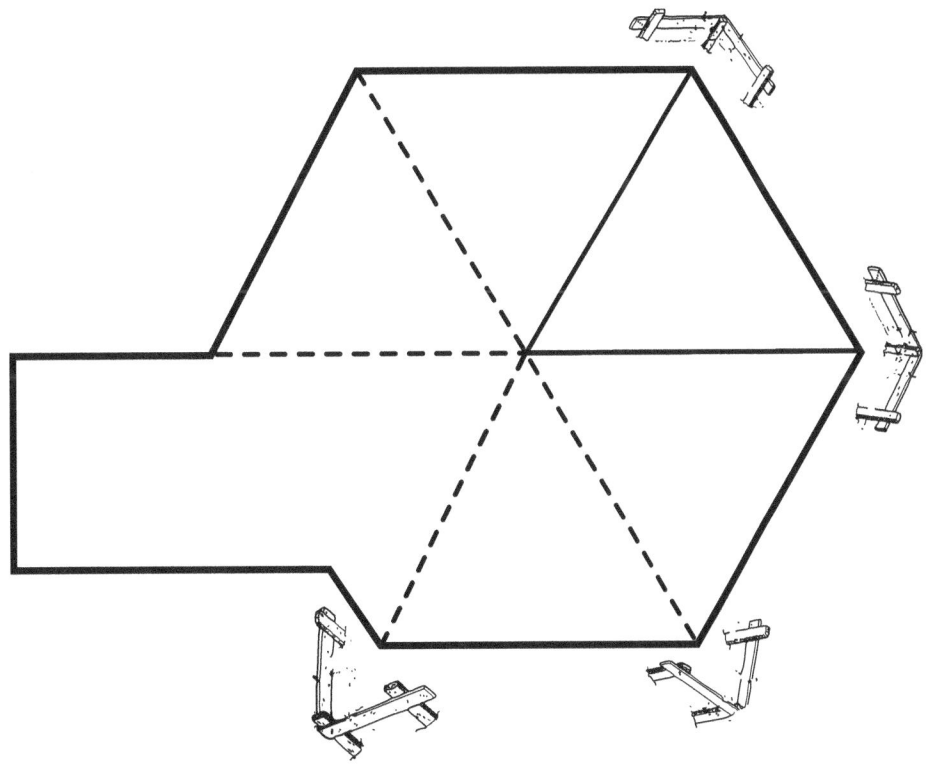

A bit more complex foundation layout. Batter boards must be at least 8' away from the outside line of the foundation wall.

CHAPTER THREE: Foundations

By lifting-up the measuring stick and swinging around the center rod, I could easily mark the next side of the hexagon. I made sure point 'A' and 'B' were lined-up. I finished the whole perimeter of the house including the kitchen section in this manner.

Build your batter boards about 8' from the outside line of the proposed house. Cross-section all of the base lines. They all must cross above the center-rod of the house. Make any necessary adjustments for better results.

With a small handsaw create a small cut to mark the position of the base line on the batter-boards. This will allow you to avoid re-measuring when you have to remove the base lines for excavation. Spray-paint the ground just bellow the base line. Remove the perimeter steel rods just before excavation. Afterwards, reconnect the lines back where they were, using the cuts you made to ensure they are in the exact position.

Excavation:

In geographical areas where severe winter freezing is likely, the excavation must extend well bellow the line of maximum frost penetration. This is because when soil freezes, it expands considerably. When it thaws, an equal degree of contraction occurs. If footing is not placed bellow the maximum frost line, frost can damage both the footing and other parts of the building. In Ontario, Canada, excavation means down to 5', including the thickness of the concrete footing.

When excavating the trench, make sure it is wide enough to allow for the footings plus several inches beyond the outside lines of the foundation. Ordinarily, the trench is excavated 2' wider than the width of the footing to allow space for the installation of the forms. Make the trench too narrow and you will be unable to move easily while in the trench.

The bottom of the trench must be level and must be of firm and undisturbed soil, in accordance with the building code. Therefore, care should be given by the back hoe operator not to excavate beyond the required depth. It is best therefore, to choose an operator whose excavator is equipped with a depth-laser.

FORMING FOR READY-MIX CONCRETE

Once excavation is finished, reconnect the base lines to the batter-boards and use a plumb bob to line-up the perimeter of the house and its six corners. Dropping the plumb bob from the perimeter base line will tell you exactly where the foundation will go. Take your time with all the steps for measuring the foundation. If you are off on your measurements here, you will be off on the rest of the house.

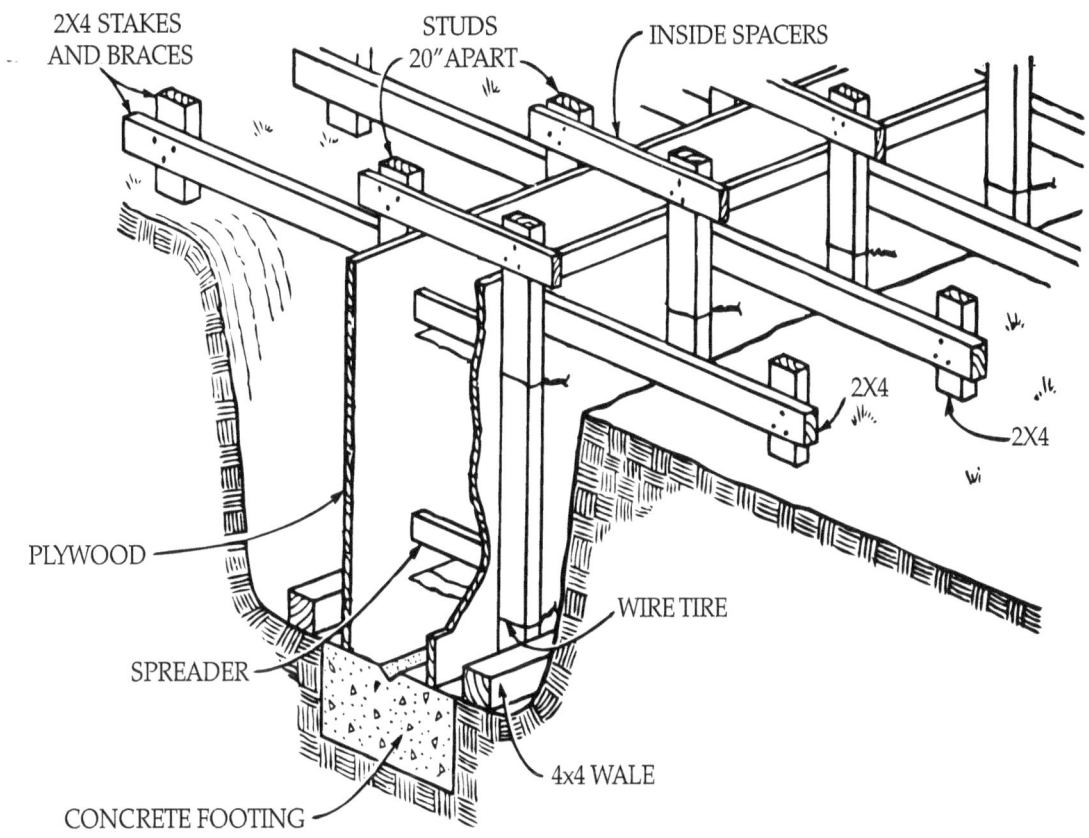

Formwork Footing:

By Building Code regulations, forming is required for all concrete footing except where the building inspector directs otherwise, such as, where lightweight structures are constructed. Forming is an aid in making sure that the footings are square, level and of the proper shape and size. In normal

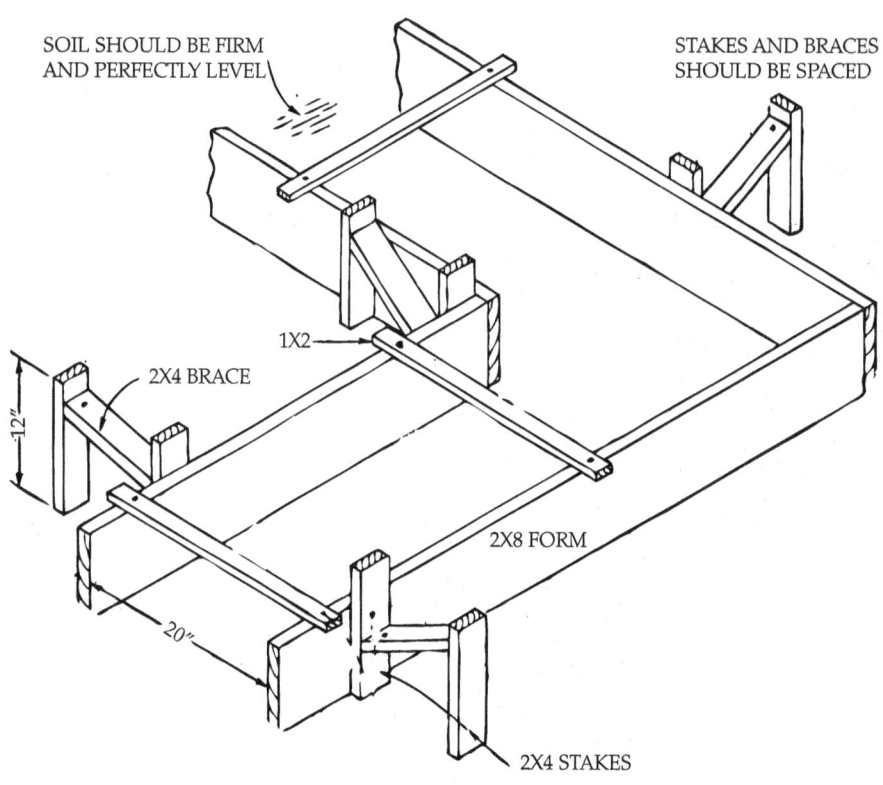

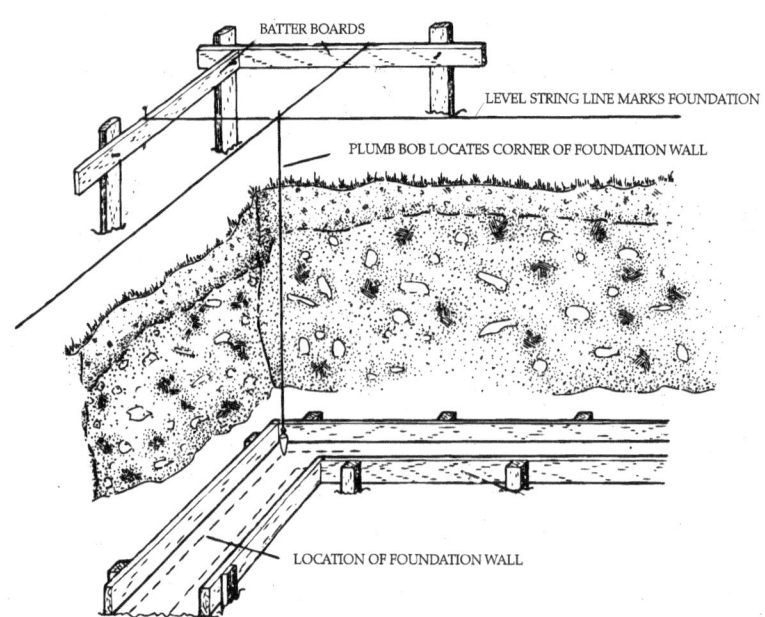

(Top) A regular forming for footings.

(Bottom) Snap a chalk line to show the outside line of the foundation wall.

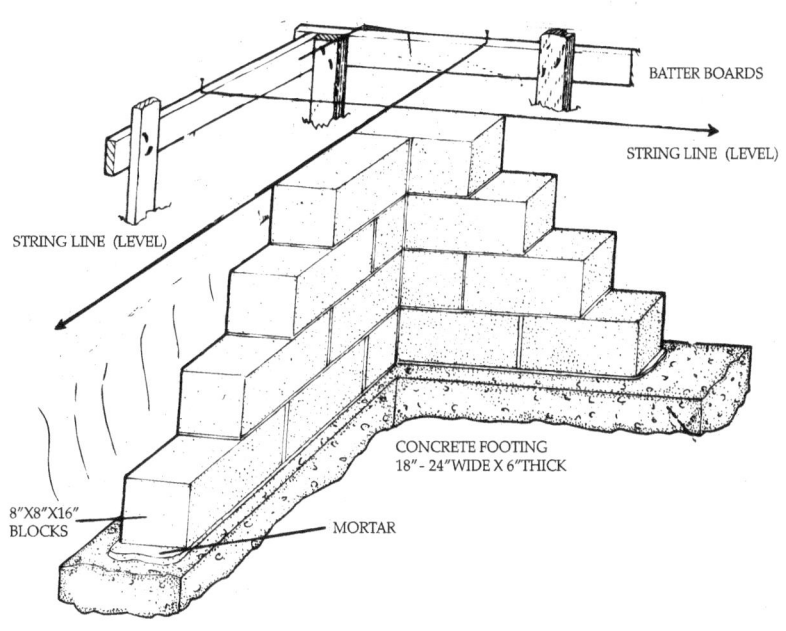

(Top) Concrete block foundation walls must begin from each corner of the home. This will give the level and height for the rest of the block walls.

(Bottom) Anchor bolts (J-bolts) should not be higher than the maximum thickness of the logs. Provide ample working space on both sides of block work.

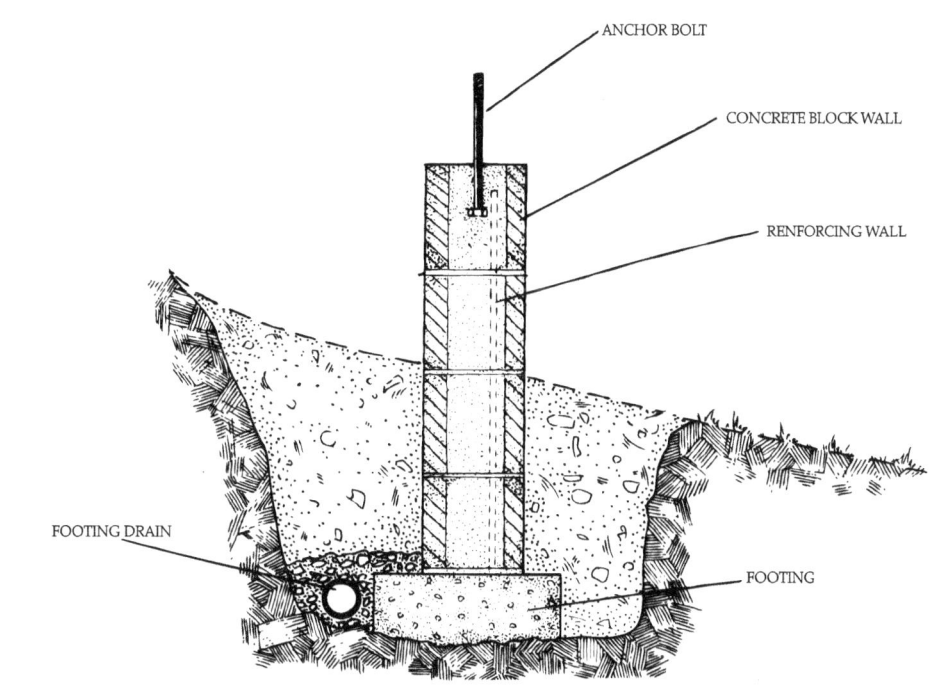

forms of footing construction, a 2" x 6" timber is used as a means of securing a solid footing. Follow the illustration to establish the perimeter of house. This illustration can serve for both conventional and complex footings. The framework must be held in place by stakes spaced out every 3' starting at the corners. This prevents side forms from leaning in either direction. As one side form is set into position around the perimeter of the house, the next form should follow the general direction, level and set into position across from the other. Make sure that they are both level and both at the same level. Follow the illustration with care.

Forming for Ready Mix Concrete: Foundation Walls:

Forming for ready-mix concrete must be built and strongly braced to insure that it will withstand the weight and pressure of the concrete. For a one story house with no basement, the more conventional method of erecting a form is the use of plywood, wood sheeting, studs, wales and bracing.

If you hire a professional, pre-fabricated panels will be used which will be assembled on the job site. These panel sections are made of various sizes so that they can be readily removed from one job and reassembled as needed.

If you decide to build your own forming for ready-mix concrete, the illustration on forming for ready-mix concrete foundation walls will guide you accordingly. Take your time and you probably can re-use forming material for other construction work.

Concrete Blocks:

Concrete-block foundation walls permit easy planning and quick construction. Though it is considerably heavy work, it can be done by beginners with little previous experience.

Concrete-block foundation walls can be economical and are used for many medium sized buildings including single story log houses. The regular size of concrete blocks is 8" x 16", unless the building code specifies otherwise. Check with your building inspector before you purchase your blocks; codes are very strict for regulations about the thickness and height of walls and foundations. Also check for building codes regarding reinforcement and metal ties placed in each layer of concrete blocks.

Any sort of reinforcement, however, is only as good as the care used in its installation and quality of the mortar. It should be noted that it is necessary to be careful in the preparation of the mortar and concrete mix. Take care on your workmanship as well. When these qualities are present, the resulting structural work will be durable.

Anchor bolts (or J-bolts) play an important role where log walls are tied or anchored to the foundation wall. It is important to provide a rigid connection between the blocks and the log wall. Common practice is to secure the first log to the foundation by means of 1/2" J-bolts which are embedded 8" to 10" in the concrete cavity no more than 3' apart. The cavity (core) on the top concrete blocks in which the bolts are set-in must be filled with concrete.

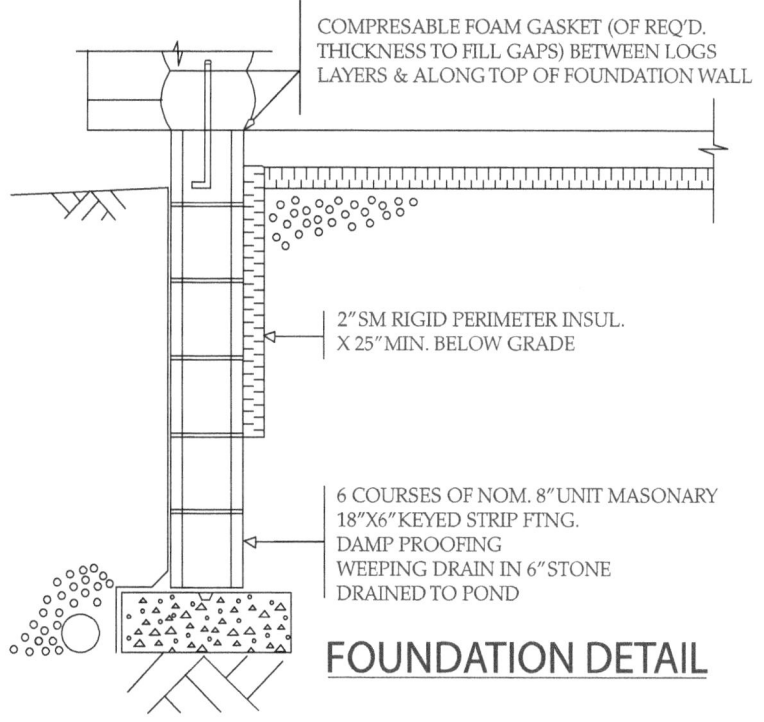

FOUNDATION DETAIL

CHAPTER THREE: Foundations

Single Story Concrete-slab floor:

For log homes without basements, a concrete-slab floor on the ground is an excellent type of construction. Properly planned and constructed, concrete floor-slabs give better results than other types of floors for one-story log houses.

Log homes with a concrete slab should not be constructed in low lands and areas that are damp or in danger of flooding from surface water. Also, the surrounding ground should slope away from the house with good drainage and ground level should be at least 8" bellow the interior finished concrete-slab floor level.

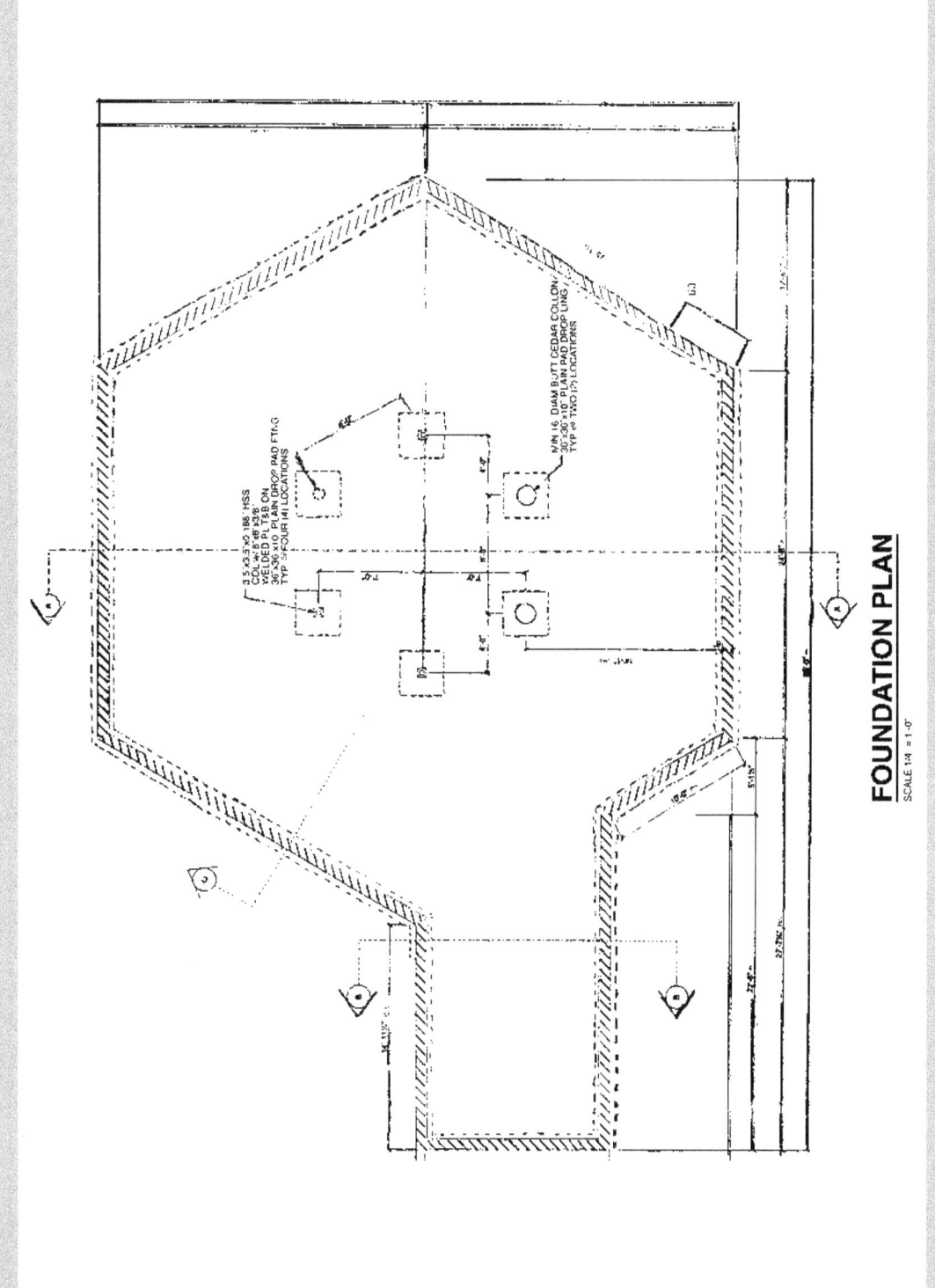

FOUNDATION PLAN
SCALE 1/4" = 1'-0"

EVENTS AND WISDOM

After the excavator left my building site, I carefully put back all the base lines now located above ground. All I had to do was to transfer the 'above ground' measurements to the footing below.

For convenience and saving time, I decided to solicit a contractor's estimate for footing formwork and pouring of the ready-mix concrete. When I received the estimate of $2,000 I asked if the price included the cost of the concrete ready-mix itself. The contractor simply laughed at my naivety! "Of course not," he said! I then asked him how long it would take to complete the job. Maximum, he said, eight hours. Imagine $2,000 for eight hours of work! No wonder they all drive big cars! I decided to do the job myself. I was not ready to start paying for convenience.

All my base-lines were in position from one corner to the other. By using a heavy nut tied to line as a plum bob, I located the outside line of the forming. Using a 4' long carpenter's level, I began to put in place the outside 2"x6" form of the footing. As I was going along I made sure that my level was correct and the forming held in place by stakes driven in to the ground. With minor adjustments, eight hours later I had made my formwork ready for the next step; to pour the ready-mix concrete.

Next day, with help of a friend with muscle, the job of pouring the concrete on the footing was successfully completed. Cost of labour was $ 175.00 plus a case of beer! Together with the ready-mix totaled $ 800. It turned out to be a good day after all!

When I finished with the concrete footing, it gave me a great deal of satisfaction. I could now see the beginning of the building process. It was no longer about planning and preparing; I was well on my way!

I now had all the necessary material; from blocks to gravel and sand, bags of cement and metal ties.

Immediately, I begin to look for someone who could handle the heavy work of the concrete block foundation wall. You see, concrete block wall construction needs at least two people inside the ditch for the actual block work, one person to bring the blocks to them and one to make the concrete-mix and supply the workers with it. I could do some of the work myself but not all.

Another problem I was faced with was this; because of the short construction season due to the Canadian weather, all or most of the 'bookings' were done during the off season, when most of outdoors workers were unemployed. I was a 'Johnny-come-lately' which meant that I would have a hard time finding help. These tradesmen were known to book various jobs ahead to keep themselves employed.

I had little or no control over the situation, so I needed to find an independent contractor. I started to seek quotes for the job. To my shock, prices ranged from $7,500 to $9,000 for the foundation wall construction. Single tradesmen were asking from $45 to $60 per hour plus two helpers at $25 to $35 per hour. This was crazy! Where would I come up with that kind of money? Regardless of whether I would pay individuals by the hour or a larger company by contract, the total cost was approximately the same. The fact that we were in the rainy season and I didn't

CHAPTER THREE: Foundations

want to have my footing covered with mudslides added to my frustration.

With only $1,200 in the bank, how on earth (this wasn't the exact word I used) was I going to manage? Of course, putting on a brave face, I was able to positively answer to Cecilia's constant question "how are things going?" The curiosity of this woman! I told her "everything is going just fine sweetheart!" Knowing Cecilia, I knew her next question would be "when will you start the foundation wall?"

Soon after, looking towards my driveway, I noticed Old-man Frank and another guy walking towards me. His name was Wayne Orr, a complete stranger to me. I invited them for a beer and as expected, the conversation soon turned to construction; beginning with the question 'how's things going'. Wayne said that he had heard of me as someone who was building his own log home all by himself. While he looked over all my logs, now drying, Wayne told me that he too had a dream of building his own log home one day. "Go for it!" I said. I told him it would build his character while he built it. He smiled and said that he actually came over to see if he could buy 500 cedar trees, 4-5' high, from me for a landscape job he was doing.

After we agreed on the price, the general conversation now drifted towards the construction of the concrete block foundation wall. For some reason I opened up the conversation by telling him of the problems I had with lack of money and with not being able to find help to begin with the construction. Much later I found out that Wayne had already heard about my perpetual shortage of money. He asked me if I wanted him to do the job.

"Would I want you to do the job? Of course I would, if I had the money!"

"Oh, I'm sure we can work out 'something'" he said with a serious face. I brought some beers and the three of us set to work on that 'something'. You see, Wayne had his own masonry company taking mainly large jobs. At the moment he was doing some landscaping, but he could still spare three or four days to do my foundation wall. When I asked Wayne for the price for his labour (since I already had all the material), he said; how about $1 per block plus 500 cedar trees for free! Does your price include all the necessary helpers? Yes, he said. I could not believe it! That same afternoon he moved in his cement mixer and forklift. I also met his father, who was Wayne's partner.

After they left, I could not wait to tell Cecilia the good news! As I was standing by my construction, all by myself, tears begin to come down! To the embarrassment of my male ego (I consider myself to be a man's man) I just could not stop crying! I guess I was getting sentimental in my old age!

Within five days, my concrete block foundation wall was constructed. Total cost: $1,000, five cases of beer plus 500 - 4' cedar trees.

One thing I remember vividly was the thought that kept going through my head during the construction of the wall: where do these people come from at exactly the time when I need them most?

Chapter Four
Log Wall Construction

73

PART TWO: BUILDING

PLAN AHEAD

Cedar trees, as with most trees at ground level, do not have the same diameter on top where the branches start to grow. A 12" diameter at the butt end will be reduced to 8" or 10" at 12' length. A 6" thick two-sided square log must have a minimum of 6" stacking surface on the top end of log. Logs must have a solid stacking base to prevent the wall from sagging inwards or outwards. Gravity pressure can be very destructive when the log stacking-base is less than 4". Rafters pushing outwards put an ever-constant pressure on log wall.

Finding the right size trees to give you the minimum stacking-base you need for a strong wall, is a matter of selection. Select trees that will give you on average an even top-log diameter. The length of logs may vary from one to another but the stacking-base must be constant.

Calculate the amount of logs you'll need to complete the construction of your log wall ahead of time. The last thing you need is to be short of logs! Count the logs you have stock-piled to dry. Get the average length of each pile and exclude those logs that would not give you an average stacking-base. Take a

CHAPTER FOUR: Log Wall Construction   75

pen and paper, if you have to, to make sure your calculations are correct. The following is an example of how I calculated my own needs; you may wish to do your own account. Take a look at your blueprint for additional help.

Make a detailed list of all the log and lumber material which will be used and note which will be supplied by your wood lot. Note the various sizes of lumber that you are going to need.

Logs Required

a) Length of house perimeter including log-corner overhang	225' per row of logs
b) Average log length	12'
c) Height of house wall	10'
d) Thickness of two-sided square log	6"
e) Each row requires (rounded number)	19 logs
f) Total logs required	380
g) Allowing 10% extra logs (for miscellaneous needs)	38
Grand Total	**418 logs at 12' length**

Roof Requirements:

a) Roof rafter at 24' length (mid-section diameter 10")	24
b) Kitchen rafter at 12' length	16
c) Center vertical support post 12" top diameter at 16' length	16 logs
d) Tied-beam support for center 12" top diameter at 10' length	6 logs

Miscellaneous Materials:
10" Galvanized Spikes every 16" space.
Insulation: Pink Plumber's Gasket,
J-bolts, nails, screws.

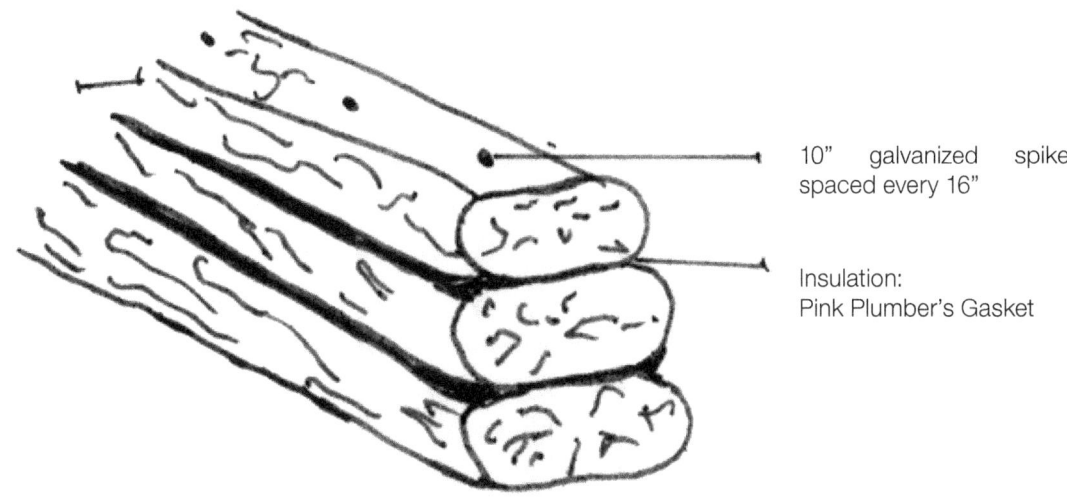

10" galvanized spikes spaced every 16"

Insulation:
Pink Plumber's Gasket

Calculate, for example, how much lumber you will need for your studs and floor, joist and purlings, planking for ceiling, doors and door frames, windows and window-frames, kitchen and vanities. Unless you are planning to buy those, I would strongly suggest making your account. Remember, this is your equity worth many thousands of dollars.

If your budget is restricted you may wish to mill your logs for lumber a little at a time by cutting them as they're needed.

CHAPTER FOUR: Log Wall Construction

Prioritize your construction work ahead of time and cut (mill) your lumber according to your priority. There is no point in milling lumber that you are not going to need until much later. This way, you can spread out your expenses and only prepare material to meet the next job in your project. Of course, there is always an exception to the rule.

For example, there was a large maple tree right next to my pond. I noticed that my three-member beaver family had eaten the bark out of the bottom of the maple tree. I decided right then to cut it down. The way it fell, it left its large trunk up in the air and remained in this position for three years. This 8' long maple trunk was sliced in the center of its length and eventually became my kitchen bar and island (see pictures of kitchen)

Lay Down the First Row of Logs:

We now had the foundation wall completed and it had been drying for two weeks. We covered it on both the interior and exterior sides with earth, making sure that no big stones hit the blocks and caused damage. All the J-bolts were in

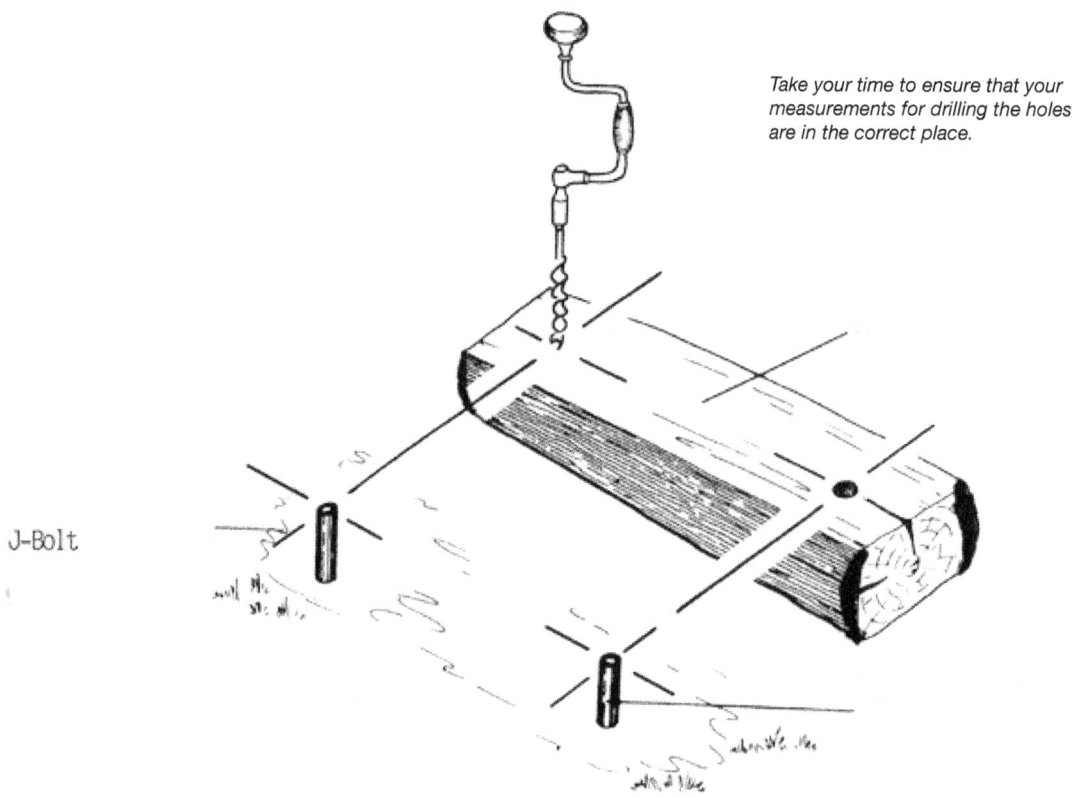

Take your time to ensure that your measurements for drilling the holes are in the correct place.

J-Bolt

place on top of the concrete block foundation wall, and we were now ready for the next step; start lining up the fist logs to be drilled and fit in position.

Before you start building your log wall, take the necessary time to select and separate your logs correctly. The shortest and widest butt-end must be reserved for between windows and between doors and windows. Choose the logs with the widest stacking-base for your first row. These first logs will rest on top of the concrete block wall. They should be placed with at least 3" of overhang to prevent rain from penetrating the space between the first logs and the concrete wall. Take your time to do this, for it may later save you a great deal of money and grief. Remember to place pink insulation between concrete blocks and logs and between each row of logs.

I had to hand drill 79 holes to secure my logs. Don't forget to place a washer before the nut on J-bolt.

Place your first log flat-side up along the top of the concrete block foundation and right next to the J-bolt. Overhang the log 24" at the house corner. Line up the position of the J-bolt with the ½" hole you intend to drill. Make sure your measurements are correct so that the J-bolt would line up in the center of the flat side of the log.

CHAPTER FOUR: Log Wall Construction   **79**

An encouraging sight to see – the log construction taking place. Provide strong support to your window frames (openings) with 2"x4"s

Drill through the log with a drill-bit equivalent to the J-bolt size. Following this take a 1½" wood drill and widen the hole on top of the log to fit-in the nut size of the J-bolt plus the socket. Drill down 2" so that the washer and nut are completely submerged and will not interfere with the top layer of logs. Have plenty of seal-gasket to place between each layer of logs. Place double seal-gasket on the concrete wall as an extra precaution on the very first layer of logs; a single seal-gasket should be sufficient for the rest of logs.

Fasten your first log on the concrete block with the J-bolt and repeat this through out the entire perimeter of the house. Where two log ends meet, do not just butt the straight end up to the next log. Joining logs in this manner will allow moisture and bugs to get in. Instead, make a 45° cut on the end of one log and another 45° cut in the opposite direction on the adjoining log, to allow the ends of the two logs to overlap. You can do this with your chainsaw. Practice before hand on unwanted logs. Make your 45° joints as close as possible to prevent moisture from entering the interior of the house. Using seal-gasket in between the joins will ensure a better seal. A note of caution; do not over tie the J-bolts to the logs. Over tightening will cause the J-bolt to 'pop-up' from its concrete cavity base. Also, do not hammer in spikes too close to the 45° cut or you will split the log.

Make sure your window-frames are level and square to provide a correct guide to the log wall.

Driving 10" spikes to secure the position of the logs.

Care should be given at this point for choosing the right kind and size of sledge hammer. Choose a proper handle grip for your palm size. Both the hammer and the short wood grip handle should be of good quality. Make sure you shop around for price when ordering 10" galvanized spikes; you will be surprised at the price difference from one supplier to another.

Lay Down Your Second Layer of Logs:

Before laying down the second layer of logs, place your insulation gasket and secure it with roofing nails (nails with a wide head). Place your log in its proper position, just inside the bottom first log. Do not spike the second layer of logs. Instead, drill holes where you are

CHAPTER FOUR: Log Wall Construction

planning to drive a spike. This drilled hole should be through the second log down to the first by 4" minimum depth. The reason you need to pre-drill these holes is to prevent mortal cracking due to the close proximity of the vibrations caused by the pounding force of the hammering. Having pre-drilled holes allows the 10" spikes to go through much easier.

Keep stacking your logs and alternate the position of the joint of logs. Spike every 16" or as needed. Always have a spike in both extreme ends of logs but do not spike too close to the end of logs, you may cause a split.

As you go higher and higher stand back a short distance to look at the vertical level of the log wall. From that position, use a carpenter's level, hold it vertical, and eye-level your wall. Should your wall lean inwards or outwards, you may need to position 2"x4" supports along the walls to keep them straight. Look at the photos to see details of how this should be done. Keep adjusting as you go higher. At this point your walls are not very stable. They will remain unstable until they are joined either by the roof rafters or by interior stud walls.

Opening of the house's main door. Notice that part of the concrete blocks are removed to allow scraper to enter and exit.

Congratulations! From here on the only way to go is up!

Allow me to get off the track for a moment. There are many log builders who drill logs to accommodate space for electrical wiring. Here, I must tell you that I'm not in favour of drilling holes on my walls. There is ample space between the natural curve of the first layer of logs and the wooden floor. You may want to hide the electrical wiring in such space and place over it a decorative base-board that would look good with the rest of the house. Electrical outlets may be 'boxed-in' with decorative wooden custom made boxes.

CHAPTER FOUR: Log Wall Construction 83

Window and Door Openings:

If you live in a heavy snow area it would be wise to have a minimum of 36" of solid log wall under the window opening. At this height, snow will not be accumulated at the bottom of your window ledge. Every log home builder has a unique method when it comes to window openings during the construction of

Grading the inside ground and preparing for the concrete base of the main posts.

walls. Some prefer to build a solid wall and have the openings cut-out later. I don't. It is a waste of logs.

Instead, if you are able to plan ahead, it is preferable to position the doors and windows that are already made. If not, temporary but solid wood frames can be put in position to guide you for wall building between windows and doors; such frames must be squared, level and cross-fastened to prevent shifting from position (see pictures for details).

Building short log walls between widows and doors provides you with the opportunity to put in use all your short logs and leftovers. These short logs must be all cut to an even size and their ends cut as straight as possible to avoid having wide gaps between log wall and window frames. If possible, have someone with a radial saw cut the ends of your short logs ahead of time. By doing this, there is no need to reshape the short logs again.

As you build up your short log walls, secure each log on its side by driving a 4" nail through the temporary window frame. This will keep the frame vertically level on both sides of the frame. Failing to keep the frame vertically level, will force you to cut off and square the opening once again. This will change the original dimensions of the window opening, which, in time, changes the size of your windows.

Short logs around window and door openings must be cut to fit a keyway. This is a groove cut in the log end in which a 2"x4" or a metal keypiece (support) will fit in position. This groove or mortise can be made with a chainsaw or large chisel. The keypiece secures the opening and prevents movement.

Logs that are placed above window and door openings must be solid logs for the next three rows high. No joints should lay in the middle of the opening. This will provide an extra protection against sagging caused by the force of gravity.

The height of your window or door will be determined by whether your logs are dried (as were mine) or if settling will take place. Green log construction of log wall and windows, roof structures and staircases are affected by natural shrinkage. Keep this in mind when working around these areas. Something else: if you are ordering custom-made windows and doors with their own frames, make sure to notify the maker that yours are for log walls and not for brick walls. This means that the window and door frames will not have a brick molding around

Time to show off for Melissa and Tobby (her dog).

them. Talk to your window and door maker of quality windows. He can advise you ahead of time about the best method for dealing with tight fitting of these areas. Avoid vinyl windows. If you can, order wooden windows and doors. They are much better suited to the style of your log home.

When the time comes to remove the temporary window frames, make sure you replace them with new frames made of 2"x6" or 2"x8" to cover most of the log ends. The bottom of your window frame should be at least 2"x12" wide plank and made to tilt with an outwards slope to guide rain water away. Putting generous portions of indoor-outdoor caulking between the short logs, windows and door frames insures no moisture penetrates between them.

Log trusses suitable for a rectangular shaped log home.

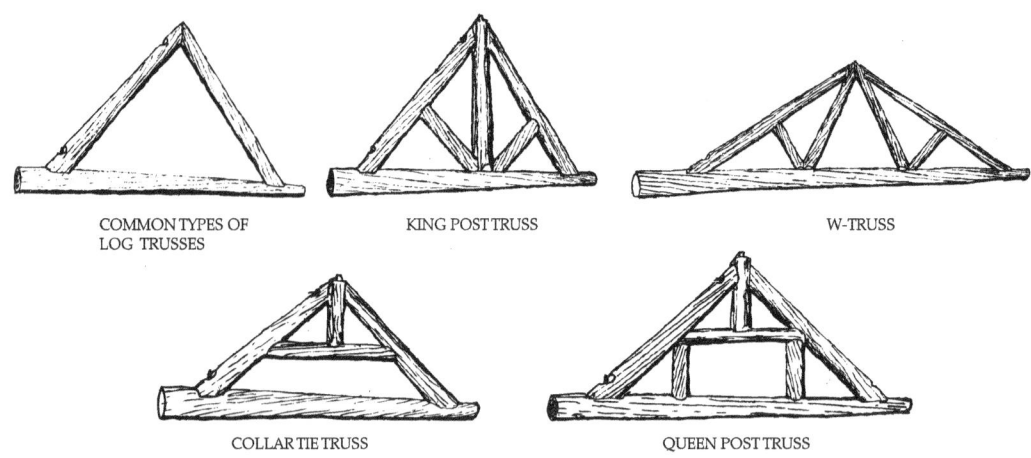

COMMON TYPES OF LOG TRUSSES

KING POST TRUSS

W-TRUSS

COLLAR TIE TRUSS

QUEEN POST TRUSS

Log walls must be strong and, at the same time, they should be esthetically appealing. Check for visible damage and split ends. Also, because cedar logs are not evenly-sized on both ends, reverse them to match accordingly. If you don't, the top of your wall will gradually start to slope up.

If a log has a bow in the center, it is better to use it for cutting into shorter pieces. Do not use long logs that have a noticeable bow; regardless how many spikes you drive into it, it will not stay straight.

Beginning of the log wall formation. Notice the pink gasket which is to be placed between the logs.

Two side square logs are not always milled exactly the same size; some variation is expected. Use extra layers of seal gasket (when possible) to compensate for differences of thickness. When you finally place your last layer of logs on top of your wall, make sure the top layer is level and even in height with the rest of wall.

Finally, take your time. And above all, keep safe at all times, especially when you are on top of a scaffold.

Sealing Corner Joints:

Special attention should be used to ensure corner logs are as close to each other as possible. Using a 2" chisel, make a

CHAPTER FOUR: Log Wall Construction

groove (female) to attach the log-tongue (male) to make a better fitting. In a two sided square log this is a relatively easy task. Scribe the shape of the log-tongue against the log end of the intended groove that is to be made and chisel out for a tight fit.

After spiking the corner log, and before you place the next on top, use caulking to fill all spaces between logs to insure that no moisture or insects will enter between them. Do not forget to place seal gasket between corner logs.

Log Trusses and Rafters:

In a race against the coming of winter season, the roof is the most important part of your construction. The sooner you finish completing it, the sooner you can rest and take it easy a little.

For a conventional log home, log trusses and purlings are the most popular style for cathedral style roof structures. Manufactured common trusses, on the other hand are considerably more expensive because they entail extra work. If you are able to use your own labour and have the good understanding of how to go about it, then the difference in money savings may entice you to give it a try!

Depending on what material is available, you may wish to build roof-trusses out of logs on the site and save the cost of manufactured log trusses. Take a look at the pictures of the kitchen roof trusses as a guide to your project. This type of log home roof trusses can be more cheaply constructed.

For a discriminating log home builder, this is the usual choice. Remember, the strength of the log trusses depends upon the firmness of the joinery; therefore, these stress points must be tight fitting in order to be structurally sound.

Lifting the main house posts. I am on top of the home-made scaffold to direct the posts to their correct location.

Log Rafters:

Some self-taught log home builders shy away from constructing their own log roof structure. Some instructional sources offer only basic information, and other sources are either overly technical and confusing or leave much to the imagination.

Here, I hope to unravel the mystery of structurally exposed (open concept) log rafters in a simple, step by a step manner.

A natural log rafter of 24' long is heavy and not easily moved around. Any work that is done on its body-structure has to be done on ground level. Roll the rafters over and rest them on two smaller logs to raise them off the ground. Uncut branches and nuts can be removed and the rafter butt-base can be leveled.

Now it is time to call your portable sawmill operator (if you have not done this job ahead of time). The aim is to have the upper longitudinal part of the rafter "shaved-off" to allow an even flat base for the roof decking to rest upon. Not all cedar log rafters share an equal diameter. It is necessary to take the average, which will allow the operator to shave an equal top surface along the entire length of the rafter. Make sure the operator shaves on the side where the hump or bow is located. The idea is to make the rafters as flat and uniform as possible.

The roof structure is subjected to two loading forces. The rest of the house walls and interior studs are subjected only to one. Vertical post and horizontal beams in the center of my log home support vertical loads. Rafters, because of their sloping, convert this vertical loading into a second force which puts stain on the walls. The amount of external loading applied to a sloped roof varies with the degree of slope.

As the roof slope increases, the snow and ice load becomes relatively less. In my area the snow is heavy at times. That is why I decided to change the slope from 4/12 to 6/12 pitch. The steeper slope makes it more likely snow will slide off the roof, reducing the likelihood of damage to the roof due to the weight of the snow.

Any and all types of open concept roof coverings can be applied to these rafters: wood shingles, asphalt shingles, steel sheeting. Remember, strict adherence to the rafter's diameter size and code requirements must be followed throughout the entire roof construction.

Main Support Posts and Beams:

The raftered roof of my log house had for its structural support 6 horizontal beams, which ties each vertical post with the next. The size of both post and beam will depend upon the loading and length (span) factors (check with the blueprints).

Under the building code, the main structural posts must rest on a 12"x12" wide steel adjustable steel plate. Bolts allow the rising or lowering of the vertical position of each of the posts. This adjustable steel plate allows for the shrinking of the log walls due to the wood drying, which is a real issue when building with green logs. The bottom steel plate is fixed and is imbedded in the concrete base under the main post, preventing it from shifting.

The concrete base of the main posts must be at least 3'x3' by 1½' deep. Positioned correctly, these concrete bases must be below the concrete floor slab. This way when the concrete slab is poured, it will secure the bolts of the plate in their permanent position. The main structural posts must rest on the center of such bases in order to distribute the overall load evenly.

Building the center scaffold that will hold the main six posts in place. Notice the concrete bases which are ready in their correct position. Melissa, of course, takes the opportunity to feel the heights of the scaffold.

Build your scaffolding in the center of the house, allowing space for each post to be inserted in that space and also to prevent accidental tilting of the main posts. The height of your scaffolding must be 4' below the beam level to allow you to work at ease. If the walking platform is too close to the beams you will find it difficult to work. Make sure your scaffolding has a safety guard all around it to prevent accidents. Your walking platform should be wide enough for you and your helper to walk with ample room.

When you are sure that your main six posts and six beams on the ground are ready to be placed in position, it is time to call your local crane operator. Last thing, place brightly coloured tape on top of the outer wall of the house where the butt-end of the main rafters will rest. Space evenly and mark the intended position, then rest the rafters on top of these coloured tapes.

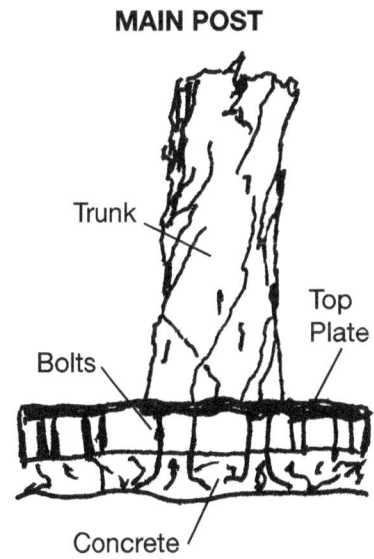

Explain to the crane operator what you intend to do. First have the operator lift the six main posts one by one and set them in place. Once in place, secure these with ropes to the platform to prevent accidental tilting. Once all six posts are temporarily in position, proceed with lifting the six beams and rest them on the floor of your platform and on their intended side. The crane operator's job is done, for now!

CHAPTER FOUR: Log Wall Construction

Once the main structural posts are in place, all within the center of the resting concrete-base, the beams will follow and you must tie one post to another. You must be very careful when you rest the beams on top of the post in order to measure and make a cut at 55° where two beams will meet. If the top diameter of the main post is 12" there will be ample space to have two beams "joint" on the post's diameter. You must cut the 55° angle to fit each corner to meet its own dimensions. This is a time consuming job, and it is advisable to have someone to help you.

When all six beams are in position, measure the corner beams angle and have special steel plates made to match this angle. These steel plates will be screwed on top of each side of the upper level. This will ensure the beams are held together firmly at the joint. You may also be able to drive 10" spike on the side of the beams to secure them on the posts top diameter. At this point you may wish to adjust the overall level (vertical) with the position of the beams and with each posts themselves. When the final inspection is done on both equal heights (from the base to the height of the beam) and the uniformity of all six main posts **(do not be off center)** you are now ready with the next step; the positioning of the house rafters.

Laying House Rafters:

Make sure that all your rafters are in the proper position on the ground and within easy reach for the crane operator to hook-up. Laying rafters is a two-person job: one on a scaffold in the center of the house and the second on a scaffold on the outside perimeter of the house. The center person's job is to spike-down the end of the rafter to the upper level of the beam. The single 10" spike will secure the rafter and will allow enough movement of the rafter to adjust its position at the outer log wall.

The perimeter person's job is to lay the butt-end of the rafter on top of the coloured tape and to make sure that the overhang is a minimum 30" length. If needed, the person on the perimeter should adjust (by raising or lowering the rafter) the overall position of the rafters on both the walls and in the center. Once he is satisfied with the position, a single 10" spike should secure the rafter on the beam temporarily. The person in the center of the house must guide the crane operator as to where the rafters will rest. Do not spike the butt-end of the rafter. Make sure to place the "shaved" side of the rafter facing upward.

The evenly spaced rafters are now secured on the wall's top log. Now, "box-in" the rafters by cutting short logs to fill the gap between the rafters at the perimeter. Keep adding logs until they are flush with the top of the rafters. You are trying to ensure that once the plywood or decking for the roof is in place there are no gaps between the rafters where moisture or insects can enter or heat can escape.

When all rafters are "boxed-in" with the short logs, begin to spike them on the wall's top plate and spike their ends sideways on the rafters. This will secure the rafters and ensure they stay in position. Next, with a commercial drill (heavy duty), drill through the butt-end of the rafter and into the top wall plate, down to 12" inside the wall. This will give you a 24" hole to place a 24" bolt, screwed and fastened on the house wall. It will prevent the rafter from rotating. Take good look at the pictures provided for guidance. Fill any space between rafters and short logs with generous caulking or spray foam. Proceed along the entire perimeter of the house. Uneven lengths of rafters in the center opening of the roof should remain as such until construction of cupola.

Steel beam provides stability to the walls against gravity. This beam was later framed with wood and drywall. Notice the lifting of rafters and the position of me in the center while Jon guides the rafter to its correct position on the top of the log wall

(Top) Steel beam tie-in support.

(Left) Let it snow...
Let it snow...
Let it snow.

CHAPTER FOUR: Log Wall Construction

EVENTS AND WISDOM

No one travels through life without learning something. How much a person truly understands depends on the person's ability to practice what he or she learns. The more you practice what you learn, the more you understand that process – it becomes part of you, not just an abstract idea.

This type of living process is not a pre-fixed prescription of how-to; it is an inner, personal experience which you can realize for yourself and by yourself. In fact, I am sure there is hardly anyone who not had this experience one way or another.

Moving to the countryside, and starting from scratch, with little money, was nothing less than a learning experience in attaining a goal; to build the best log home ever. The necessary steps towards attaining that goal could be practiced only by me. My approach may also be helpful for the mastery of your goal without seeking or expecting shortcuts and or prescriptions.

Take a look around you. We are constantly bombarded by prescriptions from how to make easy money, to find instant love, prestige and instant success for an over-inflated self-importance. We spend all our energy - and many wasted years - trying to achieve these aims. We expect success to come readily to us, while never giving a thought to making it happen. We put almost no effort or time into learning to practice fully our living process.

Once, I knew a person who could not do anything in a disciplined way unless that person was 'in the mood'. Being 'in the mood' was an amusing hobby, from one workday and the next. This person's self-discipline did not extend outside working hours. Spending eight hours a day in a most discipline way, with a task that it is best described as routine, that person was "spent", "crashed-out" or "burned-out" by the time he got home.

This person's wish for inactivity - unless he was in the mood - was a basic reaction to the stagnant routine his work forced upon him. You see, he spent eight hours a day for a purpose not of his own, in ways prescribed for him by his employer. He was not working towards his own dreams and goals. The end of the day was no different from the beginning. In short, this person's emotional life was a roller coaster, shattered, confused and lacking in focus.

This is not the case with becoming a good log home builder (or becoming good at something else of your choosing), for there is nothing routine about creating an emotion arousing hexagonal log home. Each log wall is different than the one before - even if you stack-up log after log. Each log requires your focus.

Focus is a necessary condition for anyone wanting to achieve a goal, especially if the task at hand seems overwhelming. Even more than self-discipline, focus is a condition that prevents you from leading a diffused mode of life. Lack of focus, entices us to want to do many things, all at once. Expectations for instant success, instant gratification and jumping between scattered activities, with no consistency from one to another, clearly shows a difficulty in being in control of your own destiny. This in turn prevents you and me from learning patience in the practice of living process.

I am sure that you and I have wanted - at times - to have things done all at once. It probably took many wasted hours, days and energy to recognize that doing a little of this and a little of that - in our work or studio - could not possibly achieve the desired results. Temporary lack of discipline and focus would cause us to loose patience when things were not done more quickly. We think we lose time yet, in reality, we do not know what to do with the time at hand, except wasting it with our lack of patience.

How can we achieve self-discipline, focus and patience? Should we get up with the first daylight in the morning - as our grandparents did – and not indulge in little extras, work hard and center our lives around the virtues of frugality and savings? Could this type of externally imposed discipline actually lead to a tendency to reject discipline? To make undiscipline a counter-balance to a style of life sterilized by a routine imposed upon us from the outside?

Make it your goal to create the most beautiful log home. Even if the project appears to be beyond your abilities, "go for it". If you choose this path you will not be controlled by routine imposed upon you from the outside. Your desire to achieve your goal and to become the best log house builder will be an expression of your own will. This choice will make the work feel pleasant and fulfilling. Slowly, you'll become accustomed to a kind of behaviour which, in turn, will be good for your body and soul.

It takes a great deal of effort and self-discipline to become an exceptional log home builder. Learning to focus on a task of supreme importance is beyond simply describing how to build your own log home. It is a devotion, a relationship that becomes an instrument in the practice of living process. Good luck!

* * *

For weeks, last summer, I was looking for a solution to how I would finish the ceiling of my cathedral roof. From the inside, I wanted the rafters to be exposed to give a rustic look for my ceiling.

At times, I considered using plywood as a roof covering and finishing the interior ceiling with drywall and plaster. I kept rejecting the idea of using plywood because of the triangle shape formed between rafters. While the widest span between rafters is 6", as you are building towards the center of the roof, more and more of the plywood would be cut-off in odd shapes, making the remaining material useless. At 6' space the 8' plywood would be cut-off at the center-line of the rafter to allow the next plywood space to rest on the "shaved" area. On the next piece of plywood, as the triangle narrows, the excess cut-off would be greater as you follow towards the center. In my calculation more than 50% of the plywood would have been wasted.

Another problem to consider was this; in order to dress-up the plywood from the inside, I had to use drywall sheets and carrying them up to 18' high. The measuring, cutting and accurately fitting drywall pieces between round log-rafters in a triangular space was too big of a project for a single worker. When cutting drywall-based on inside to inside measurements - the round shape of rafters would not allow for an exact fit. Hiring extra labour was another cost factor, for this task needed one person to cut drywall on the floor and two people to fit the large and heavy drywall pieces on the ceiling.

My second solution and the one I was most inclined to was to build the roof ceiling with 2"x6" cedar decking. This would give my ceiling a rustic look. It would also save me the extra cost of labour and material. I knew that I was planning far ahead (to build my roof for next spring) but I needed to have the cedar planks cut to the correct sizes and have them dry. September was coming soon, which meant the rain and eventually snow was not too far in the future! By mid September, I came to realize that I was not going to have my material for my ceiling cut and dry in time for the next building season (all because I had no spare money to buy the cedar logs needed to provide me with the lumber).

It was about this time that Ralf Kuhl came to my place. Ralf was a fence installer for local farms and was looking to buy a bush-lot of small diameter cedar trees for posts. I needed the money, so I invited Ralf to take a look at my small cedars and see if we could make a deal.

After the normal touring through my building site and Ralf's old stories about log home building, we decided to take a walk through the bush. Between walking and talking (with ideas floating back and forth) we made a deal for me to sell Ralf 3" to 4" diameter trees. We agreed to begin harvesting them next spring.

A couple of days later, Ralf returned with a written contract. It was then that I asked Ralf if he could advance me a down payment in a form of one hundred and twenty logs, 12' long with 10" diameter, instead of cash. He agreed to take me to his open air storage site to select the logs and take what I wanted. I could, he said, come anytime and remove the logs. Driving back to my place, some ten km from Ralf's, I was struck with an idea; what if I turned my new equity of 120 logs into a larger equity of lumber decking for my ceiling!

Back to Ralf's place, I asked him for permission to bring a portable sawmill and cut these logs into planks. From there, I went to find Lynn McKenzie to book his portable sawmill, still not knowing how to pay him for his work. By the time I got to Lynn's place I'd formed this idea; would he take about 40 cedar trees that I had in my place in exchange for milling 120 logs? He said yes! By the end of the next two days I had over 600 pieces of cedar decking; enough to cover my entire house ceiling. I stored and covered my precious lumber in my property, ready for the next building season.

Imagine my excitement: no plywood to waste, no drywall to cut and no extra labour to pay!

The next spring I called Ralf to remind him of our written contract. When someone else answered the phone, I was told that Ralf had decided to retire somewhere down south and that the fence business was no longer in operation! This new person knew nothing about the 120 logs Ralf had

given me as a down payment on the trees. I had received the logs I needed but had no way to "repay" Ralf with the trees he had requested.

To this day, I have never heard from nor seen Ralf Kuhl again!! He, like others, came at a moment when I most needed a solution - and left behind a good deed!

Is there a moral to the story? I don't know! ... maybe !

102 **PART TWO:** BUILDING

Chapter Five
Building Your Roof

103

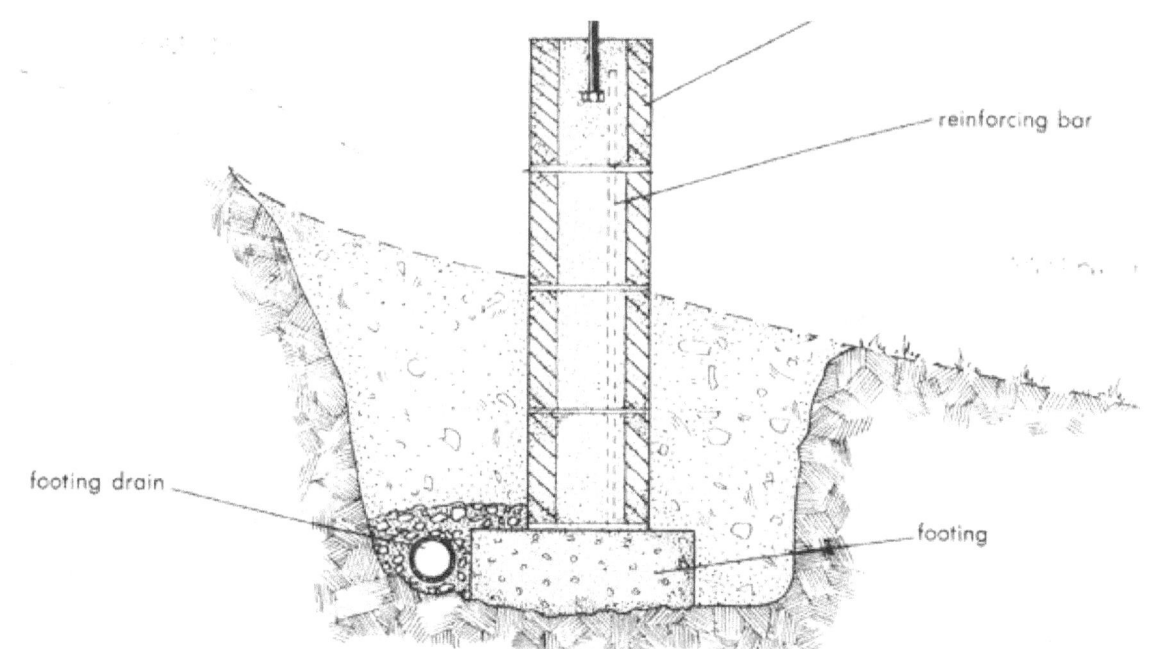

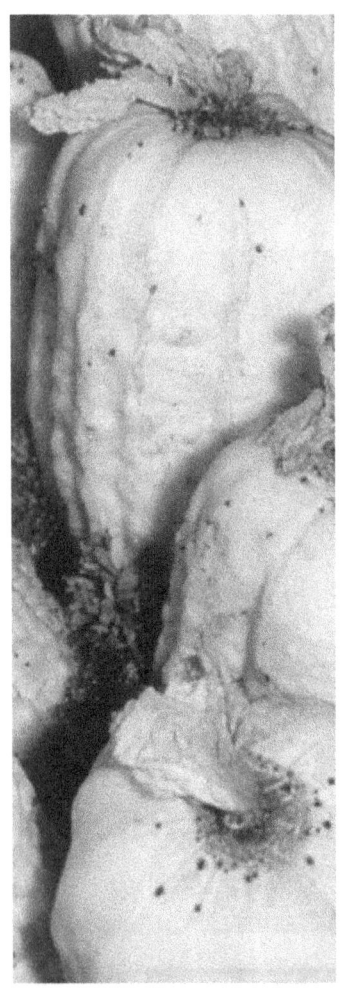

BUILDING YOUR ROOF

Start by renting or constructing a scaffold in the areas where you are planning to do your roofing work. If you have electrical power, you may wish to place a small table saw on top of the scaffold for cutting your ceiling decking.

If you have a planer, plane the underside of the decking (the side that will be seen inside the house) and bevel the edges for a better look. Make sure the decking is straight so there is not a large gap between the decking pieces which will be visible from the inside

Start by nailing the roof decking on the rafters. Finish one whole side of the hexagon. Then run a chalk line along the center of the "shaved" corner of the rafter's surface and cut along this line the extra lengths with an electric saw or chainsaw. It will make the job go much quicker to cut afterwards; the choice is yours. Make sure you do not cut any nails and ensure the blue chalk line is visible while you're cutting.

As you are building your decking closer to the peak of the roof, use the shortest pieces of decking, saving the longer ones for the widest part of your roof. You do not want to run-out of these, at the time when you would most need them. Make sure that all decking pieces are in line with the next section

Save your largest decking pieces for the widest section of your roof.

line of decking. Every once in a while, take a look from the inside to see the general direction of the lines and the degree of evenness. You don't want the decking to be slanting on one direction.

Build your roof decking close to the opening of where the cupola will be constructed. Finish the entire decking of your roof before you begin with the construction of the cupola.

When the decking is in place, it is time to put on the tar paper, as required by building code. Tar paper comes in rolls of 36" wide by 50' long. Start from the lowest point of the roof and work upwards. Do not step on the tar paper or you may rip it. As you are laying the tar paper horizontally (overlapping the next layer), nail strips of wood strapping over top of it and use these as stepping-blocks. This allows you to walk over the tar paper without damaging it.

Remember to overlap the tar paper at the hexagonal corners of the roof. Overlapping at these corners gives extra protection from moisture.

When the tar paper is in place, you may begin placing the vapour barrier, which is also required by the building code. You must do this simultaneously with the installation of the purling. Vapor barrier is a plastic sheet 8' x 50' long, which must be used to cover the entire roof. Gaps in the vapour barrier will allow moisture through and can lead to mould.

Decking over the kitchen roof: These long pieces served me well.

Since the plastic is slippery and thus very dangerous to step on, you must lay it down to only cover short sections of the roof at a time. Install the purling one at the time over the plastic sheet. Start from the lowest point at the roof and work upwards. However, if you feel safer, you can start from the cupola and work downwards. Unroll the plastic sheet near the last purling you are nailing to ensure you do not step on the plastic sheet. As you are preparing the next section of purling you should unroll the plastic sheet at the same time.

Before you start with the roof purlings make sure that you have installed the main purling which is located on the corner of the hexagonal triangle. This main purling is the section where

CHAPTER FIVE: Building Your Roof   107

Notice the short logs between rafters.

the horizontal purling would be attached on it. Remember to always walk on the wooden strips so as not to damage the tar paper.

When rafters are exposed, a roof structure must be composed of material having the required insulation value and tar paper and vapour barrier to meet standards of R-value. In some areas where roof decking is used, a rigid insulation of a required R-value must be applied to the top of the deck. Check with your local building inspector for details.

Rigid insulation can be sprayed on top of the cedar deck and overlaid with suitable vapour barrier to protect both the insulation and the roofing space from moisture damage. Wooden straps of at least 1½" square must be installed in the opposite direction of the purling, to permit unobstructed air flow between the insulation and the roof sheathing. This air flow or venting is required by the building code.

Roofs over cathedral ceilings generally require a minimum total area for the inlet and outlet vents by locating half the required ventilators on each eave.

Once strapping and insulation are in place you will want to install your roof plywood "painted" with asphalt and have the roofers finish the roof as soon as possible so that rain does not damage the insulation.

Remember that strapping is very important and serves two purposes; it provides space for air flow throughout the roof and provides extra support to the purlings. When securing strapping, make sure to place them so that the ends of plywood will land in the center of a piece of 1½"x 1½" strapping. This will allow the next piece of plywood to be nailed securely.

Construction of the Cupola

To build the cupola you must cut a straight edge along the ends of the rafters at the peak to form the cupola's desired opening. Build a base that follows the hexagonal shape of the house roof. Stud walls, complete with opening for the windows, should be completed along with the cupola roof.

Build the cupola's roof to follow the general slope of the main roof. This work must be done before the roofers arrive so that they can finish the cupola's roof at the same time as the rest of the house. Install the cupola windows now so that the entire roof will be weather proof and protected once the roofing is complete.

Roof plywood "painted" with asphalt.

Finishing the Roof

Although I am mainly a do-it-yourselfer, for finishing the roofing of your entire house I recommend you contract a professional. I feel this type of work needs experienced hands. However, if you feel you can tackle the job, go for it!

With the purling, blocking, strapping, plywood and cupola in place, it is now time for the roofers. Since roofers are very

Roof Purlings under construction.

busy and you do not want to be held up waiting for them, you must make arrangements with the roofers ahead of time.

If you are buying asphalt shingles, make sure that all the bundles have the same production number and code. Colour mixing is not an exact science - if you buy two bundles of shingles with different production numbers and codes, the same color may have a different tone or shade. Having the same production number and code will ensure an even colour of shingles. If you do not take this precaution, the finished roof may have sections that are noticeably different shades.

If your roof has a high pitch, you may consider cedar shakes. Hand-cut them by using any scrap pieces of short, 18" cedar logs. Avoid using wood shingle shakes if your roof has a low pitch. With a low pitch roof, snow will remain on the roof for a longer time. Like all wood products, the shakes will be affected by the constant moisture, heat and cold. Choosing asphalt shingles with a rustic look will provide a satisfactory appearance for a roof with a low pitch.

110   PART TWO: BUILDING

Your Gutter System

The basic function of the gutter system is to carry rain water, from both flat and pitched roofs, directly into the down pipe and then into the drain, or in some cases, drain into a well.

During a rainstorm the amount of water flowing off your roof can be considerable. It is important to channel that water away from your house walls. If you don't keep the water away from the house you will find it seeping into your concrete foundation walls.

Also, in the areas where water can be in short supply, collecting the rain off your roof can help with low water levels.

Most house builders use plastic gutters because they are light-weight, and not affected by corrosion. They require virtually no maintenance and are easily installed. Plastic gutters can be clipped or screwed to the fascia board. Visit your local supplier and follow the written instructions (see illustrations).

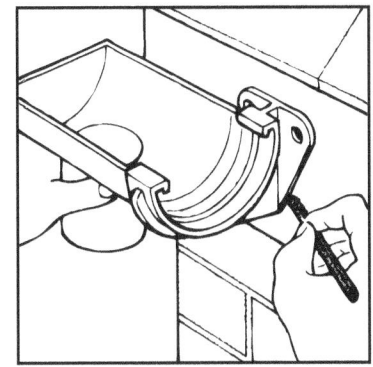

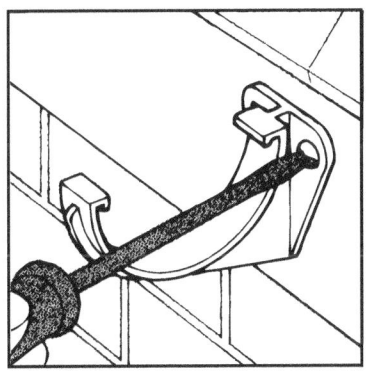

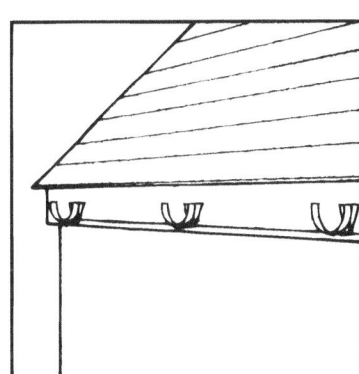

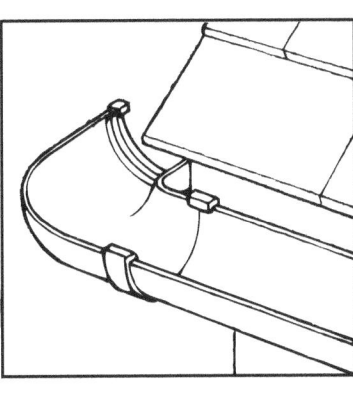
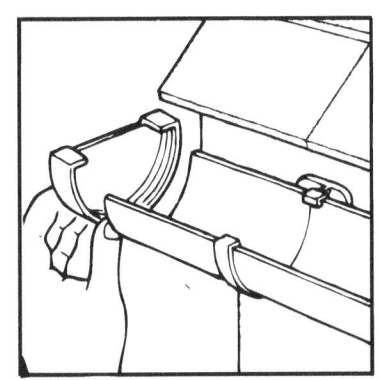

CHAPTER FIVE: Building Your Roof

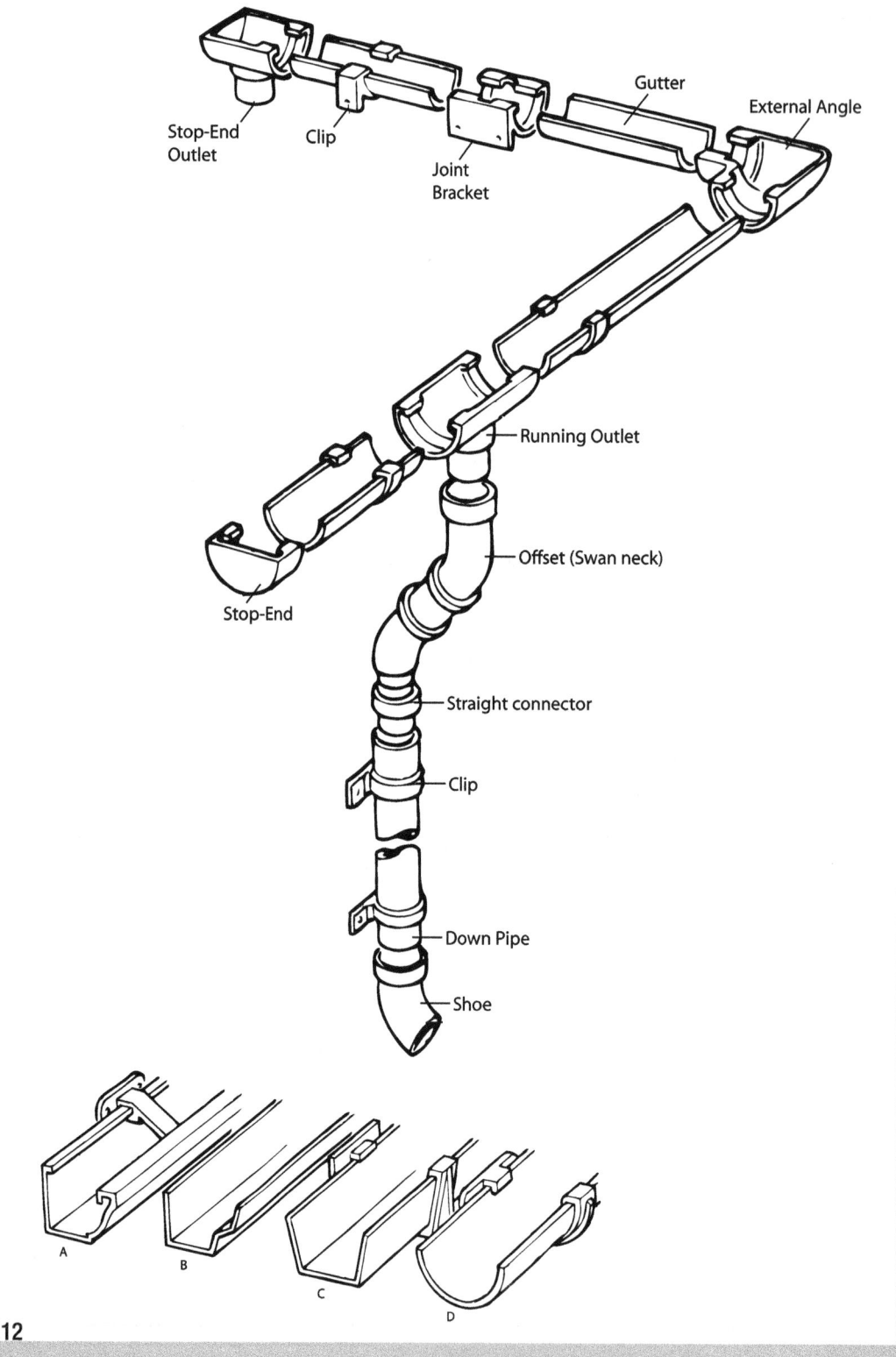

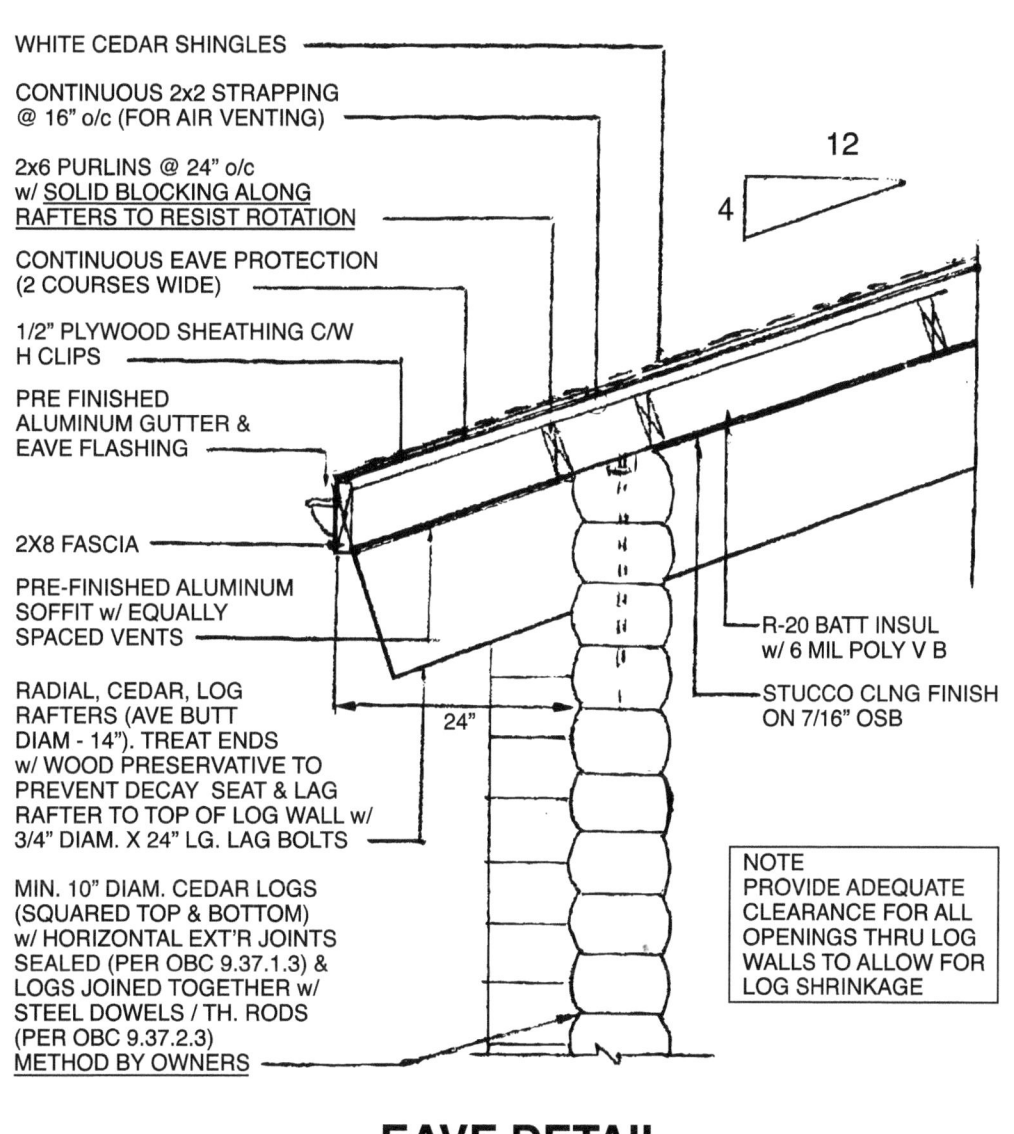

EAVE DETAIL

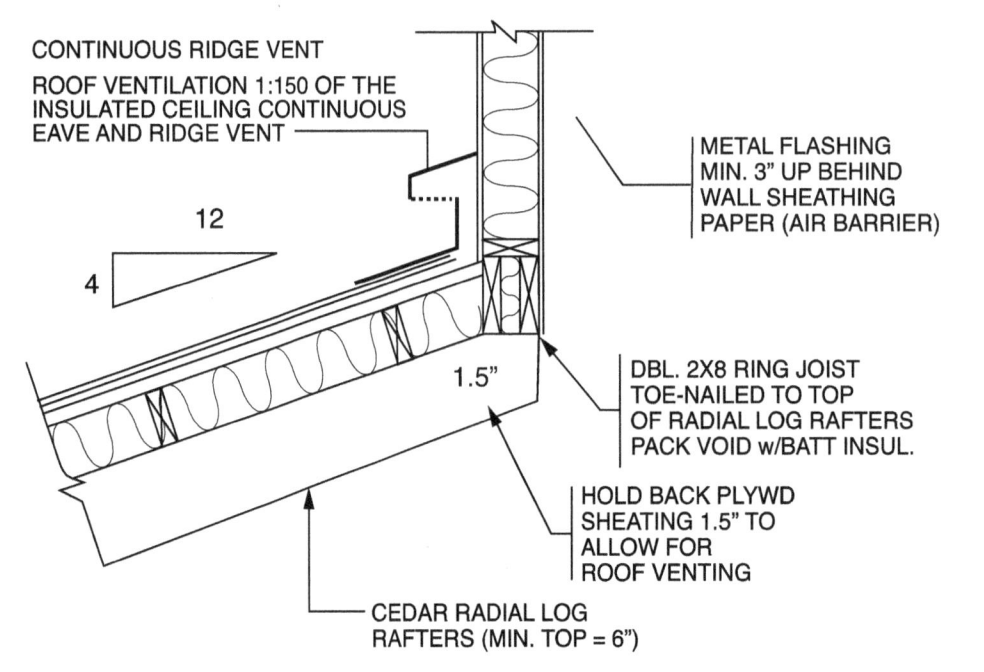

DETAIL AT CUPOLA BASE

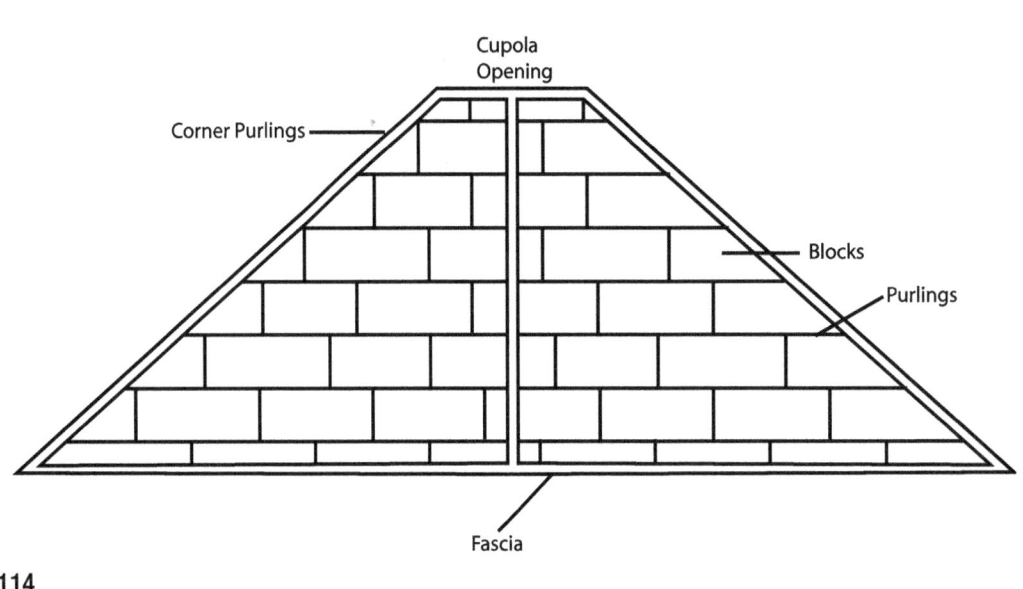

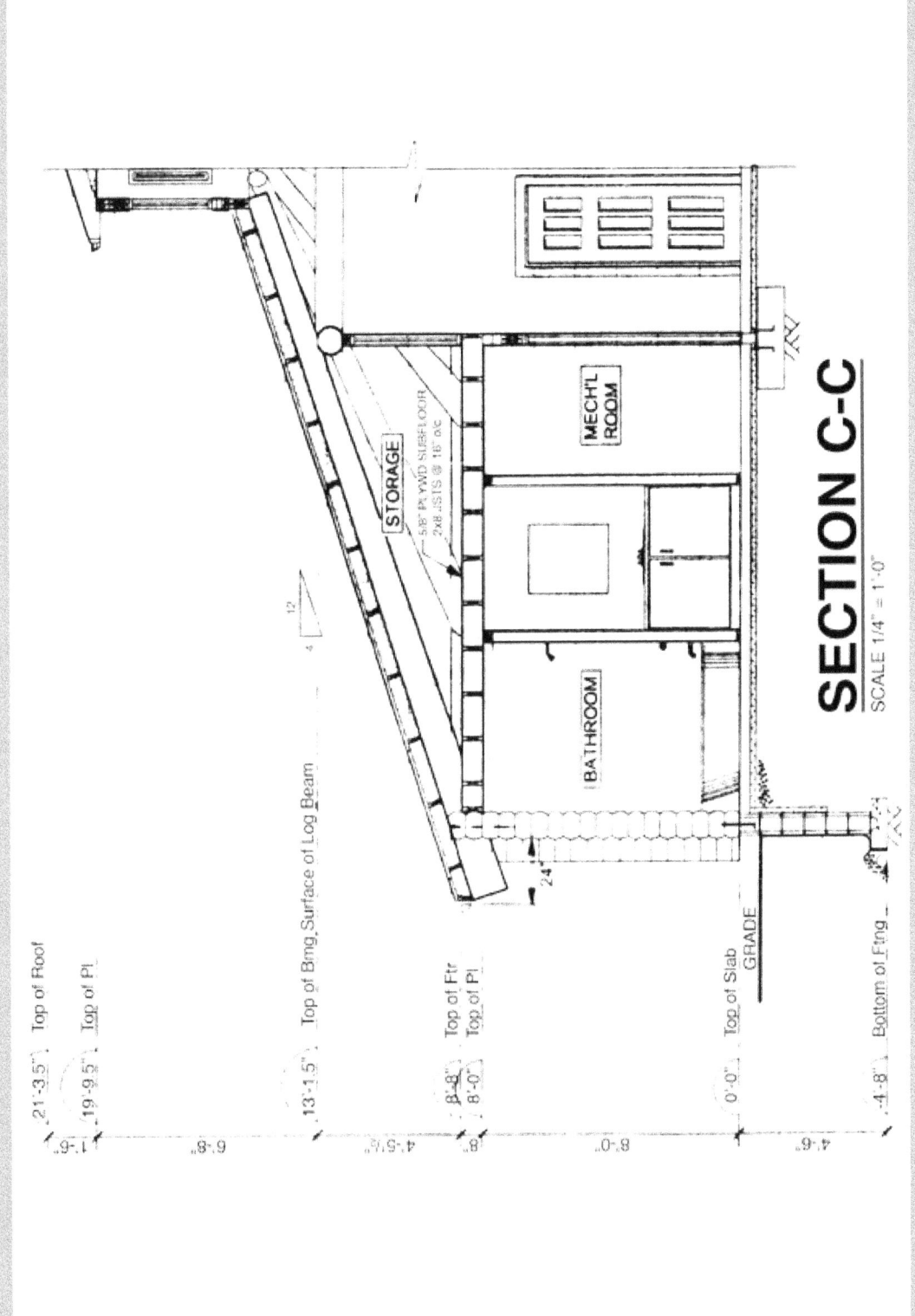

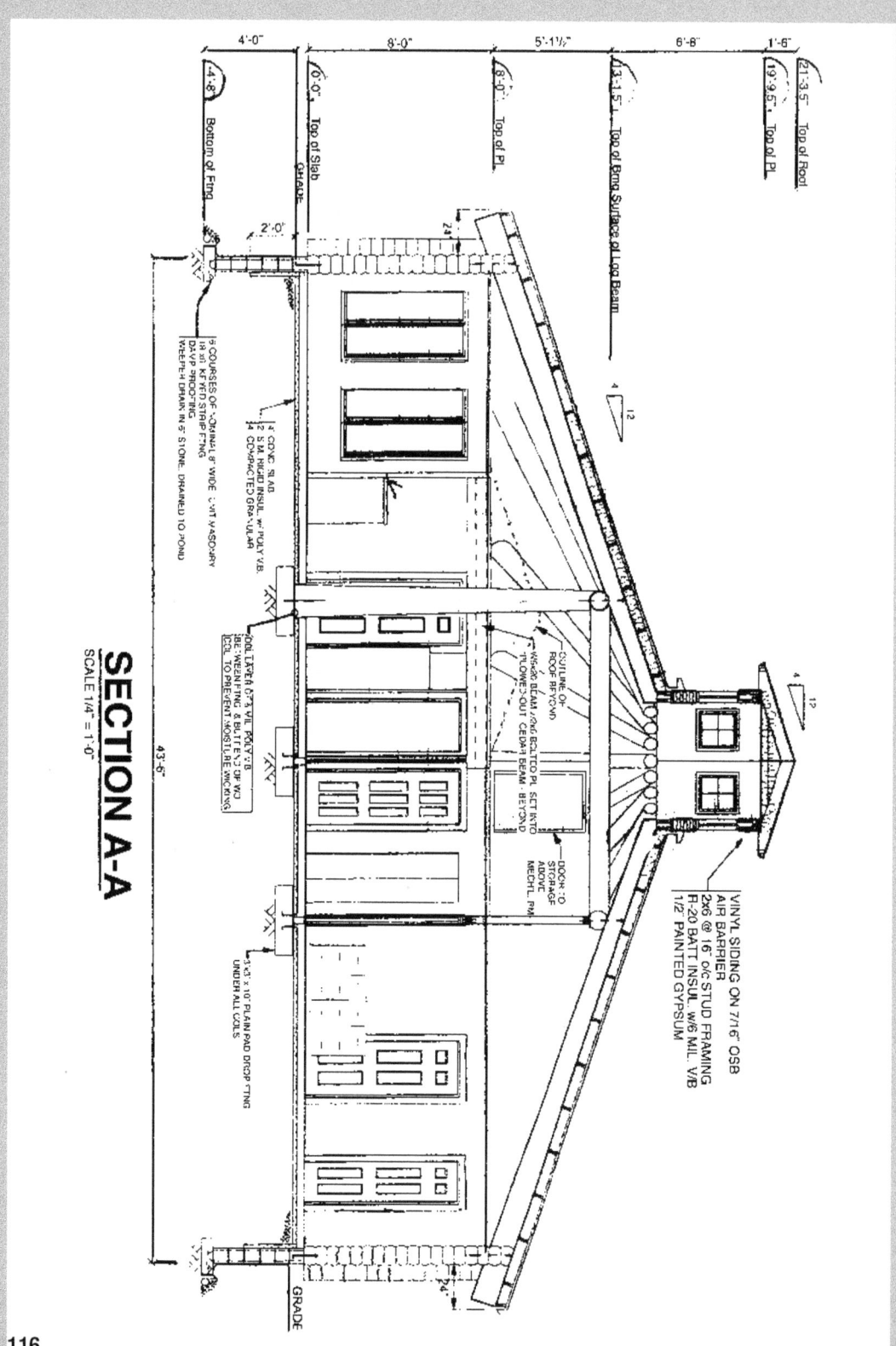

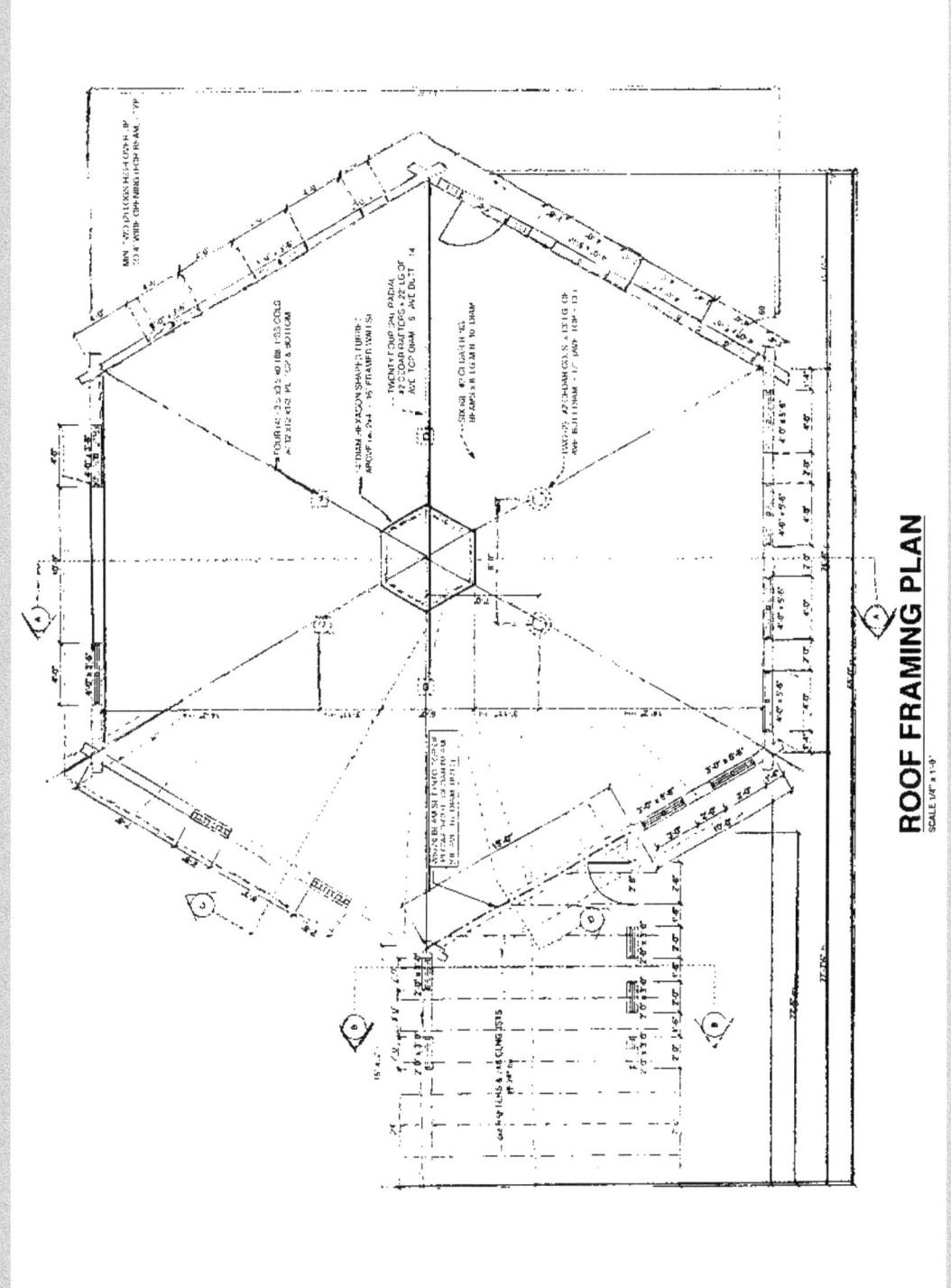

ROOF FRAMING PLAN
SCALE 1/4" = 1'-0"

EVENTS AND WISDOM

I was just about to finish with the sub-grade and was spending time figuring out the proper installation of the rough plumbing. I started visiting the big box store's plumbing section to view their model plumbing piping system. Still, I had a hard time (I'm a very visual guy) understanding the entire rough-in plumbing system with its drain, venting, hot and cold water lines and so forth. I kept asking questions and got short and fast answers from sales staff and a final advice to hire a professional! I thought to myself, "That's a good idea, but who has the money to pay for that professional service?"

I began to prepare my sub-grade with layers of sand and gravel, and had still not solved the problem of installing the rough-in plumbing. At one point, I thought about not pouring the concrete slab in the kitchen and bathroom areas until the rough-in plumbing solution was solved. Although, this would have cost me extra dollars, the idea eased somewhat my concern about the plumbing problem.

But, Ray's visit altered my plan for the better!

Ray's curiosity, like many others, enticed him to visit my construction site. He had just finished building his own stick home and had it for sale. At 70 years old, Ray was not exactly a "spring rooster" yet this man had more energy than most twenty year olds. His neighbours told him to go and see that "funny looking" house that some crazy guy was building.

Ray was very pleased to meet me, and asked if I could show him something about building log homes? I looked at him right there and made up my mind that he was crazier that I was. I said sure, stick around and I'll show you all I know.

Ray (who loved talking and advising everyone) noticed that the floor's sub-grade was finished with sand and gravel and ready for pouring concrete. He also noticed that there was no rough-in plumbing in place. Looking at the neat gravel, he asked me the location of the toilets, bathtubs, sinks and washer and so on. My reply was somewhat vague! I simply pointed the general area in question; from this reply, Ray gathered that I knew little about rough-in plumbing! Would I agree, he asked, to teach him about log construction, in return he would teach me about rough-in plumbing? Would I ever, I thought!!

We spent the next few days installing rough-in plumbing and talking about life, travel, women and how to solve the world's problems, all at the same time.

We now had the rough-in plumbing ready for inspection. I could continue from here to finish my plumbing on my own. The basic rules of plumbing; what to do and what not can be made simple. Sewer pipes must have a certain diameter, toilets and venting another; that sewer pipes must have a gentle slope to where the solid waste must travel slowly so that solids do not break down. Venting pipes must always be above water lines; that all septic pipes are placed below water lines and all white color pipes are placed outside the house towards the holding tank and septic bed.

My rough-in plumbing passed inspection. A few days later we poured the concrete slab. Ray and I have since become good friends. Some months later, Ray started to build his own log home. I helped him by lifting his logs onto the walls using my tractor. When he had finished with his log wall, I was more than satisfied with the fair exchange of knowledge and work.

It was always a pleasure to have Ray over for coffee and exchange of friendly insults, as guys normally do when they get together!

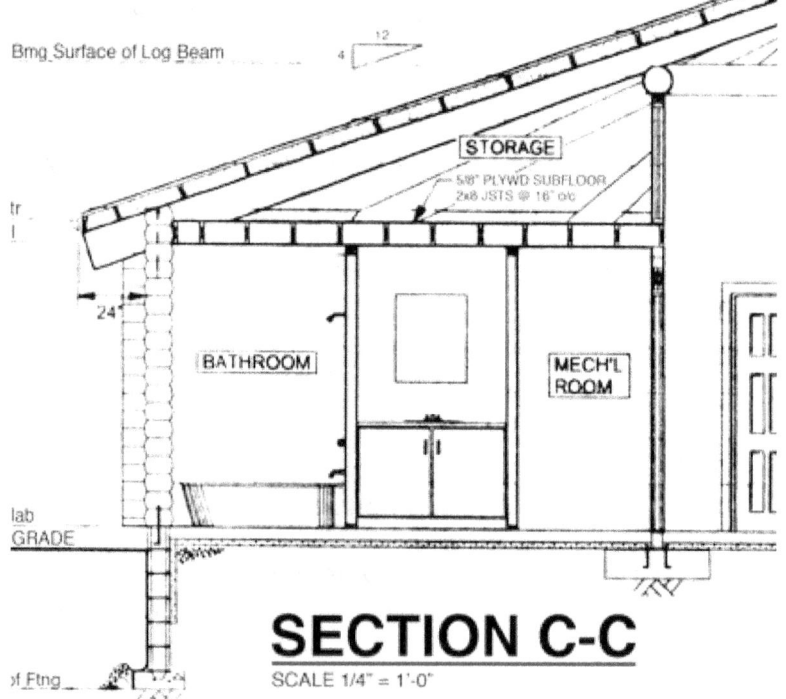

SECTION C-C
SCALE 1/4" = 1'-0"

120   PART TWO: BUILDING

Chapter Six
Inside Construction

121

PART TWO: BUILDING

INSIDE CONSTRUCTION

Most of the outside hard work was now over. The most exciting part is about to begin with the preparation of the ground for pouring the concrete slab floor.

Let us start from the beginning - from the undisturbed soil. From this level you must calculate the total height of your floor, that is, from the sub-grade, concrete slab, floor joist, to the hard wood floor or carpet. This height must end about even with the first row of inside logs.

virgin soil and add 4" sand, 6" gravel, 6" concrete slab, 6" floor joist and 2" for plywood and hardwood decking, total 24". At this height the floor level should be just under the first log on the inside wall. Floor insulation must be placed between joists.

Notice the rigid insulation around the perimeter of the foundation wall. Also the rough-in plumbing for sewer pipe. Sand, gravel and concrete will cover all of these pipes to floor level.

In cold climates you must place rigid insulation around the inside perimeter of the foundation wall. This will prevent ice-cold entering the sub-grade. Sheets of 8' x 2" rigid insulation is the material you'll need.

At this stage, outline your 'rough-in' plumbing and place pipes under the concrete slab.

To get started, on top of the soil add 4" of washed sand and level it accordingly, making sure when settling occurs it does not cause irregularities. It must be perfectly level.

On top of the sand, place 6" of washed stone (gravel), carefully compacted by tramping or rolling. Ensure this is level as well. Finally, a vapour barrier should cover the entire floor area. The building code states that in freezing climates compact 2"x8' insulation must be placed along the entire inside perimeter of the foundation wall. The upper level of this compact insulation will be at the finished level of the concrete slab itself. A hard wood floor or a carpet will cover the edge of this insulation.

For large floors, a read-mix concrete truck should deliver your calculated amount of concrete. A 6" concrete slab should be ordered. Be sure to specify what the concrete is intended for and order at least 10% more than the estimated load. Provisions for utilities for plumbing lines under the concrete slab and connections to such lines must be brought to the desired point (location of toilets, bathtubs) above the concrete floor. Rough plumbing work must be complete prior to the time of pouring the concrete slab.

Pouring Ready Mix Concrete

Plan ahead to synchronize your time with the time the concrete truck will arrive. The day of the pour, the truck is likely to be late, so don't panic, for it always happens. When the truck arrives, explain to the operator what exactly you want.

Make sure, if you are doing the pouring and directing the work-load, that you have eye contact with the truck operator to direct him when to start and when to stop pouring. This is important especially if you are pouring by using a belt or pump. You do not want to have a great amount of concrete in one side (or spot) when you do not need it. If you calculate the volume of concrete as closely as you should have, the last thing you want is to waste it!

A critical aspect of pouring concrete in large areas is to make sure that no spaces are left unfilled in the walls or around posts. The concrete must be vibrated so it settles everywhere. There are several methods of vibrating: by electrical vibrator, by tapping the sides of the forms with a hammer or packing the concrete from the top with a 2"x4" attached to the end of a stick.

CHAPTER SIX: Inside Construction 125

After the concrete has cured, you can hand-pack mortar into spaces that were difficult to fill while pouring. Have someone with experience help with the pouring. But remember, pouring concrete is not rocket science - you can do it yourself with the help of a few hands for that day!

Remember to mark (with a brightly coloured paint) the level of the concrete slab all along the perimeter of the foundation wall. For the center level, use a 10" spike in the gravel, to mark the 6" depth of the concrete floor. When you reach that desired level, start pouring in the next area.

When pouring over rough plumbing, make sure that you do not move the position of the sewer pipes!! Let the concrete cure and when it has hardened you can proceed with the next task; building your floor joist.

Floor Joist and Insulation

You have now installed your rough plumbing and your concrete slab has cured. You are now ready to construct your floor joist, place the insulation material and install the floor covering.

Floor joist with compact insulation.

Compact floor insulation of 4" was cut to measure.

Whether the floor joist rests on concrete slab or on the stud walls slightly above the slab, its elements are the same. Joists are typically 2"x6" or 2"x8", laid out on 12", 16", or 24" centers and nailed on the edge. They are held in place on their ends by 3" nails to the plates on a perimeter joist and thus, are blocked in between. The same principal is equally similar with roof purlings and stud walls.

Using blocking (same as the roof purling blocks) stabilizes a floor, a stud wall or roof purlings, preventing the joists from twisting over time. If you omit this step you may find the floor eventually becomes uneven.

Check that all joists are straight and all are the same size. Start building your joist, meeting the building code as far as size of material used. Secure the joists and level the entire section you are building. Make sure that the joist sits solidly on the concrete slab.

Notice any up or down movement as you step on it? Correct any deficiencies by placing a wedge under the joist without changing the joist level. If movement still occurs, place a wooden block next to the joist and drive concrete nails through the block and afterwards secure joist onto the block using 3" nails. Place compact insulation between joists, with additional insulation around the perimeter of the floor where the cold from the outside will be felt more.

The last element of any floor joist system is the material (plywood or decking) used on top of it which adds a structural continuity to any wood floor. The choice of material and how to apply it is yours.

Using tongue and groove plywood, cover the section you are finishing now. Now that you know how to do one section, you may want to finish with the whole floor.

Before you finish your floor in the kitchen and bathroom with plywood, make sure that all the plumbing that goes under the floor is completed. You should now have all the black pipes coming through the floor as well as any water lines. If the rough plumbing is not completed as yet, leave the plywood on the side and start making your outline and layout of your water supply lines.

At this stage, plumbing requires careful planning. For air venting and drain pipes, it is best to place them on top of the concrete slab. By cutting off sections of the joist you can fit these lines within the floor system. Furthermore, these same lines will be placed in the stud walls for proper installation. Venting pipes can also be fitted within the wall system all the way to the roof.

Layout for Stud Walls

Once the floor is finished, clear all garbage from the plywood floor. This way you can see the chalk lines on the floor for easy identification. Doing a layout before hand increases the speed and accuracy of framing. The blueprint is simply an abstraction of the interior wall to be constructed. The layout translates your blueprint into a full size set of templates, the top and bottom of each interior wall on a specific level of the house. The section then can be cut and framed.

Within each framed section the builder has to deal with wall height, location of doors and windows, corners and partitions. Study your blueprints and note the information you need to determine the best section to begin building. You are now in position to make any changes on the floor plan, and note these on your blueprint. In my case, I altered the plans to include the steel spiral staircase.

Mark a chalk-line on the floor to position where every wall will be framed. Next, cut the lumber for the top and bottom plate for each wall. Use a square and plumb to make your job and that of the dry waller much easier.

Where possible, do the layout of the interior walls all at once using a chalk line. Cut and fit the plates against each other and you can be sure that the partitions will be done correctly. Any changes can be done now **before** the walls are put together and become troublesome.

Stud Walls

Studs are normally 2"x6" on 16" centre and provide the nailing surface at regular intervals for interior or exterior finishings – such as drywall, decorative material and siding. In most cases, studs provide an avenue where electrical wiring and water pipes can be installed.

The emphasis with framing is accuracy. Speed, or course, is no less important; speed, however has to dictate a certain level of care. The problem

CHAPTER SIX: Inside Construction

created by sloppy framing – studs that bow in or out, walls that will not plumb up and rooms that are out of square – have to be dealt with later when a new layer of material is added. At this stage, it requires little problem-solving since most of the thinking has been done at the layout.

As long as the layout is done with care, nailing together and raising the stud wall is relatively easy. Start with the back walls of the interior, avoiding having to overcome obstacles. Plumb your walls as you are building them. Start at one end of the house and work your way through. You will develop a good sense of order as you go, and not long after the remaining walls will be nearly plumb. The stud walls will begin to become rigid and act as a unit. Check all your corners for straightness; this precaution means that when the time comes for you to do the drywall, you will not have to do multiple measurements and worry about your walls being out of plumb.

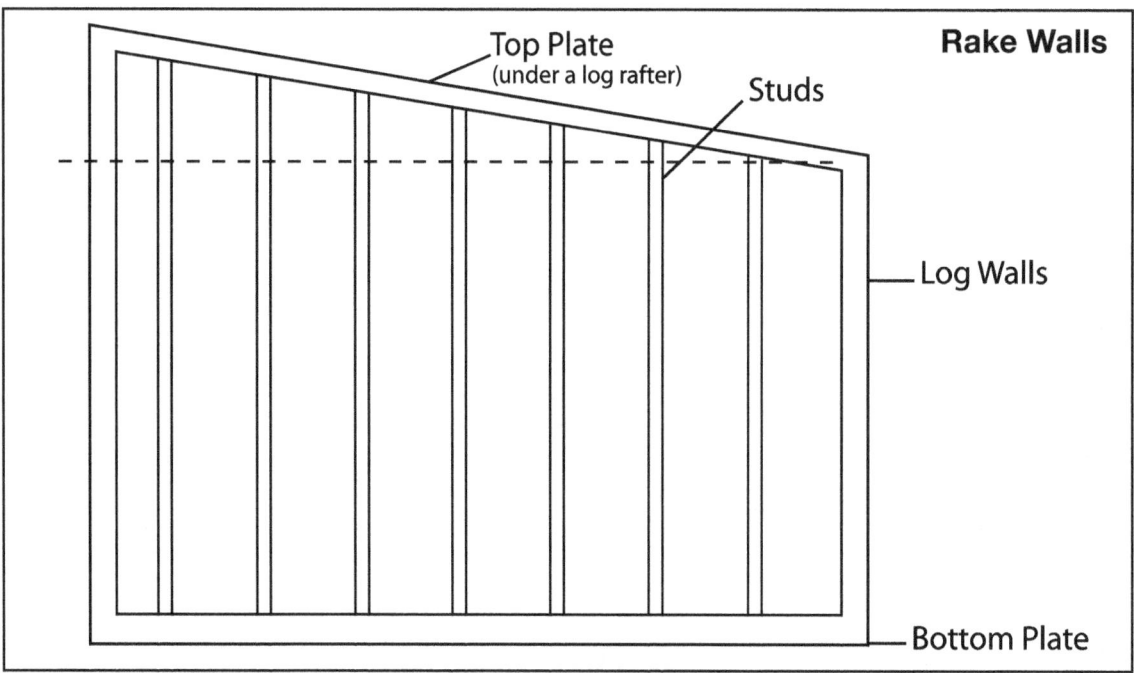

Rake Walls

Rake walls, also called gable-end walls, require the framing to fill in up to the bottom of the pitched rafters. This means, that each stud will be a different length and will be custom cut at the rafters' pitch. Typically, a log rafter will sit on the top plate of the rake walls. Beginning at the lower end of the interior stud wall it can be built as one unit with continuous studs of different lengths.

Rough Door Opening (Interior)

The building code requires that door openings have headers to shift the weight of the roof in that area to both sides of the door. This is called structural section. My stud walls are non-structural because they do not carry more than their own weight. The center posts and rafters are structural because they support the entire roof structure.

Rough door opening is the rough-opening width, measuring between the trimmers, by the rough-opening height, which is measured from the floor to the bottom of the header.

To determine the height of trimmer requires you to work backwards; from the dimensions of the size of the door. Followed by the width of the door-frame, the rough opening height must be about 4" from the height of the door. The same measurements apply with the rough-opening width. The door trimmers should be framed very plumb.

To recap then, interior construction begins when the log walls (shell) and roof has been completed. Roughed-in

plumbing, concrete slab and wooden floor is in place; weather protection is placed over your outside door and window openings. To have a well proportioned partition, it is important to do some careful measuring and make adjustments before you start building your interior walls. Use a chalk-line and mark where your walls will land. By simply erasing the chalk-line you can easily make adjustments. **Chalk lines must represent the inside or the outside of the stud walls, not the center.**

If you are building your stud walls on top of the concrete slab (instead of on top of the floor joist), place insulation gasket similar to the one between the logs, directly under the lower plate. This will prevent wood decay caused by the concrete's moisture.

Many builders make this fundamental mistake when it comes to some basic prevention. The concrete slab takes many years to completely cure and harden. It will be wise to place an insulation gasket under your wooden floor joist as well. Finally, have all interior layouts chalk-lined on your floor, or slab, and then take time, if needed to reconsider your options.

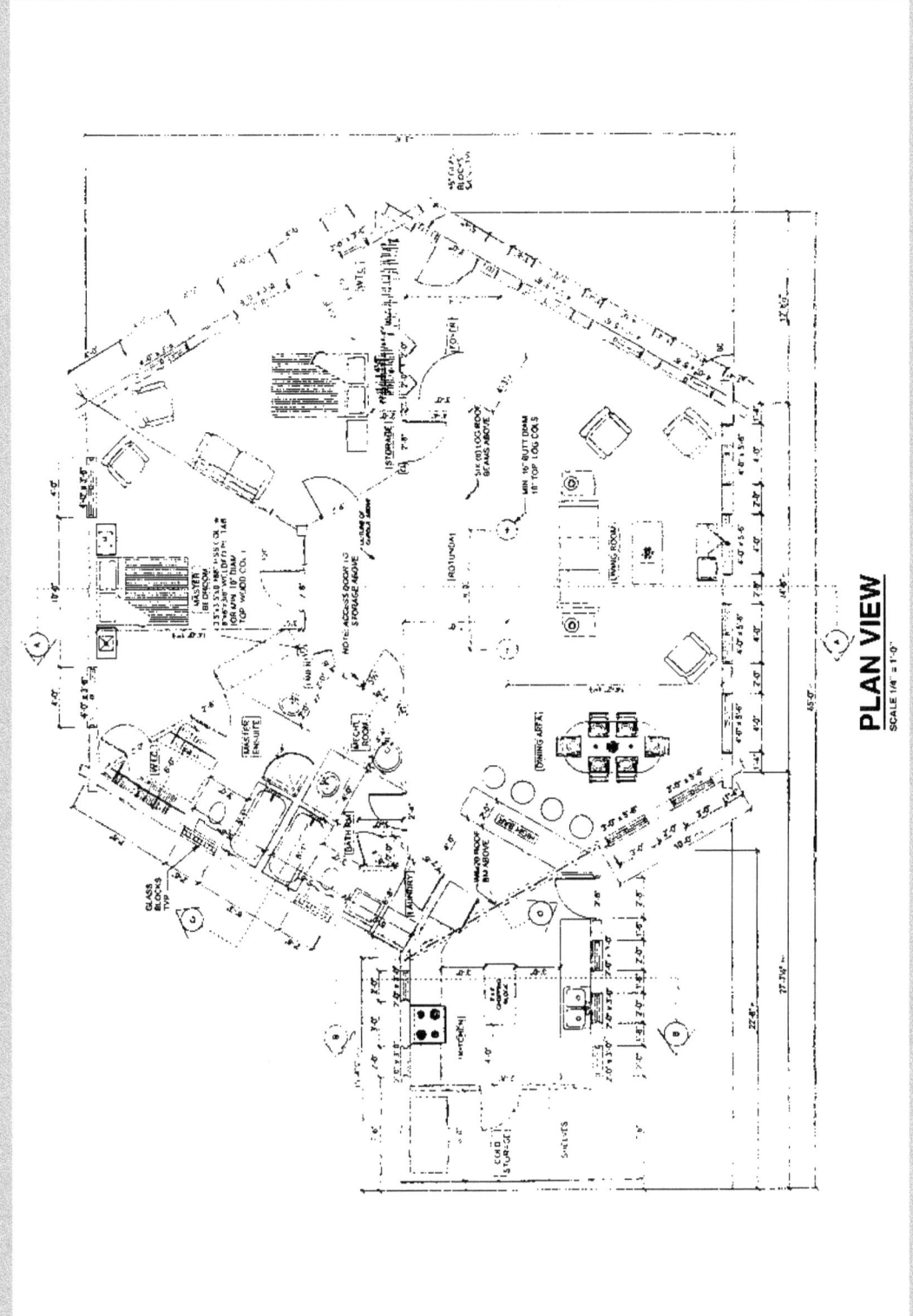

PLAN VIEW
SCALE 1/4" = 1'-0"

EVENTS AND WISDOM

My problem, as usual, was the constant shortage of money. Insulating the entire house floor with compact insulation was an expensive proposition. I needed 150 pieces of 2'x8' sheets at $23 each. This would cost $3,450 an amount that I didn't have. My only consolation was that I still had about 45 days before I needed to solve this problem.

Not long after, I was driving on Highway #10, not far from Markdale, Ontario, when I noticed a large industrial reconstruction site of an ice cream distribution center. Workers were taking apart the insulated floors to expand the freezer area. These were the large freezers where ice cream was stored before distribution.

Instantly, I noticed a large pile of pink compact insulation located on the inside of the construction site. I asked the workers what they were planning to do with the insulation. They were waiting for the dump trucks to remove the stuff. I asked if I could have it and was directed to the foreman. When I found him I was told I could have it all as long as I took it before the dump trucks arrived. The price: a bottle of booze.

I only had a few hours to remove the insulation. I drove as fast as I could to find Ray with his van. He agreed to help transport it. For the next two hours, Ray and I made five trips in his van loaded with insulation. We made sure to collect the best 2'x8'x4" compact insulation.

Tired from loading and unloading, I'd made my final trip to the liquor store to buy the man's whiskey! By this time I've forgotten the brand, so I chose the one with the best looking label (I should tell you that I do not drink at all). When I delivered it to the foreman he said, "You know, when I saw you driving away with your last load I thought I would never see you again! But here you are with my booze. You are a gentleman!" I was surprised he even thought that I would skip out on 'paying' him.

Total cost for the insulation came to $85 for gas and whisky! I now had all the necessary insulation for my entire floor of my log house. It turned to be a fine day after all!

* * *

The second winter had come and gone; April was a welcome sign of better things to come as well! I was beginning to recover from an accident that I suffered last September. My foot was placed in a solid orthopedic boot to keep it in a fixed position. Still, at least for a while, I could not put a load on it; it simply could not take it. A walking stick provided some stability which I very much needed.

I was hoping things would speed up a bit. I had all my lumber - for my floor joists and stud walls - ready and dry since last August. The only draw back was my injury which prevented me from going up or down the step ladder. Here I was where I could finally put my work experience as a framer-carpenter to a good use. Soon, I needed to start with my partitions. By now I had all the necessary tools and electrical power to do the construction, and all I needed was someone to work with me to finish with the interior of the house.

Chances of finding a good helper at this time were slim to none. In my area, you must book contractors and helpers, landscapers and plain labourers well ahead of time. Also, construction workers tend to go back to the same contractors each year. Due to my injury, I was not on top of my game when it came to looking for helpers! By the middle of May I still had not found someone reliable.

I began visiting small towns and villages in my area, offering tradesmen free transportation and free lunch, but nothing changed my position. Doing as much as I could did not advance the construction of my house. My frustration was now getting the best of me!

One day I looked up and asked "Who the heck is driving up towards my house?" The visitor was approaching and I was not in the mood to play host and give a tour to another stranger.

The young face was somewhat familiar but I could not place from where. "Hi!" he said, as he approached. "Do you remember me?" Politely, I said that I've seen him before but could not be sure. "I'm Joseph Trudell," he said. 'Dave's son!"

I had not seen young Joseph for quite a while. He turned out to be a 6'2", 180 lbs, 16 year-old robust young man. I remembered that his younger sister Laura and my daughter Melissa were classmates. Joseph's father, David, was the architect who had made the blueprints for my log home.

Well, young Joseph was looking for work in the construction industry to get some experience, and he was willing to work after school and weekends, going fulltime when school finished for the summer!

Good God, I thought where do "they" come from when I most need them?

As it turned out, Joseph was a conscientious helper who did more for me than one would expect from such a youngster. We began work the following weekend. Step by step, I guided Joseph through every aspect of construction work; from stud walls, dry walling, to flooring and insulation. Joseph proved to be a fast learner and a good worker. When he paid no attention to my instructions, it was because I tended to over-explain things to a point of confusion.

It was, basically, Joseph and I who built the whole of the interior of my house; and he worked with me until the end.

It was about this time, when Joseph and I were putting up our stud walls, when Ray came up with the good news that he had sold his house. He had to move out within 30 days. His intentions were to build a small log house in a lot not far from mine. As things were, I told Ray that he could move into my trailer and use it as a temporary shelter until he is able to move into his new house.

Ray's visits became more frequent. He got along well with Joseph, although he tended to over advise the youngster. It was something to look at a 72 year-old, opinionated man, and a 16 year-old, exchanging ideas about construction methods, plumbing and electrical solutions.

It was through one of these verbal exchanges that I learned that Ray had done his own electrical wiring in the house that was just sold.

A week before Ray had to move out of his house, he came with a better solution to my offer; in exchange for my trailer, he would do my house wiring - all I had to do was supply and pay for the material. Since my knowledge of wiring was limited I agreed (with no additional delay) to the barter. Both Joseph and I helped Ray with the rough-in wiring; drilling holds and passing wire through the studs.

I was beginning to believe that "Living Angels" do really exist!!

138 PART TWO: BUILDING

Chapter Seven
Interior Finishing

INTERIOR FINISHING
Plumbing

The basic rule of plumbing (a professional told me) is to remember that "human waste runs down hill and pay day is on Friday." This means - I think - that plumbing is not too difficult to install.

Plumbing in a log home is the same as in any other type of conventional home, large or small. First, is the rough-in plumbing - the main system of disposal of human waste passing through it; with it comes the installation of the ventilation system.

Second, is the installation of water lines - hot and cold - connecting the household to main water supply source and the supply of hot water.

Plumbing work requires careful planning. Venting pipes and water lines are best placed within the stud walls. You can save money if you align the kitchen and the bathroom back to back, using a common stud wall and single set of lines to serve both areas. For second floor or basement, the plumbing lines should be located above or below each other.

Strict building codes govern specifications of drain, vent, and water lines. P.V.C. plastic drain and venting lines are the

CONVENTIONAL DRAIN AND VENTING LAYOUT

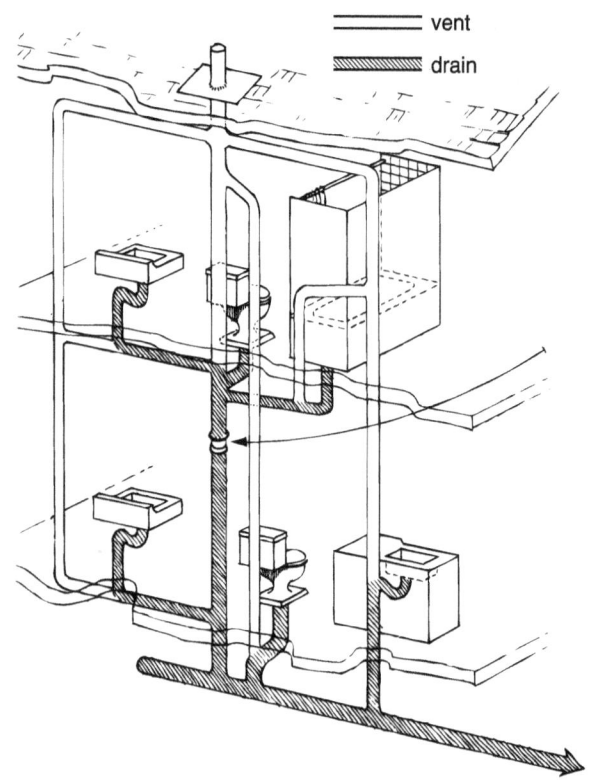

CONVENTIONAL HOT AND COLD WATER LINES

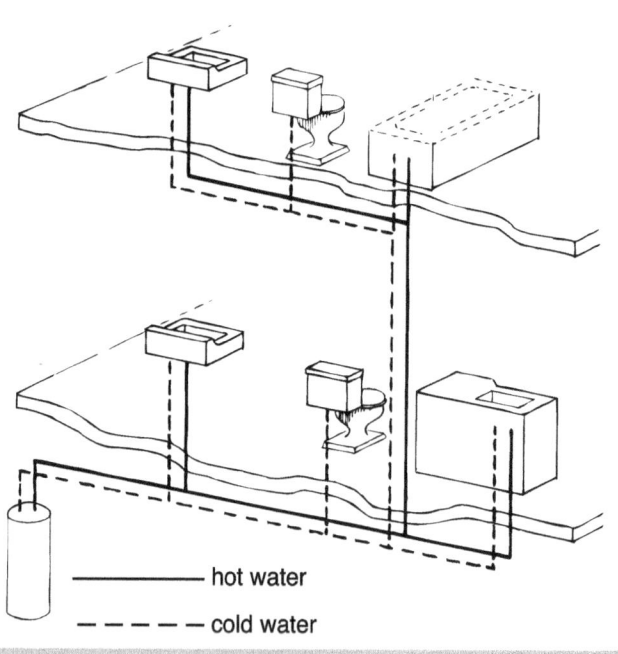

black pipes used within the house and under the concrete slab or sub-flooring. A.B.S. plastic pipes - white in colour - are used for an underground septic system.

The acceptance of P.V.C. plastic pipe as a plumbing material has dramatically increased the number of people who can install their own plumbing. For the budget minded, this means a large savings. Of course, having a well functioning drain, venting and water system, depends on how well you can do the cutting and joining of pipes and fittings. Take your time; all depends on approaching the task at hand in an organized and professional manner.

Joining P.V.C. (Black) Plastic Pipe

Plastic P.V.C. pipes come in 12' lengths and are light enough for one person to handle. Using a common hand-held saw you can cut the pipe at desired length. Once this is done prepare the fitting (figure 1) for joining. Remember, because the fittings and pipes are joined with a fast-drying solved cement, you can not adjust them after they are set.

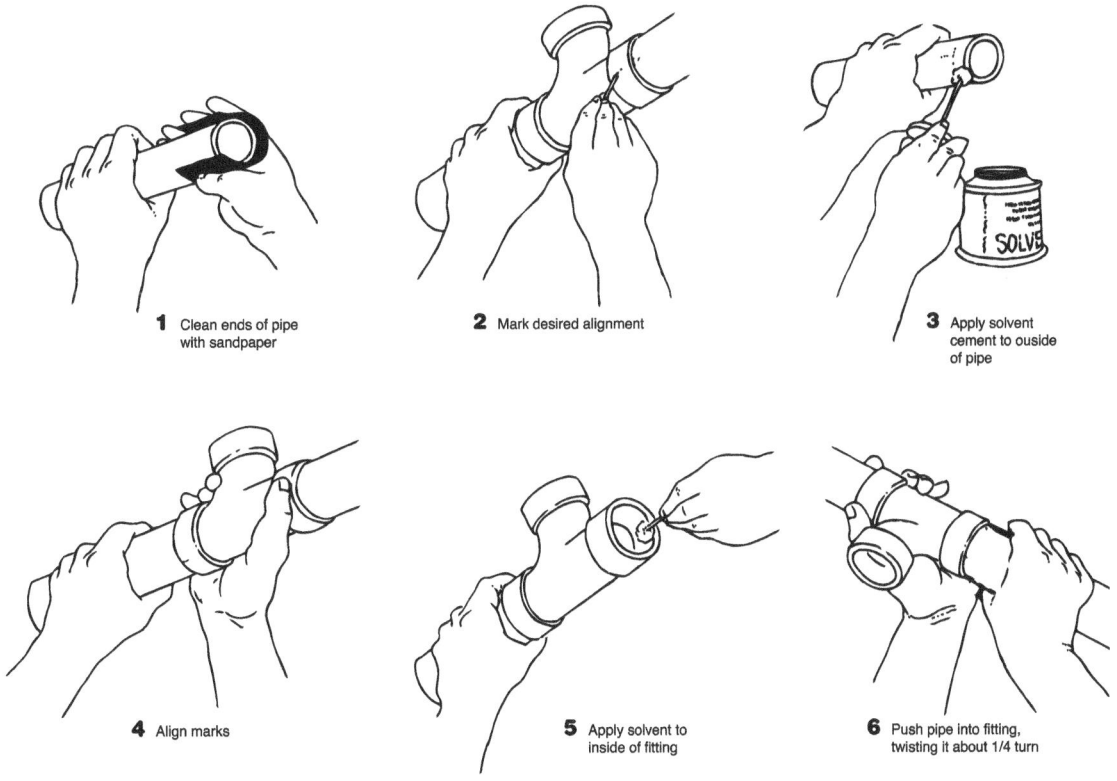

1 Clean ends of pipe with sandpaper

2 Mark desired alignment

3 Apply solvent cement to ouside of pipe

4 Align marks

5 Apply solvent to inside of fitting

6 Push pipe into fitting, twisting it about 1/4 turn

CHAPTER SEVEN: Interior Finishing

Venting

Venting pipes can be positioned vertically or horizontally. Toilets and showers normally have vertical venting while sinks may connect to vertical pipes with a horizontal one. Under a floor, horizontal venting will rise through the stud wall connecting to main venting pipe leading to the roof. Venting pipes located on the roof should not be too close to the skylight or a roof window because sewer gases may enter the house through those openings.

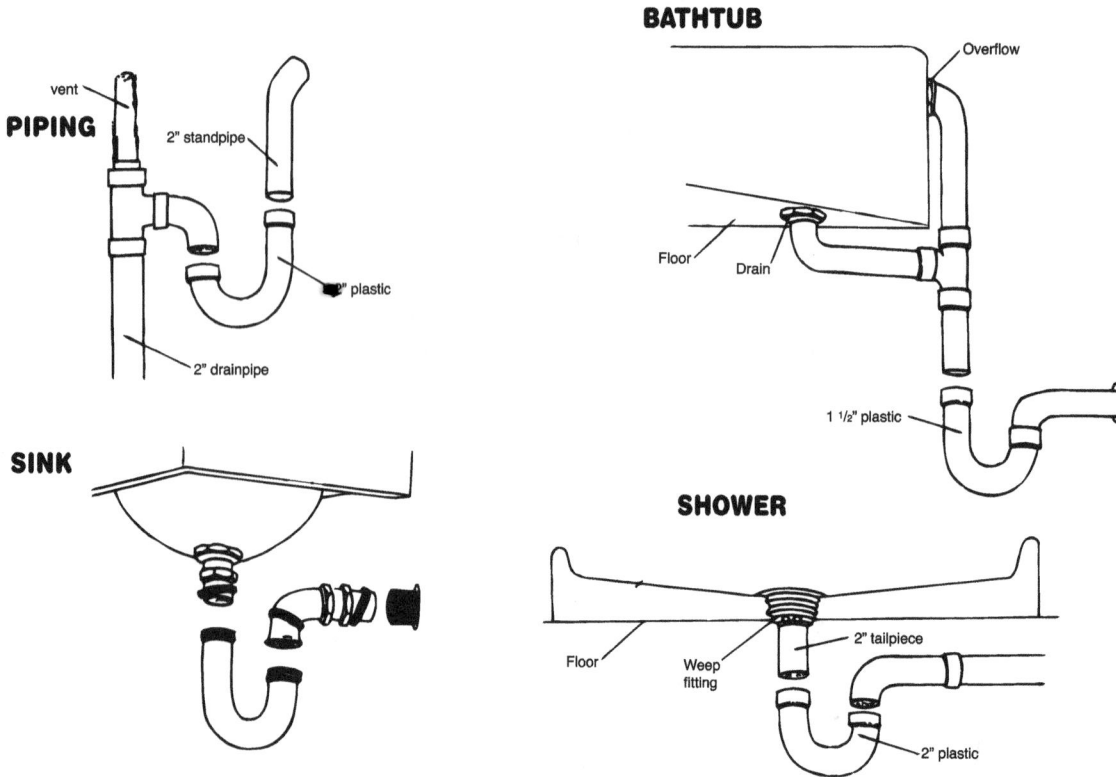

U-Traps

The primary function of the U-Trap is to keep the sewer gases from entering your house by keeping water level in the pipe. Instead, gasses are forced to exit through the venting system into the roof. A U-Trap is and must always be full of water because it takes a dip downwards thus 'trapping' water every time water runs through.

A U-Trap can be of 1½" of diameter, but you must check with your local building code for your requirements.

Installing Your Sump Pump

By building code all homes with a basement or crawl space must have a sump pump installed. The sump pump discharges water out of a flooded basement preventing damage to home equipment.

The most popular style of sump pump is the vertical one consisting of a raised motor that does not make contact with water. A sump pump operates automatically. It does not require a switch to turn it on when it is necessary.

If you have a building lot that retains water and you are planning to build a basement, you may be faced with a regularly flooded basement. In this case you may want to connect the sump pump into a set of back-up batteries. The sump pump, since it is electrical, will not work during a power failure, which is likely when you will need it most.

To make life easier, plan the location of your sump pump. Preferably it should be close to the pressure tank and main water lines, where floodwater will be pumped out quicker. Before pouring your concrete slab in your basement, place a

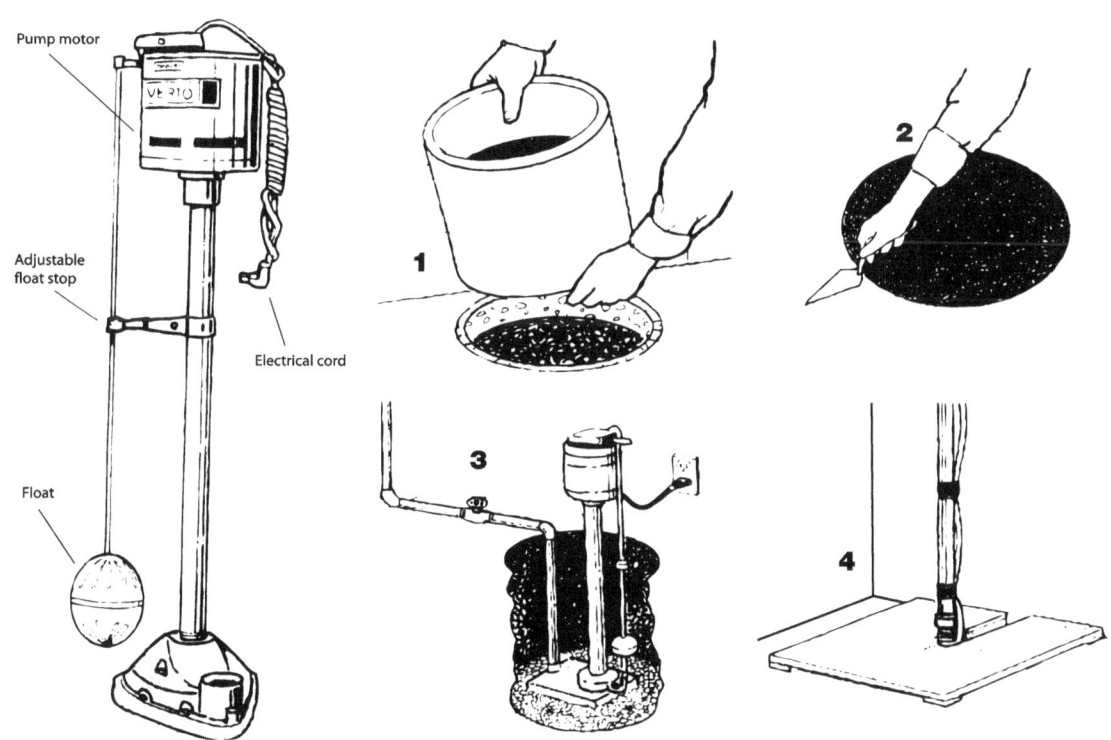

CHAPTER SEVEN: Interior Finishing

wooden forming where you plan to position your pump. If you decide to install your pump later, you will not have to use a jackhammer to open the required hole.

When the sub is dug at about 24" place a sub-liner in the hole (figure 1). Finish the edge of the sub-liner with concrete making sure to level the inner edge so that the water will flow towards the hole (figure 2).

When the time comes, place the pump into the sub and connect the discharge pipe and plug into electrical outlet (figure 3). Make sure that the discharge pipe has a check-valve to prevent water from backing up and flowing into the sump.

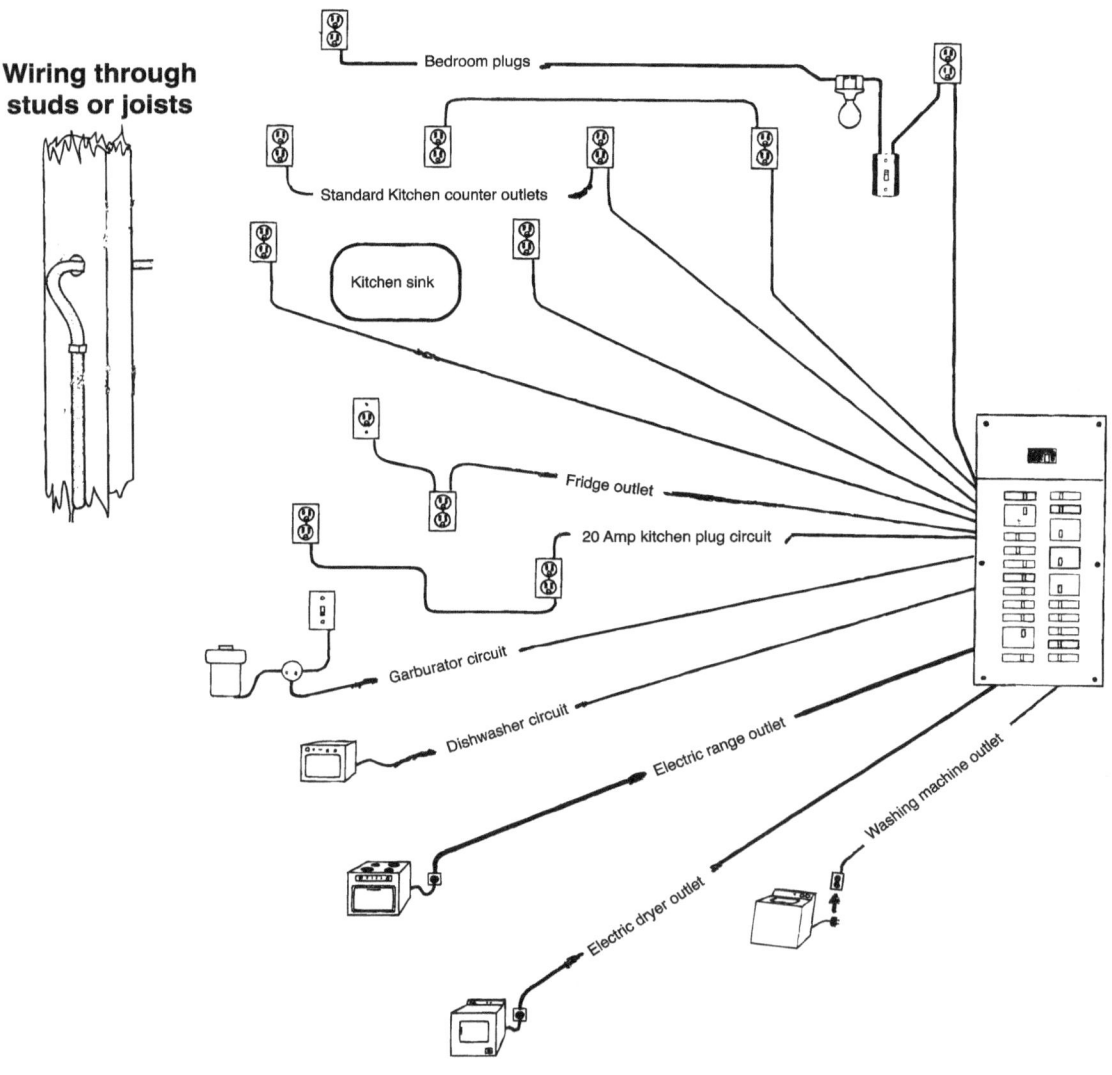

Finally, make sure to build or buy a cover for the sump. Secure the cover to prevent children's accidents (figure 4). Check the discharge pipe connection for leaks by pouring water down the sump.

Layout and Electrical Rough-in

I strongly advise you to plan your layout of your electrical outlets very carefully. Make a long list of your family's activities to place an electrical outlet where it is most needed. This way you avoid using long extension cords, which maybe in your way or dangerous. Ask yourself simple questions: where will you put your TV, your microwave oven, toaster and telephone? Where does your wife want the washer and dryer?

You'll have a better idea where your outlets will be placed once your stud walls are up. Go from room to room and place a marker where plugs will be. Mark these on your blue print so your electrician will be able to give you a better estimate. Once you finish with the inside rooms, do the outside front and back door for flood lights and outdoor plugs.

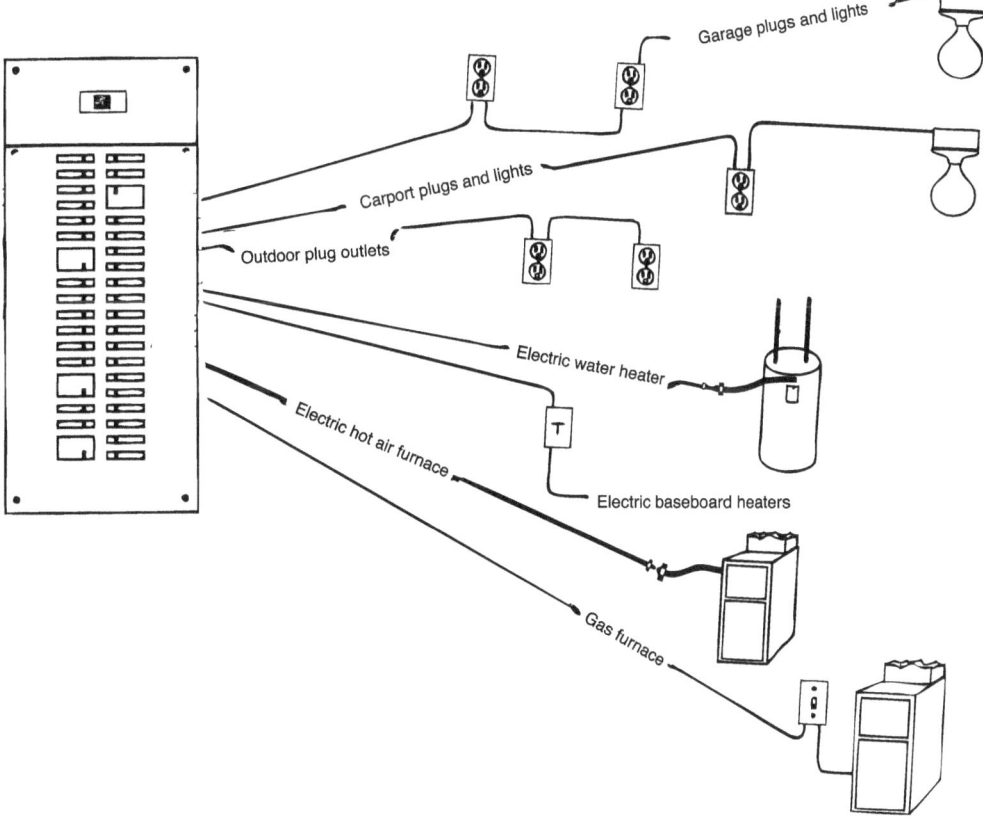

Go around, once again, check where there are switches required for each room and lighting needs, such as staircase and outside lights. Mark their positions using different colours from the plugs. Make sure your blueprint has correct information.

If you live in a cold climate, I advise you to construct an entry room at the outside entrance. Don't forget to include a heating panel, lighting, plugs and switches to such an entry.

Staircases are an area of frequent activity. Should you place one or two lights? This information must be incorporated in your overall layout of your electrical needs. Poor planning and lack of input from other members of your family should be avoided. Kitchen and bathrooms must be your focus point, because most household traffic originates in these two areas, especially if you have a large family.

Unless you are a qualified electrician or at least an electrical handyman, I would recommend hiring an electrician. However, if you want to save some money, you can always do the rough-in; that is, drill holes and pass wire in the stud walls. Most electricians would be glad to have you doing the rough work leaving the electrical connections to them.

If you decide to drill and pass wire, get solid advice from the electrician about at what level from the floor you'll drill the holes, the height of your plugs from the floor, and about the colour of the wires which are different from living rooms and bathrooms or kitchens.

Remember, electrical codes change from time to time as far as colours, level of plugs and switches.

If you pay attention you can do it well. Once again, talk to your electrician; see how he does things so you'll know for the next time. Finally, choose ahead of time where you'll put electrical baseboard heaters and their location; these outlets would require a different colour of wire than the rest of the house.

Alternative Energy and Heating Systems

Heating systems used in log homes are no different than in the city or in conventional homes. You may choose natural or propane gas, oil or electrical power as a heating medium. Choosing the right kind of heating system demands a considerable attention. One thing to consider is; whatever system you'll choose you must have a back-up system that does not depend on electrical power to function. In cold areas where a winter storm can cause a black-out, back up heating will be a life saving. Attention must also be paid on heating cost. Latest indications predict the steady cost increase in oil, propane, natural gas and electrical power.

Solar Panel

As mentioned above, if you are planning to build your log home in a cold part of the country, it is important to install two kinds of heating systems. If one of your systems depends on electrical power to heat the house, the second must function without. This is not only to heat the house, but to be able to heat water and cook while the power is off.

Heating system, like baseboard panel, oil and gas furnace, will shut down in the case of a power failure; although some gas furnaces can work without electrical power. You may want to check this out with your local supplier. If the house is left without heating for a time, frost would cause the water pipes to freeze or split open when temperatures drop bellow zero.

Installing a back-up system which does not depend on electricity would save you from potential problems. Natural or propane furnaces which do not require electricity is an ideal back-up heating system. Put your back-up system on a thermostat that will turn on if the temperature inside the house drops below normal levels. Installing a back-up system with a controlled temperature costs much less than repairing damages to the plumbing system.

If you live in a geographical area where the sun shines almost daily, solar power in an option to consider. There are many manufacturers of solar heating and components, as well as, solar collectors, regulators and pumps of all sorts that are available to you. Make sure that your supplier of solar equipment will also be the one who will do the service required.

Solar collectors are used to heat domestic water tanks and pools; they could save you a considerable amount of money. In sunny geographical areas installing sufficiently large solar collectors make good economic sense. Check with your relevant environmental agencies for grants or subsidies for saving energy.

In the part of the country where I live, the sun is a precious commodity; for five months of the year it does not appear very often. Having to install a large solar collector for heating my house makes little sense. The only time the collector would be of any use would only be in spring and summer months. The rest of the year, the solar collectors would remain inactive due to lack of sun. In winter the solar collectors would be covered with ice and snow, blocking any of the sun's rays.

I am all for using an alternative source of energy. Still, do the math and take a reasonable decision.

Wind Power

Like solar power, the power of wind is unlimited. Producing energy from wind power would depend on the speed of the wind and overall diameter of the windmill. In my area, most Amish farmers use windmills to pump water out of wells. Such windmills do not need high wind speed to pump water in the surface; but do not produce energy for electrical heating.

Wind Power

If you live in an area where the average daily wind, at sixty feet altitude, is over 28 miles per hour, then you may wish to consider wind power. If you live some distance way from a conventional source of power, it also makes sense to go for wind power with solar energy as a back-up. Combine these two sources of power along with additional back-up electrical generator would make your life easier.

Airtight Wood Stoves

A decided visual asset to many a log house is a freestanding airtight wood stove for heating and cooking.

Airtight wood stoves are the most common heating system found in good quality log homes. They provide a warm heating glow and create a unique environment.

With the rapid increase in fuel costs, as well as, the possibility of future shortages, wood-burning stoves have made a noticeable comeback. Most new models are equipped with electrical hot air blowers. If you want to save energy or you find the air blower noisy; or in case of a power failure, you can purchase a free-stand heat propelled fan which stands on top of your stove. As heat increases, this free-stand blower starts spinning, sending hot air for up to 12 feet radius.

In today's world of appearance, cost and convenience, a wood burning stove's efficiency may be compromised. The old saying "put another log on the fire" is understandable, but the principles of efficient wood burning can lead to the putting of far less logs on the old fire.

How well will the heating stove do the job you want it to do, will be determined primarily by its size. For obvious reasons, a very large space cannot be heated by a small stove. On the other hand, would you want a large stove heating a tiny room?

Much can be learned about airtight stove burning efficiency from the weight of the stove. Generally the more massive the stove is, the more efficient it is, but only if the weight contributes to keeping the combustion zone hot.

Once you have decided what size heating stove your household needs, the efficiency is the next logical consideration. Be informed about how much heat will it deliver? What are the BTU's per hour? How long will it burn? Much of these questions can be answered by how well can you control the draft and how tight the door latches.

Positioning Your Wood Stove

Heating stoves are best located in a central part of the lowest section of your log house. Location must follow all necessary building codes with respect to kind of floor, walls and other inflammable material.

Strict regulations have made fire prevention and the use of wood stoves much safer. The set-up area must follow installation of non-combustible material: the firewall.

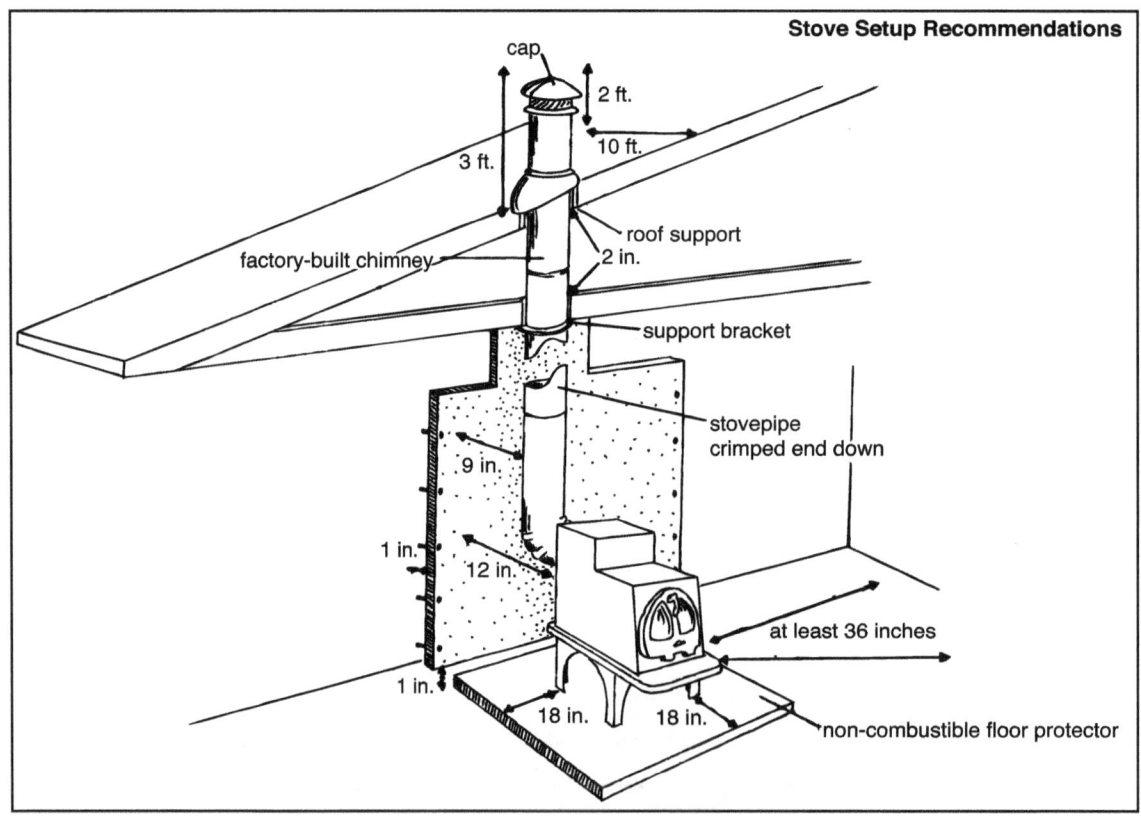

Stove Setup Recommendations

152 PART TWO: BUILDING

A firewall is made of non-combustible material, such as stones, concrete block, bricks or pre-fabricated 4x8' concrete sheets. These protect all combustible material, such as stud walls, panels and ornamental material. Plan ahead so the location of your wood stove will allow the best fire protection.

First, cover your stud wall with 5/8" drywall. This is the wall that will be located directly behind your wood stove. For extra protection add a pre-fabricated concrete firewall sheet over the drywall. Mortar spaces with concrete mix to exposed stud wood.

Next, start building your decorative concrete or stone wall. Allow 2" air space between the two walls for extra protection. Building codes will permit you to position your wood stove closer to the firewall than if you do not have the 2" air space. Air space does two things: it gives extra protection by not permitting excessive heat to pass, and allows you to place your wood stove at least 50% closer to the back wall than the manufacturer's specifications.

Make sure your building inspector inspects and confirms every step of the construction of the firewall. You don't want to have to redo anything.

I would recommend that you hire a qualified stove installer. Your house insurance may want to see the installation receipt as proof it was installed correctly.

Airtight Wood Stove

CHAPTER SEVEN: Interior Finishing

Layout of a Functional Kitchen

Begin by drawing possible layouts, by observing the movement of a person who does different tasks when the kitchen is in use. Follow the basic rule of movement between three areas of the kitchen: the sink, the cooking stove and refrigerator. All must be within easy reach of the user to avoid unnecessary steps. When possible, avoid obstructing the flow of movement and arrange the work areas to correspond to uninterrupted work sequence. Have the travel path between the sink, stove and refrigerator, exclusive for walking to and from.

In the pictures of my kitchen, for example, you can see that the half-log maple island is abstracting the flow of movement between the sink to the left and the stove to the right. The stove and refrigerator are located on the right hand side, with the sink and dishwasher to the left side, between the island table. To solve the problem of going around the island to wash vegetables, I simply put an additional sink between the cooking stove and the refrigerator. Within easy reach, one can cook, wash and use the refrigerator within a distance of 8' reach.

Different kinds of kitchen work are summed up into three distinct work areas: the clean up, the preparation, and cooking.

The clean-up area requires water for both the sink and the dishwasher and ample counter space for dishes and utensils.

The preparation area requires room under and on top of the, counter for bowls, mixers, blenders, baking dishes, spices, oil and grains to be stored.

The cooking area is the third major area. It includes the stove, refrigerator, sink, and necessary utensils. You'll probably need extra counter space here, either all on one side of the stove or in section on each side. In my kitchen, I have the island maple-block directly in front of the cooking stove with ample walking space between them. The island maple block can also function as a preparation area with the refrigerator near by.

While it is convenient to have all your bowls and utensils handy, it is essential to have the most frequently used immediately at hand. Items you use constantly should be available with a single motion if possible. This short reach must be accessible without your having to stoop or stretch.

Finally, your kitchen layout, from the location of your electrical plugs and switches, to storage space for extra large pots and pans and large utensils, must reflect the way your family moves throughout your home. Consider the way you and your family cook and clean up so it will work better for all.

Take a close look at the pictures and you may wish to adopt or modify the general layout.

Layout of Bathrooms

Your bathroom is your personal space, so it is wise to plan it carefully. Whether you do the work or give the job over to a professional, a written plan will guide you to complete the task successfully.

Your planning should depend on your budget. What do you really want your bathroom to look like?

Get your wife and family involved and ask the right questions:

- Do we prefer a shower or a bath?
- Are there elderly person's, young children or both?
- Does your family have a disabled person?
- How much storage will be enough for the whole family's needs?
- How many members need to bath and shower at the same time?
- Should there be a second bathroom?

Once you decide what you want, keep your notes together for a final discussion with your family. Next, transfer your requirement into a layout and add the fixtures - or explore different options by visiting bathroom stores. A good layout for a full bathroom will have the sink near the door or shower. If you have plenty of space, locate  the toilet in a separate compartment where it cannot be seen from the door.

If more than one person has to use the bathroom at the time, your layout should prevent a traffic jam by having the sink and vanity as far away from the tub and shower as possible. On the other hand, if you have limited space, it is hard to maintain

CHAPTER SEVEN: Interior Finishing   157

recommended minimum clearances around the fixtures, but try to adhere to them as closely as possible.

Remember that building code stipulates that the switch for turning on the jet-air in the tub must be out of reach from inside the tub itself to avoid possible electric shock.

Your Utility Room

The utility room is the nerve center of a country home. Its veins are spread to reach areas need be served with water to bathroom and kitchen sinks, electrical power to the main water supply hook-up to pressure pump and distribution of hot water where is needed and central clean-up for the septic system.

It also functions as a storage room for brooms, cleaning supplies and household items out of children's reach.

Common utility room.

Small space under stairway hiding the hot water tank.

It is also an area to fit-in your laundry, drying as well as an area to pot your plants and keep seasonal garden tools in storage.

If the electrical inspector permits you, you may consider installing the main electrical panel in the utility room and safe storage of your breakers and provide you with a quick shut-off for both the main panel as well as the sump pump.

Any sort of emergency can be dealt from here where all main outlets are located in a concentrated area. Keep clear all house garbage off the utility room so as not to attract parasites and other unwanted guests.

Installing Your Windows & Doors

A building's windows serve a double purpose; they allow solar heat to enter the house in the winter and provide you with a view of your surroundings. But the true connection is more than a view; it is a true but subtle balance of the separation from and connection to the outside. One may say that windows and doors are an expression between the part of us that wants to be outside and the part of us that would rather be inside. As a result, everything about your doors and windows will have a huge influence on the feeling your log house creates for your family.

A set of well placed windows and doors may by designed to give access to the scents of a flower garden and as a special place that 'frames' a specific view.

For this reason, you need to layout your windows in a way to allow for easy communication

CHAPTER SEVEN: Interior Finishing

between those on the inside and elements of nature on the outside.

In thick walls, you have a lot of choices when it comes to window placements where the window rests relative to the inside of the wall surface. A slide tilt of the bottom sills would direct rain water way from the window frames and towards the outside.

If your windows are fixed you must carefully design a location for windows with openings to create the best ventilation and the most natural flow of fresh air.

In cold climates, building codes require that you install a basic double-pane glass (two pieces of glass separated by air space), having at least double R-value than single-pane glass.

Putting On the Finishing Touches

A) Take a walk around your house and note some of the things that need to be finished. For example if you see insulation sticking out of place in your log walls take a box-cutter and trim it. At the same time pay attention to gaps

Panoramic view of the cathedral ceiling.

CHAPTER SEVEN: Interior Finishing   161

between logs that may permit air flow into the interior of the house. Be sure to take transparent or white outdoor caulking and caulk the hole of the outside of your log house. This will insure your home has weather protection from moisture and stops insects from entering.

Special attention should be paid around doors and windows where large gaps in the side of the wall should be covered. When you finish you may go into the interior and do a visual inspection of your log wall. You may have missed a spot with your caulking. If you can see light penetrating space between logs you should plug them immediately on both sides of the log.

B) With your chain saw it is now time to even the outside corner log extensions that are longer then the rest. Take a length that you will want all your end logs to have and cut the rest to meet your requirements. You may want to also check the lengths of all your rafters for uniformity with one to another.

CHAPTER SEVEN: Interior Finishing   163

C) Having done your trimmings it is time to brush the ends of your rafters and corner logs with wood preservatives to protect your logs. Wait a day or two and repeat the process.

D) One of the best methods for protecting your walls, especially under the overhang where insects tend to build their nests, is to place individual birdhouses within 3' from each other all around your house. Place those just under your overhang of the wall and watch the birds getting fat from eating all those nasty insects.

E) On ground level around the house, check that there is a slope grade outwards and away from the wall foundation. At the same time check the front and back steps making sure they maintain their level. Special attention should be paid around the eave and fascia. Make sure that your venting is in place and that there are no holes for mice to enter into your house. Prime and paint your fascia every year to get a long lasting life out of them.

F) Do not let grass overgrow around your foundation wall. This is the place where insects tend to live.

G) On the interior start by checking your drywall for cracks caused by excess dryness. Correct those as soon as possible.

H) Sand down and urethane your wooden floor. Do the same with your doors by taking off of their hinges and placing them flat on a wooden horse, repeat again when they dry.

I) If you have flag stone floors like mine you may want to clean them well and cover them with special agents to maintain a shone surface.

J) Leave painting of the interior for the end when all other tasks have been completed. Choose earthy colours complimenting log homes and to the surrounding environment.

K) Check under all sinks and tubs for possible leaks of water. Special attention should be paid to the utility room where most of the pipes are located.

(Top) Interior view from kitchen.

(Right) A convenient place to hang your pots and pans.

(Below) French door of the under room (Door on right).

CHAPTER SEVEN: Interior Finishing 167

EVENTS AND WISDOM

As I mentioned before, the economic potential of your land is more than its standing trees. To take advantage of this economic potential I had purchased a homemade cedar-shingles sawmill. Since I have plenty of cedar logs and cedar cut-offs lying on the ground, I thought that a cedar sawmill would be profitable. In my area there is a relatively good market for natural-cedar shingles because of the number of log homes and

unique home structures. There is no question that cedar shingles are much more attractive than conventional asphalt singles.

I made some modifications on the cedar-shingle sawmill to make it run more smoothly. When I finally got it running well, I got too busy to work on both the construction and the sawmill. So it stood idle for about a year, until Chris Kiuphen, a local Amish cabinet-maker, took a notice of the sawmill.

I had known Chris for a while since I always bought my eggs and fresh vegetables from his family farm. I hired Chris to build my kitchen and bathroom vanities. I was going to supply the cherry wood and pine for the interior of the cabinets and Chris would supply the labour.

Chris came by to take measurements of the vanities. Shortly after taking the measurements, he returned with an estimate that almost caused my heart to stop: $ 6,000 for the labour. This price was quite reasonable for the quality of workmanship

Chris provided. In a big city, the same work would have cost many thousands of dollars more. Even so, it was a price too rich for me.

At one moment Chris saw the cedar sawmill sitting in the middle of the bush not far from my log home. Out of curiosity Chris ask me about it. I told him that "it" was a cedar-shingle sawmill that cut shingles for roofing. In turn, he asked me if it works and could he take a closer look. On both questions I answered yes!

After examining the sawmill he asked if I wanted to sell it. I was not sure. I suggested he make me an offer and I would think about it.

The next day, Chris returned with a horse-drawn flat-bed wagon full of family members, all wanting to take a look at the sawmill. After taking a good look, we started it and everyone watched very carefully how I cut shingles from left over logs. I explained the basic economics of operating a shingle sawmill.

They all started to talk in a language that I did not understand; but I concluded that they were all in favour of buying the sawmill.

Now it was up to Chris! Horse trading back and forth, we were getting no where, so I decided to change my strategy. I said that I didn't want cash. Instead we should use the price of the sawmill as partial payment for the cabinets.

Chris, after consulting with his family, made me an offer of $4,000 - take it or leave it. I took it because the sawmill had only cost me $800. We shook hands and the deal was closed. They loaded the sawmill, the cherry and the pine wood and off they went. I looked up at the sky and gave my best smile and a big wink!

CHAPTER SEVEN: Interior Finishing   169

170   PART TWO: BUILDING

Chapter Eight
Outdoor Construction

PART TWO: BUILDING

OUTDOOR CONSTRUCTION
Installing Your Septic System

The general purpose of a septic system is to store and distribute household waste. This includes both water and human waste. To get a good return on your investment and satisfactory service, you must know something about the design, operation and maintenance of your septic system.

A septic system has three main sections; first the watertight septic holding tank, second the distribution box, and third the leaching bed or field.

These days the holding tank of a pre-cast concrete unit is the most widely used. This pre-cast concrete tank is generally cast in two sections, top and bottom. Both sections are delivered to the building site as one unit and set in place. The top and bottom are sealed together with a mastic compound to make the holding tank watertight.

The distribution box is also a pre-cast unit with a number of outlet holes. Their purpose is to distribute the fluids evenly to the leach field. Invariably, some leach pipes will receive more than others.

Sewage, like human waste with brown water, flows through the main drain pipe into the septic holding tank. As sewage enters the holding tank solid waste and brown water separates. Solids remain in the holding tank and brown liquid enters the distribution box to be led to separate lines of the leaching field.

This liquid in turn, percolates into the ground. The solid waste remains into the holding tank. The sludge must be leaned - pumped out - so it does not overflow and clog the system. Normal cleaning time for an average household is 1½ years of full time use.

Delivering the holding tank. Work is supervised by Joseph (to the left) and by Ray (at center).

As a home owner, and for the sake of a good and clean environment, you must detect problems with your septic system by observing the following:

- If toilets and pipes back-up, it means that the holding tank is full.

- If the grass above the holding tank is a darker hue and growing more rapidly than the surrounding lawn, it means the tank has cracked and sewage is escaping.

- If the ground above the drain field erupts, it means that there is a build up of gas. If this happens, the contractor has installed the septic system improperly and therefore he should be held responsible. Notify your local health authorities immediately.

Keep the following out of your septic tank,

- Grease
- Coloured toilet paper
- Drain cleaners (lye)
- Toilet bowl cleaners
- Bleach
- Coffee grounds
- Chemicals that kill bacteria (you need bacteria in the septic tank to break down solid waste).

Common Septic Layouts

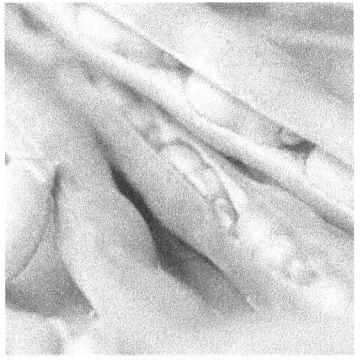

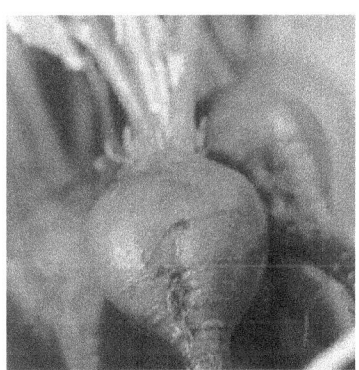

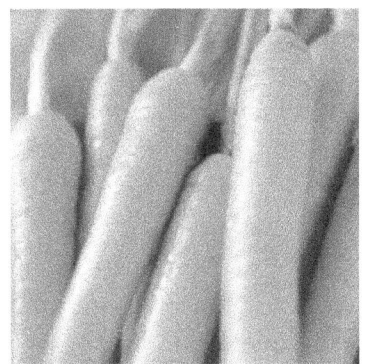

Installing a simple septic system is quite easy if you have the right tools, equipment, and knowledge. The first step in the installation of a septic system is the septic layout. You begin by visiting your local supplier of septic equipment. Take with you the information given to you by the soil testing firm that analyzed the sample you supplied. With this at hand, your septic equipment supplier will calculate the length of your pipes; from that you will be able to determine the area of your septic field. In my area a normal two bedroom house will need four hundred feet of pipe. Depending on the size of your septic field you have the option to divide this length into four 100' sewer trenches which equal 400' or five sewer trenches of 80' or any combination that will total 400' of pipe length.

In some areas you need a septic permit which your local building inspector will provide you. In other areas only those with special license can install septic systems. You can install your own by having the permit issued in your name and seek the aid of outside sub-contractor.

Experienced contractors can do a good job installing your septic system. But the contractor, like other house contractors tend to be expensive. A normal installer of a septic system may cost you from $5,500 to $ 7,500 including labour and materials, depending on where you are. Your contractor-installer should begin with the excavation of the septic trench and a hole for the holding tank. Dirt and stones will be removed around with the front bucket or the backhoe. He must follow

the septic design to the letter. It is advisable to check his work periodically to make sure that everything is going according to the requirements of the design.

After the excavation is done, your installer will install the septic components starting with the holding tank. When the septic holding tank is set, your installer must make sure that it sits in solid ground. If the ground is soft, it might be necessary to install a layer of stone under the tank. Your holding tank must be at least 20' from your nearest house wall and your well 150' from the septic field.

By this time the dump truck should have delivered 2 loads of crushed stone which needs to be distributed evenly in the bottom of each trench.

Lay the perforated pipes (white in colour) on top of the gravel and in the center of the trench. Your installer will cut and joint them to the corner pipes with adhesive. All field lines will be connected to the distribution box. All pipes must be placed correctly with the required slope.

Once the tank is in its place, your installer will need to make sure that is level to accommodate the level of the distribution box. The holding tank is then connected to the house main line which is not perforated. An elbow fitting will be attached to the end of the drainpipe that protrudes into the holding tank extended into the liquid level of the tank.

When all pipes are joined together, level them with a carpenter's level to the required slope. Talk to your building inspector about the required degree of slope; in my area it is 1/2" per 10 feet.

When the pipes are in place and all are leveled up, call your building inspector to inspect the septic system. Adjust any level as needed to the inspector's approval. Next, cover the entire length of the pipes with "filter cloth" to prevent soil from entering the holes as you fill the trenches.

Cover the filter cloth with crushed stone and you may now want to call back the backhoe to cover the trenches but not the extreme ends of the pipe system. This will allow the building inspector (if he wants) to inspect the septic system once again; he may want to see the pipes, gravel and "filter cloth." A note of caution, ask your building inspector if you can do what I am advising here before you begin to cover the septic drainpipes.

Have the installer of your septic system do a good job, and do not allow anyone to look for speed and convenience which may be a costly ending.

If you are willing to do the work yourself, the cost may be reduced considerably. In other words, if you are under a strict budget, work is work and it can also help to save some money. Talk to your neighbours to see if they are willing to help.

DO IT YOURSELF TRENCH SEPTIC SYSTEM

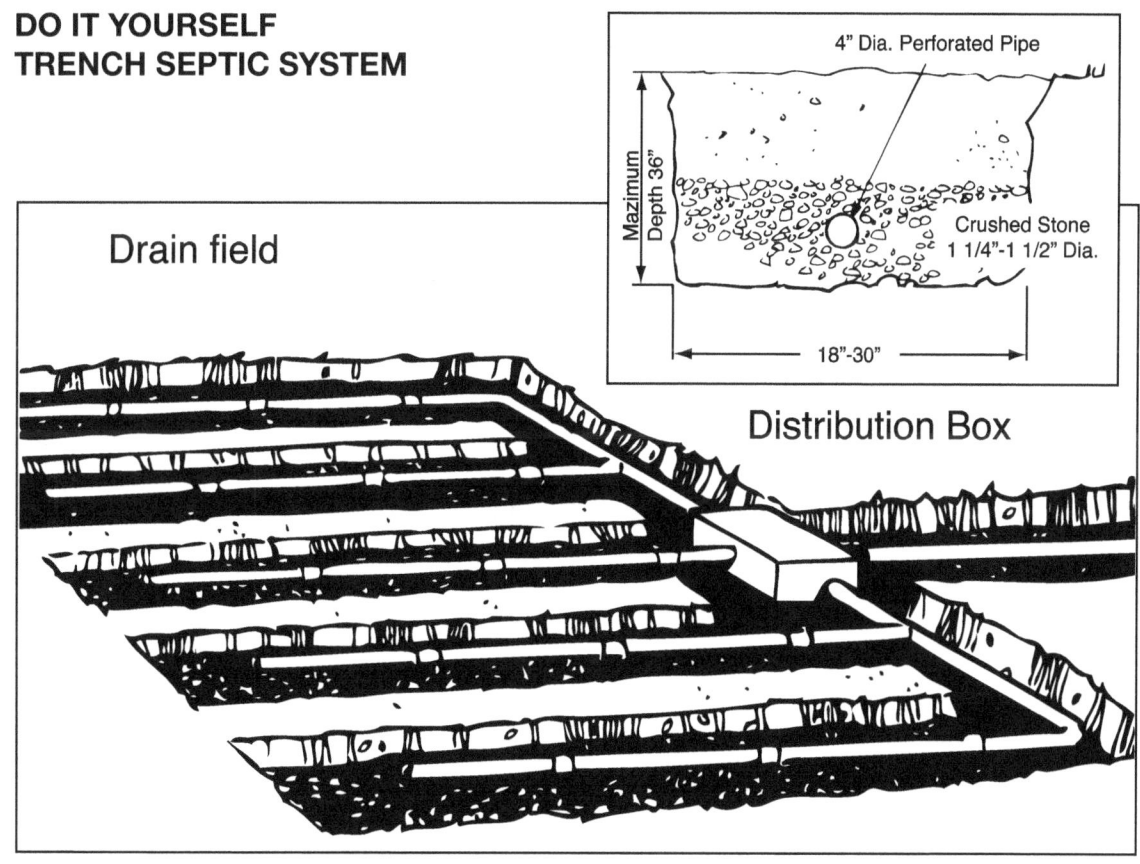

If you own a large building lot, a trench septic system is the least expensive version of all other existing systems. A typical trench system sets the pipes into trenches that are between 1 to 5 feet deep. The width of the trench tends to run from 1 to 3 feet. Perforated pipes are placed in these trenches on a six-inch bed of gravel, with a second layer of crushed stone placed on top of the perforated pipes.

Because of its design a trench system uses both the sides of the trench and the bottom of the excavation to provide an outlet for liquid. Only one pipe is placed in each trench. This is the reason it requires more land area than other types of systems. This can be a problem on small building lots, which can be solved by adding to the expense of clearing land for a septic system.

A trench system is ideal for hilly landscape where the trenches can be dug out to follow the natural slope of the land. This will give your system a maximum utilization of the sloping ground. At times, you may be able to place your trenches between trees so long as these trees are an acceptable distance from the pipes. This method reduces your clearing costs and permits your trees to remain in place for aesthetic purposes.

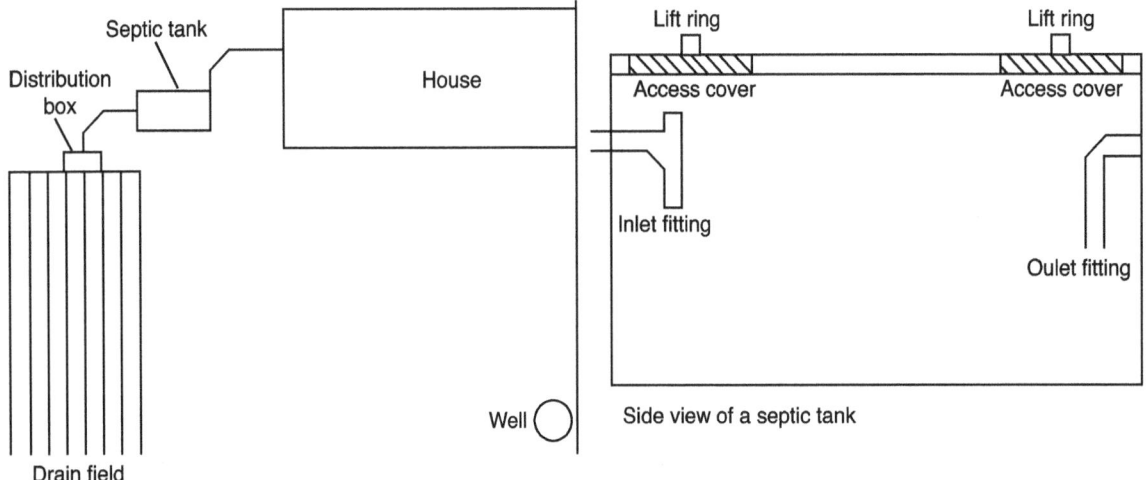

Constructing Your Driveway

The layout of your driveway must be related to your building site. After all, you are constructing a driveway that will help you arrive at your log home. Once you choose your building site, your next task is to construct your driveway. Two questions must be asked at this point. How long will the driveway be and how wide should it be?

CHAPTER EIGHT: Outdoor Construction   179

The length of the driveway determines the amount of dug out material to be removed and stored. Do a rough calculation of the amount of imported material you will need, such as sand and gravel.

Will your driveway accommodate one or two cars passing? Will it be wide enough for a delivery truck to turn around in order to exit?

Removing top-soil.

Once you answer these questions, it is time to begin with the construction of your driveway. It is very important to have a solid driveway. A solid driveway is one where the topsoil has been removed and replaced with more solid material. A mixture of sand and stone and later crushed stone or gravel are the material used to construct a firm based driveway.

Concrete ready-mix and construction delivery trucks must have a firm driveway to be able to provide you with their service. Some drivers may refuse to enter your property with the topsoil still in place, especially the propane delivery trucks that provide regular service. Topsoil is a soft element which is both slippery and easily gives in to excessive pressure when driven over.

Removing and storing the topsoil is the first thing you should do. A bulldozer with an

8' or 10' long straight blade will do the job well. Go down as deep as needed to remove all the topsoil, roots and stumps. Slope the perimeter to avoid mud re-entering your driveway.

Either you or your bulldozer operator must call your local gravel-pit to deliver the first of many loads of mixed sand-stone (pit-run). Spread the material evenly over the entire length of your driveway.

If time permits, let rain and the heat of the sun settle your sand-stone mixture. Check for areas or spots on your driveway where drainage is slow. This means that you must put more sand-stone on top of these spots.

This first layer of sand-stone will allow you and others to drive without fear of getting stuck in the mud. Also check for soft spots where the ground has sunk. You'll have to keep adding larger stones and sand until there is no more sogginess.

In time, add another layer of sand-stone mixture and hire a grader to level the entire driveway. Once the sand-stone is packed solid, it is time to place gravel on top. Depending on general conditions and climatic elements you should check your gravel-driveway frequently and add more gravel as needed.

Drilled Water Wells

The most reliable water source is the drilled well. It extends deep into the earth and reaches water sources that a dug-out well can not come near to tapping. This is because a drilled well taps into the water found deep in the earth. It is very unusual for drilled wells to go dry. For this kind of dependability, drilled wells can be expensive.

The difference in price between a dug well and a drilled well can amount to thousands of dollars. Shallow wells (dug wells) can run dry or become contaminated which gives an unsuitable supply of potable water. When all the factors are weighed, drilled wells are worth their price.

Geographic location will determine the depth of a drilled well, ranging from 50 feet to 250 feet or more. Call your local well driller and ask for your area's average depth of drilled wells. By law, a well driller must keep records of all drilled wells in the area and the recorded depth. With this information and the cost per dug foot you will be able to determine the approximate cost of your drilled well. In my area drilled wells range from 125 to 175 feet of depth. A bedrock supply of water will give you much cleaner water than a depth nearer to the surface. At 160 feet, our well reached bedrock which gave us cleaner water and more gallons per minute.

From the builder's point of view, when it comes to drilling a well, deciding the well location is the main issue. Building code requirements address issues pertaining the minimum distance from the septic field. An experienced driller can provide you with solid advice when it comes to choosing a spot for a well. He will also look for access to the drilling site. Drilling rigs require driving over solid ground and need a lot of room to maneuver around and exit the property.

ANATOMY OF A WELL

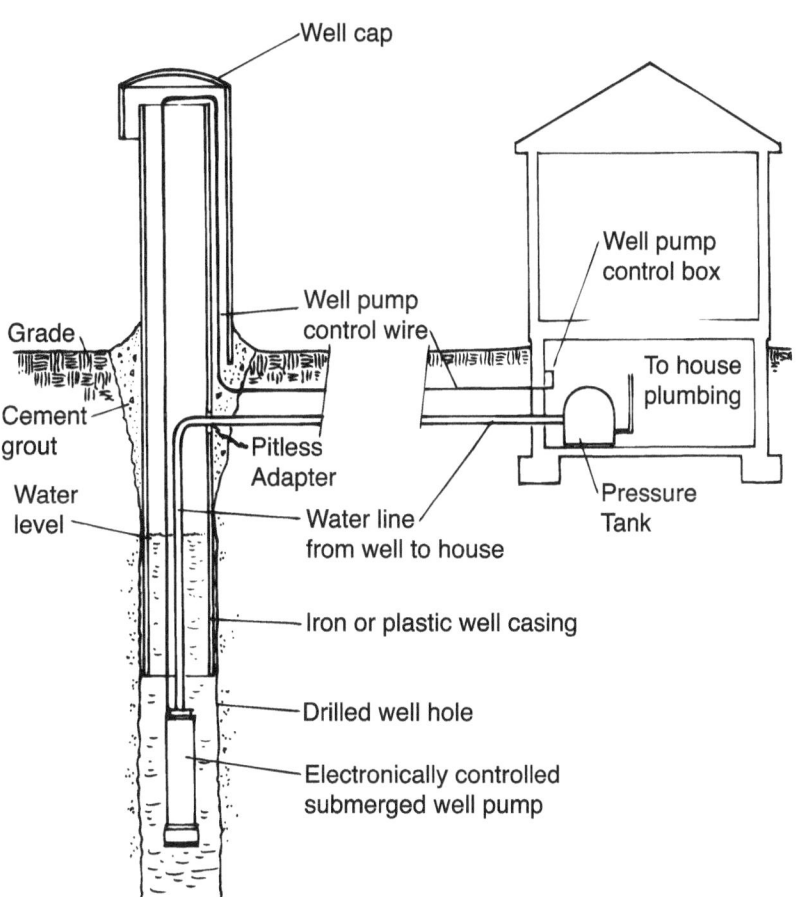

Along with these considerations, you also have to evaluate where the dug-out trench for your underground well services will go. That is the water pipes and electrical wiring connecting the well sump-pump to the utility pressure tank.

Once you have your well driller working on your property, there is not much for you to do but wait. Periodically you may want to check with the driller of the current depth and current rate of water flow in gallons per minute. Ask your well driller or your local banker for the minimum gallons per minute that a household needs to qualify for a mortgage. In some areas, the minimum requirements are 2-4 gallons per minute. Of course, the quality of water is also important. A shallow depth, even if it is getting 4 gallons per minute, is not a preferable due to cleanliness issues.

When the drilling is done, the driller, in most cases, will insert a 6-inch steel casing down to the well's depth touching the bedrock. When the ground is not solid there is always a possibility of the hole collapsing and plugging the hole; the bedrock does not need steel casing because of its solid material.

While most of the well drillers are hard working and honest people, ask for references or talk to your friends to recommend a driller. Some drillers tend to drill deeper than is required in order to add to their invoice. It happened to Ray whose driller reached 30 feet more than was needed. At the time when we both needed a driller we chose a reliable one.

When the job is done and the steel casing is in place there will be a 6" pipe 3' above ground. The top of the well casing should be tapped with a cover where the legal registration of the well is recorded and the registered depth is inscribed along with the name of the driller. In turn, the driller must provide you with a certificate for your well. Keep these records in a safe place for future use.

Protect the exposed well pipe from accidents. It is now time for the final step to connect your well to your house.

Installing Your Drilled Well Sump-Pump

Whether your driller or your plumber installs your sump-pump, you must make arrangements for a trench to run the water service pipe and electrical connections from your well to your house.

In cold climates the trench must be four feet below the frost line to protect the water lines. While the trench is exposed, take a safety precaution that nothing larger than leaves fall into the trenches.

This trench should start from the well-casing to the house just outside of the location of the utility room. This presupposes that you already have an appropriate opening on the side of the house (below the frost line) leading to the utility room where the water from the well can be attached to the pressure pump.

Next, get your supplies from a reliable supplier. Explain to your supplier the following:

- The length from your utility room to the position of the sump-pump.
- The type of sump-pump that will not over-work to supply you with water
- The appropriate electrical wiring (three or four prong) that is appropriate to the kind of sump-pump you are planning to buy.
- The water line (pipe) that's diameter fits the opening of the sump-pump without the need to buy addition adaptors.
- The right kind of pitless adapter and safety valve.
- Miscellaneous fittings and clamps including the big-"O" pipe which will protect your water line and electrical wiring from stones in the trench.

Utility Room

Following this, make a clear arrangement of how far the sump-pump installer is going to take the job. Will it include the installation of the pressure tank and all the accessories and electrical connectors? You need clear answers to questions before you need to award the job to a sub-contractor.

Installing a sump-pump involves lots of steps and material. If you are signing a contract, check the fine print or you might wind up paying a lot more than you planned for a well system. Remember installing a well functioning sump-pump takes careful planning and a lot of patience, but it is not a rocket science.

I am going to take you through a step-by-a-step description of how to install a sump-pump that you can be proud of! When there is something that you do not understand you can always go back and reread instructions.

We begin at the empty trench and at the side of the steel casing is located; and I assume you have all your supplies including the big-"O" pipe.

1) Go down into the trench on the side of the well casing. Drill a hole on the casing 3 feet bellow the frost line. It is in this hole where the **pitless adapter** will be installed from the inside of the well casing. A pitless adapter is the unit that connects the water line of the sump-pump with the water line outside the well casing. Installing the adapter on the side of the casing will give you a hanging support. Adjust the drilling hole to the size of the adapter.

2) The hole size is determined by the pitless adapter's outgoing water line; the side of the water line that is outside of the casing. When you are finished, cover the hole to prevent dirt from falling in.

3) Take your pitless adapter to your local hardware store and purchase a galvanized pipe with a thread at the end that will screw into the adapter to the top part. The length of this pipe should be about 6 feet long with a stopper welded on top to prevent accidental dropping of the pipe down the well casing. Make sure that the adaptor and the thread of the galvanized pipe are the same size.

4) It is time to assemble the sump-pump, the water pipe from the pitless adapter to the location of the bottom (where the pump will stop) and the electrical wiring. The water line fits between the adapter and the sump-pump - cut the water line to fit. The electrical wiring should measure from the bottom of the sump-pump to the inside of the utility room. The assembling should be done above ground; one extreme end is at the sump-pump and on the other at the pitless adapter and between the water line and safety protection of the pump.

5) Have a qualified person connect the wiring on the sump-pump. Make sure the connected wires are done right and are solid. You may also read the instructions that come with the sump-pump.

6) Connect the water pipe on the sump-pump. Secure the clamps tight. Secure a nylon cord on the body of the sump-pump to prevent accidental dropping of the pump into the deep end.

7) NOTE: the black water pipe has a permanent state of hardness. To insert fittings into it is, therefore, very difficult. For example, to fit the opening of the sump-pump to the water pipe is hard. To achieve pipe flexibility dip the end into a bucket of hot water for a couple of minutes. This should make the end soft enough to allow a metal fitting for easy fit.

8) Connect the pitless adapter to the other end of the water pipe. The water that is pumped out will go through the adapter and out to the underground pipe and in the pressure tank located inside your house.

9) Take duct tape and secure the water line with the electrical wiring at various locations to prevent loose movement.

10) This next job is for two persons. Lay the entire length of the water pipe on the ground with the sump-pump at one end, the pitless adapter on the other and the galvanized pipe inserted (screwed) onto the adapter. Keep the part of the adapter that screws on the out side of the well casing apart to be used when the adapter is in place.

Cordwood tool shed covered with log-slabs.

11) With care drop-in the sump-pump all the way down to its designated position. Hold on to the galvanized pipe and drop in the rest of the length into the position of the drilled hole in the side of the casing where the adapter will be placed. Your helper with the remaining adapter part should go down to the trench and screw in the fitting.

12) Position the pitless adapter in its place and tighten the nylon cord on the well casing. Tighten the outside one half of the adapter in place. Remove the galvanized pipe.

13) Your job is now done as far as the inside of the well is concerned. Connect the horizontal underground water pipe to the adapter (using hot water to soften the hard end of the plastic pipe).

14) Using duct tape, tighten the electrical wiring and the water pipe. Pass through these in to the big-"O" 6" flexible pipe to provide protection from dirt and stones when the time comes to cover the trench. This big-"O" pipe should be the length from the well casing to the foundation wall. Call your building inspector if it is required.

15) Water pipe and electrical wire should now be inside the foundation wall and into the utility room through an under flooring opening.

16) Call back your local backhoe operator to cover the trench, making sure that the opening in the foundation wall is sprayed with foam and outside stones to prevent unwanted visitors from entering your house. Make sure the dirt is well packed.

Inside the Utility Room

The rest of the work takes place inside the utility room. Here, the pressure safety valve is installed between the pressure tank and the water pipe from the well. This pressure valve stops the water from returning back into the pipe, when the sump-pump stops and starts. It is best to have this valve inside your utility room for an easy access in case something goes wrong. Some would place this valve inside the well casing - the choice is yours.

The pressure tank that you see in the picture refills itself when at a certain pressure, the sump-pump is required to run and refill the tank again.

An electrical or plumbing qualified person should take over from here on to insure quality of work. However, I would advise you to hang around the job if you want to see how is done for next time.

Landscaping Your Grounds

In most cases log home owners are the kind of people who associated the idea of log home in the country, with tranquility and harmony; away from noisy crowds. They seek a simple retreat.

Landscaping is very important in creating the right kind of retreat, for those who enjoy being close to natural environment.

Like everyone else, I too have my own preference of the right kind of landscaping for a rustic natural-log house. I have, yet, to make sense of people who landscape around the log house, as if it was a conventional house in the suburb of some city.

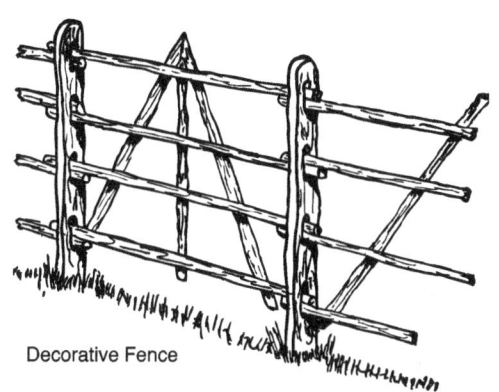
Decorative Fence

Post and Rail Fence

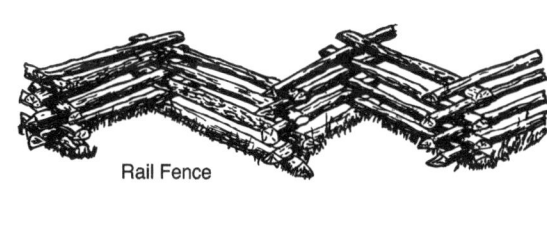
Rail Fence

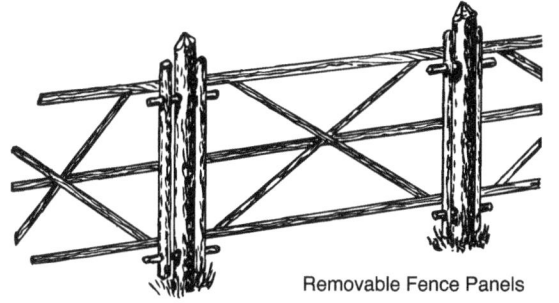
Removable Fence Panels

Snake Fence

CHAPTER EIGHT: Outdoor Construction

My property fence constructed with log slabs.

Wood, stones and iron structures for your garden are suitable for log homes. As with vinyl windows and doors, garden structures made of the same material should be avoided.

Likewise, I am not in favour of having a log home yard unkempt or surrounded by old tires, forest debris, rotting old tree stumps and left over construction material.

Neither would I recommend an overly cosmetic landscaping because it will look like replica of an architect's blueprint.

Design a living space for your garden of plants that do well around rocks that like to live in sparse soil. Choose to use a variety of perennial plants because they are hardy, love direct sun and do not need much of soil or water.

Stone walls in a large or medium garden with walking paths laid with flag stones compliment your log home. Make sure when you buy stones for indoor or outdoor use they are in a natural state and not polished; accidents happen when one walks on a shining stone floor that is wet.

With a good green lawn that is kept clean will go well with log or wooden structures. Fences, old cedar rails made from left over log slabs or old cedar rails, is much more attractive than lumber yard fences made of treated wood.

EVENTS AND WISDOM

For obvious reasons, the best way to learn about building a log home is to build one. But how do you go about getting experience? Or rather, is experience necessary in order to tackle with a project that could become at times, overwhelming? I honestly hope to answer this question further on!

I recently picked up a very glossy book about building with traditional material. A whole 600 pages devoted mostly to construction pictures. Yet, what was surprising to me was that the author found necessary to knock-off something that he called the *male answer syndrome*. In short, he claims that a man will offer an answer to a question or offer an opinion even though he does not know anything!! Yet, as a warrior-philosopher once proclaimed "Knowledge begins from ignorance" which allows a person to try and experiment or "search-in-the-dark" for solutions to the task at hand.

On the last pages of such a book there was a list of about 15 people (man and woman) who have helped this author put the book together. The pictures of the construction were staged and were taken by a professional photographer. The writing was taken over by someone who "took confused scribbles and turned them into actual sentences with punctuation ... and meaning." Another who is "a natural builder, writer, and photographer" added his expertise, next person added, "her sublime art direction", and another did "the amazing colour illustrations" and so on.

Finally, when one looks at the pictures of those who do the construction itself, there is little evidence of the author's building experience who is suspiciously absent from most of the pictures taken. Yet this author offers a load of psychological mumbo jumbo advice about "mental stress" and "decision making process" when one is building a house. In my humble opinion, this author provides answers through other people's experience, which in his opinion, it is okay to do so since these answers were given by someone in the know, dished-out by the "author" as if these were of his own. Whatever his problem is, I refuse to accept his *male answer syndrome* because the later indicates trial and error. This "author's" book is then an outright deception, dressed in glossy pages.

★ ★ ★

While a certain degree of planing is necessary to build a log home, you can be over-planning by confusing attempts to capture the whole image of the log construction in your head.

We all do things based on a logical sequence of events; the necessary steps we need to take followed by another in order to arrive to a desire point. But the physical world that exists outside of our minds, has its own governing laws and conditions which, at times, conflict with our perception of these laws and conditions. In most cases, we modify our perception in order to harmonize our ideas with the physical world. This is what trial and error is all about. When at times, we miscalculated something it is because most of our decisions are based on intelligent conclusions which at times can be wrong!

Case in point; my logical perception of the physical world concluded that if I take a piece of plywood on top of the scaffold and then climb up, the next step is to take this plywood to the roof. The problem with this intelligent conclusion was that while I was planning this, the physical conditions changed (ice on the roof) which were not conceptualized by my mind, which caused my accident. On the other hand, had I harmonized my perception with the physical world I would not have climbed onto the icy roof (in other words, I would have modified my ideas to fit the reality). From the moment we get up from bed through our daily activities, we practice trial and error whether we are aware of it or not.

The more experience accumulated, the more the physical world imprints upon our mind the proven or tested, by trial and error, our intelligent conclusions as a guide to future actions.

The starting point of every future decision we make is always based in some theoretical conclusions we have accumulated in the past. Books and magazines about building log homes can only become functional if we put what we learn into practice. Otherwise it will always remain at the stage of "it is easier said then done."

Whatever you have learned from reading this book, and whatever I learned from Ray's explanation about rough-in plumbing, is a starting point for doing the rest "without experience." And the physical world that exists outside your mind, will forever be your guide to the things that you do, correctly or not. Trust the real world, for it will never lie to you because it simply cannot lie!

194   PART THREE: OUTDOOR PROJECTS

Chapter Nine
Additional Outdoor Projects

More Projects and Suggestions

In this chapter. I will try to present you with a healthier life style and some projects to match; some simple and some more complex. You may have a few reasons not to try them out. But if you persist and take one step ... and then another, you may get hooked!

This sensible approach to life is the main reason people seek to find a non-competitive but physically and mentally challenging lifestyle. In seeking a more traditional lifestyle, I hope you will be encouraged to adapt some if not all of these projects. They are meant to give you some ideas and possibilities for something new, a change we all need and seek - to adopt a more wholesome lifestyle!

Backwood Settee

Old Dutch Settee

Closed and used as a table

CHAPTER NINE: Additional Outdoor Projects

Horseshoe Court

A horseshoe court for men has the stakes spaced 40' feet apart, for women, 30' feet apart. The stakes are placed in the center of a 6'x6' foot square pitcher's box. This is a box raised 6" above the ground and filled with playground sand. The top of the stakes stand 12" above the level of the box and have a forward lean of 3".

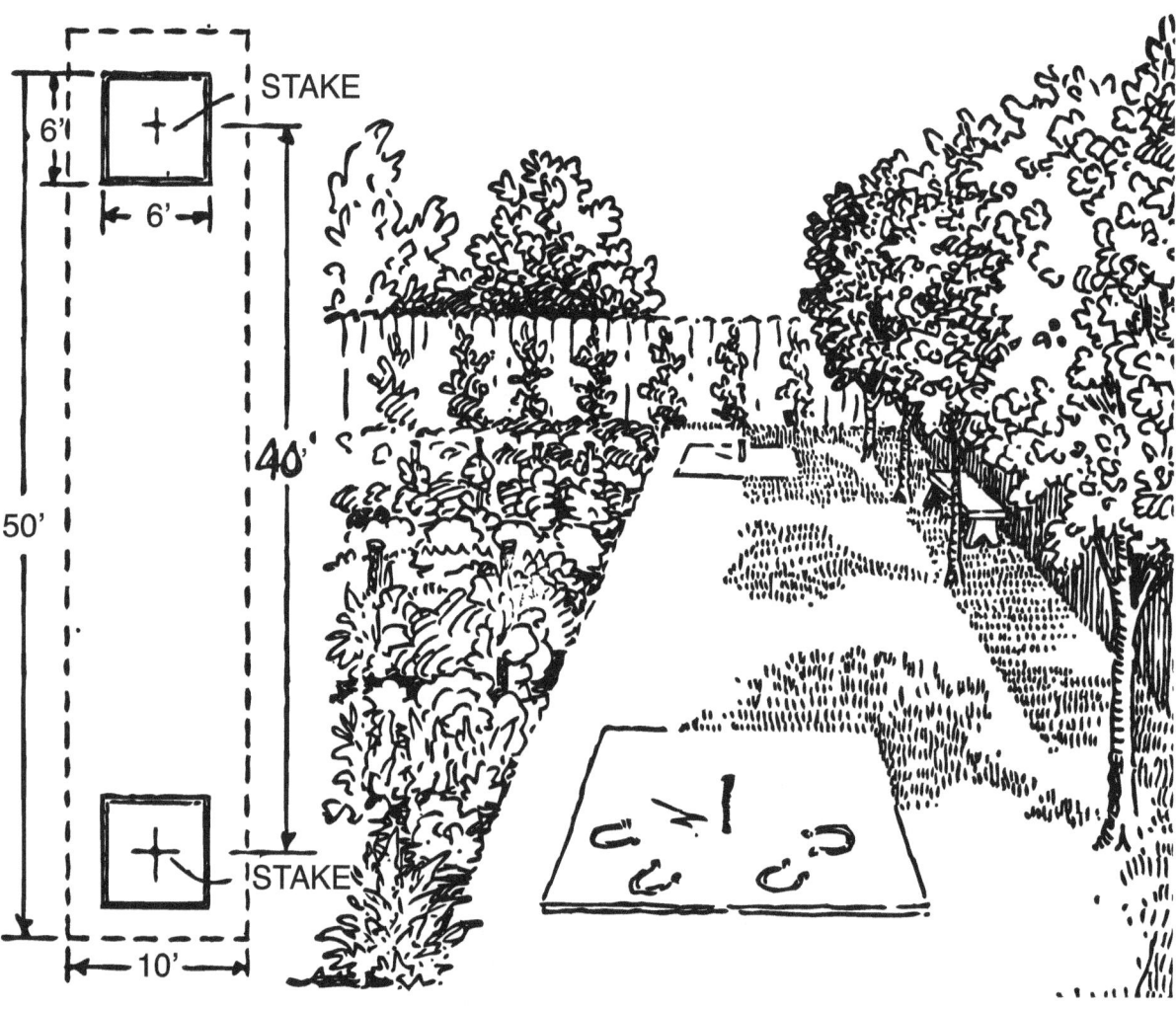

Half Log Bar and Kitchen Island

My kitchen bar and island are made of a maple half-log. After cutting it to size, these two half pieces are 6' long by 2' wide.

I cut down this maple tree when the local beaver family in my pond decided to eat the bark about two feet off the ground. It became a matter of time before the beaver family would have the maple tree down on the ground. The way it fell, the maple tree had its trunk off the ground. It stood there for about three years until it was dried.

When the opportunity came, I cut the trunk in half and left it drying for a summer under cover (see picture below).

Because of its heavy weight, it took considerable effort to bring each piece into the house. Each piece required a steel support bolted in the concrete floor slab. A steel base was then cased into the trunk's cavity and bolted secure.

The steel support was cased with good quality wood 1"x8" allowing a clear view of the trunk's original shape. Do not over-finish a round-log surface. Leave it as natural as you can. Clear finishing is preferred.

Two Styles of Outdoor Barbecues

The exact dimensions of the barbecue will vary according to the size of the material used – brick, cut stone, concrete blocks or field stones.

Footing: Excavate below the frost line for a 4-inch footing. This footing must be 4 to 6 inches wider than the dimensions of the barbecue base on all sides. Install 2" of gravel under the footing. Reinforce the footing with a grid of 3/8-inch rods. Allow concrete to cure for a week.

Construction: Using a snap-line, mark the outline of the barbecue on the base wall. Dry lay the first course of concrete blocks on the base. Lay the first course for the perimeter then for the dividers in the center. Build to the desired height. Make sure to build your exterior and interior sides course by course instead of building leads.

Filling the Firebox: After the firebox is high enough, fill it with sand and stones. Make sure the sand is dry and leveled. Allow 2 to 3 inches space for the layer of concrete using the side walls as a level guide. Trowel smooth.

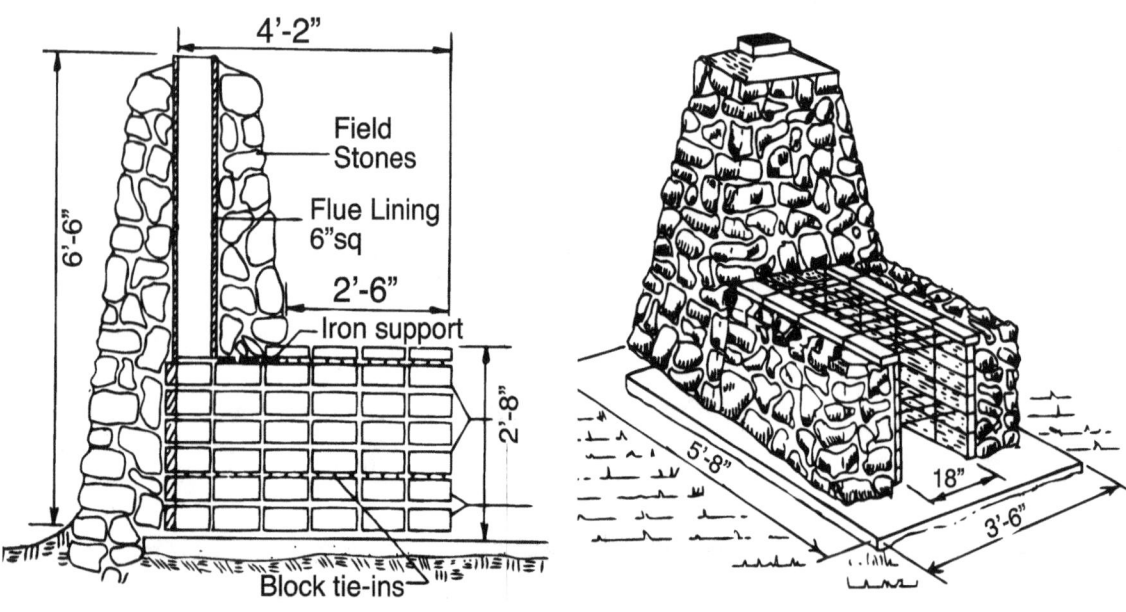

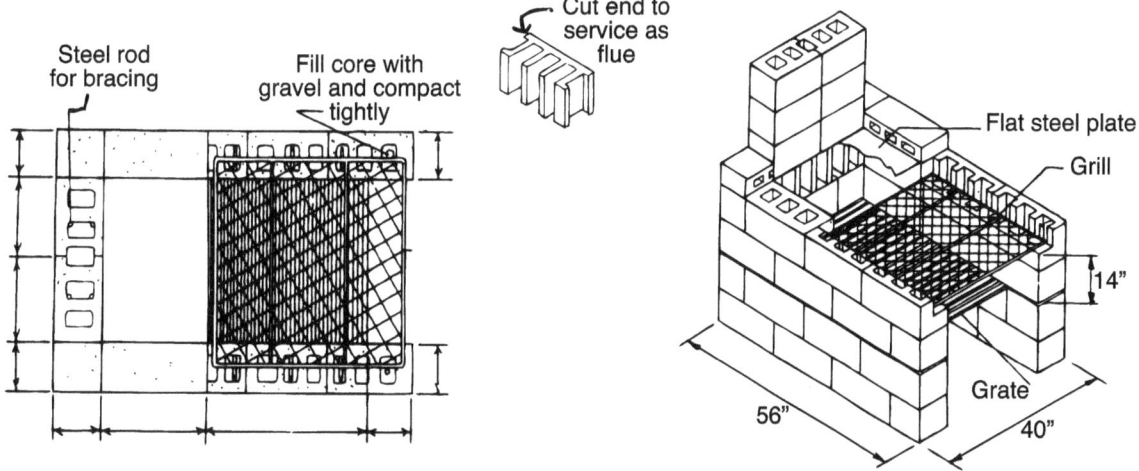

Construct the Upper Level: Construct the outer and inner walls until enough space is there between the grill and the firebox. Install the rods across the firebox to form the grill and lay enough mortar on top for the next course of concrete blocks. Build two courses of concrete blocks.

Construct the Chimney: Build two courses of concrete blocks then embed a 3x3 angle iron for a lintel across the front of the opening. Lay mortar on the lintel and continue building to your desired height. Finish with a mortar cap.

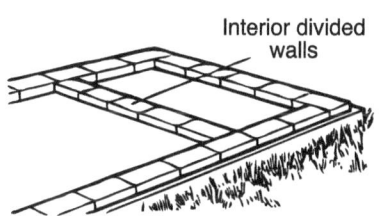

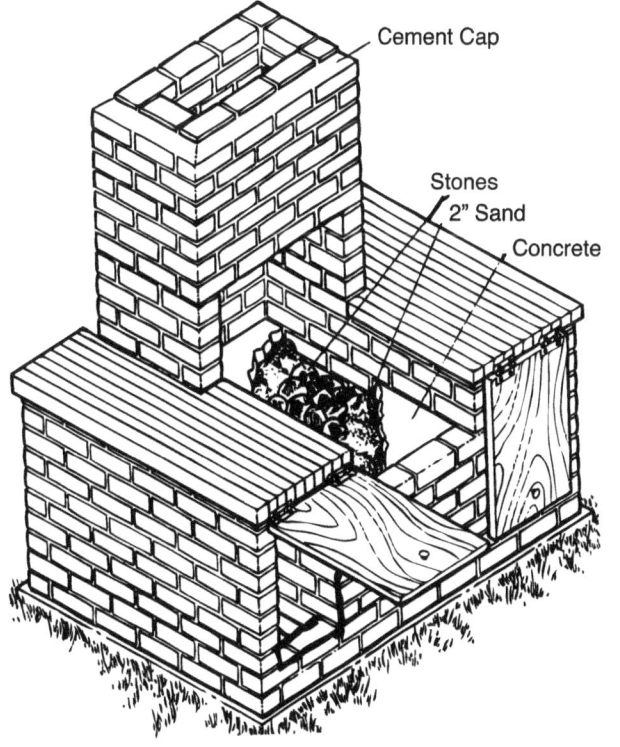

CHAPTER NINE: Additional Outdoor Projects   201

Natural Fencing

A 200' long property line fence made of 8' cedar posts and cedar cut-offs.

A Classic Smokehouse

A smokehouse is another avenue to explore to generate income or for personal use. On my land for example, I have about 80 apple trees whose branches I can use to give flavour to smoked meat and poultry. Once people get to know your fresh-smoked meat they will come to buy.

Most commercial or homemade smokers share a common structural mistake; they do not separate the firebox from the smoke chamber through a cooling medium. Whether you use an old fridge or commercial smoker, the basic method is the same; the firebox is at the bottom (perhaps separated by thin metal) and the smoke chamber directly on top.

If the smoke chamber gets hot, the fat from the meat begins to melt and the meat dries out. Therefore, the half-cooked meat is prone to rapidly spoil.

Best Design

The enclosed chamber of a smokehouse helps get the smokey flavour into the meat without actually cooking it. Whether you re-adapt your fridge or current smoker, this will show you a more reliable way.

I should point out that I am not a typical consumer; I would rather look to improvise than to walk into a store and buy a new smoker.

The idea is to separate the smoke chamber from the smokehouse. With little effort you can do it. Look at your local classifieds, talk to your neighbours or friends or perhaps you have a used firebox insert from an old fireplace. Make sure it has a proper door, with a draft to control a slow burn. The interior must be lined up with firebrick. (see illustration)

When you find the proper place make sure you surround it with a generous mass of stone and masonry to soak up the excess heat. The stovepipe must be also surrounded in the same general structure leading up to the mid-section of the smokehouse.

CHAPTER NINE: Additional Outdoor Projects 203

If the smoke pipe is exposed to the winter's temperature it will become unreliable for maintaining the proper heat. Run the smoke pipe through square concrete blocks to moderate the temperature inside the smokehouse.

Attention must be paid to the smoke chamber. It needs a proper vent to let the smoke in easily. You control the venting by the amount of air you let in from the firebox. Smoke leaking into the smoke chamber creates a back pressure for greater affect. The smoke will concentrate on the upper level of the chamber (where the meat is located) near the ceiling.

Having the exhaust release close to the bottom of the smoke chamber will cause the smoke to hang around longer where it is most needed.

If smoke backs up through the firebox it means that the air venting is open too far, creating uneven pressure between the exhaust and the intake.

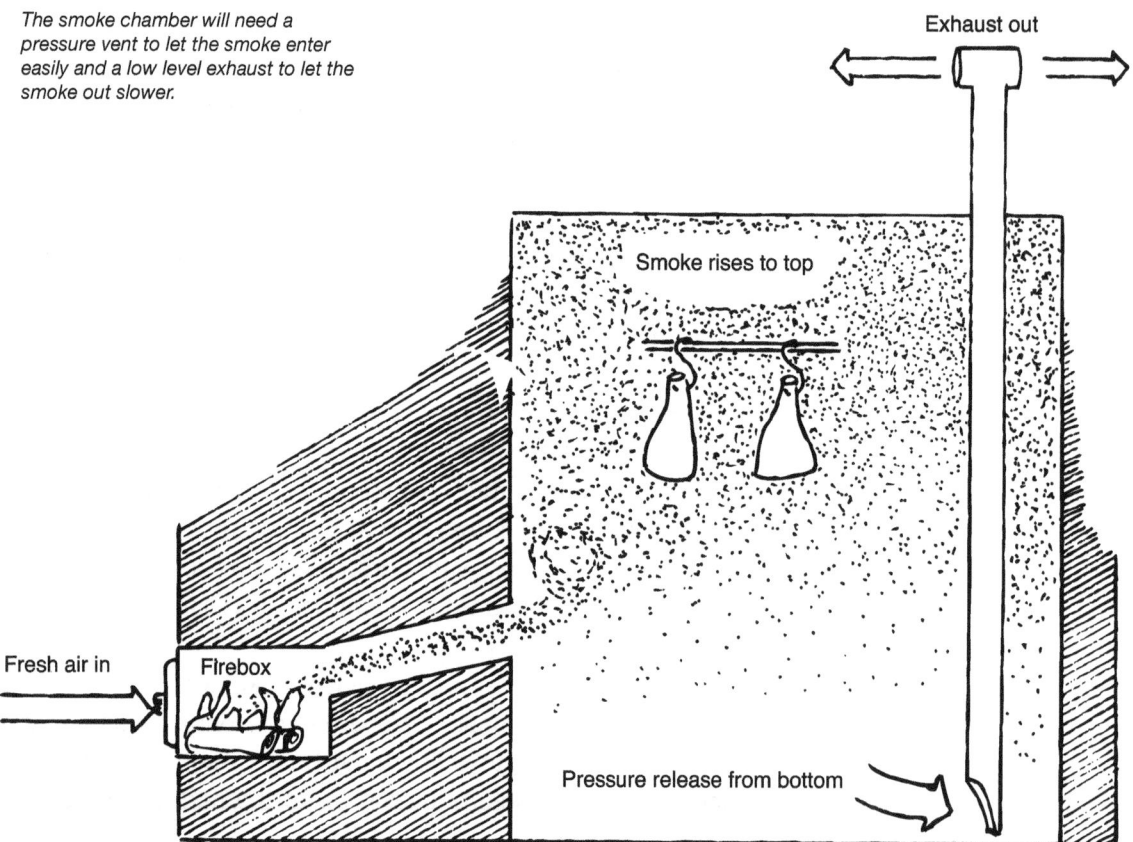

The smoke chamber will need a pressure vent to let the smoke enter easily and a low level exhaust to let the smoke out slower.

Building a Smokehouse Chamber

A 6' x 6' x 8' smoke chamber is the appropriate size to have plenty a room for all your smoke needs. Making the interior with 1" x 6" and 2" x 6" stud walls with plenty of insulation this will prevent heat escaping when you most need it. Slope your roof with a shingle pitch and ensure the door is insulated and flame shielded with thick weather stripping. Make the door no more than 28" wide by 6' high. For better insulation of the smoke chamber, spray foam insulation between the studs and cover with natural decking. The floor should be well insulated and made of wood.

Thermometers

It is a good idea to make a thermometer panel that has two thermometers. A chamber thermostat to stand on the rack and show at a glance the inside temperature of the chamber for cold and hot smoke. This is a great asset for a thoroughly controlled smoking process that will turn out a high quality smoked product every time. The second thermometer is for the meat. Stick the sharp end of it in the meat and it will show when the inside of the meat is done. You may want to choose rare, medium or well done.

Best Wood For Smoking

Do not use resinous woods or bitter flavours will be absorbed into the smoked meat. Use woods that will burn slowly and steadily, requiring the minimum of your attention and produce low heat level. Oak, Beech, Ash, Sycamore, Hickory and dry Apple chips are all suitable woods.

You may wish to experiment with Pear, Plum, Damson and Hedgerow woods such as Hawthorn and Blackthorn.

Most of the above woods add colour and flavour. Take a look around your area and ask fruit growers for pruned branches and sawmills for oak and other types of suitable left-over woods.

Building With Cordwood

There are many stories of the origins of building with cordwood; those range from how the Vikings brought the idea to the Americas, to how primitive man discovered the value of wind-breakers by stacking cordwood against winds. Whatever building historians and cordwood builders write about this environmentally friendly green-construction, one thing is evident; this is one of the cheapest ways to build your own home.

A simple pile of firewood that gives you heat when you need it, can become a protective shelter. Properly constructed cordwood-walls and an enclosed unit with a sod-roof can give you a superior building insulation, rival to none. Cordwood builders prefer cedar-wood to other varieties of wood; the common denominator being the mud.

As with other types of construction, cordwood construction must be adjusted to suit a variety of environmental conditions, particularly temperature and humidity. Each one must meet certain standards and be combined with others in a particular way; all depending on requirements for insulation, thermal mass, insulating core between mortar in around the cordwood ends that form the walls.

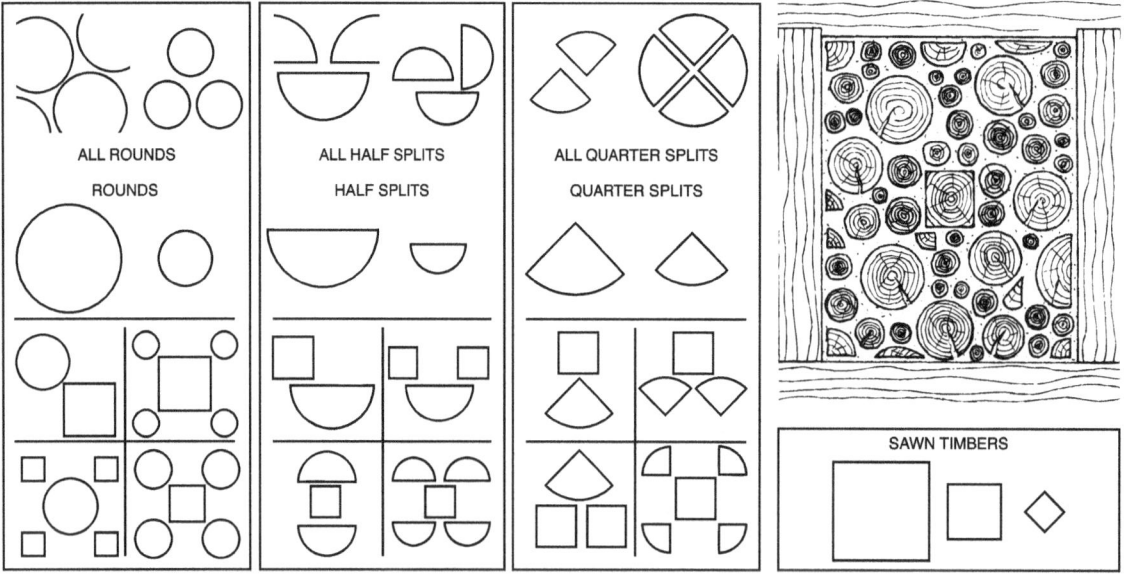

Unlike contemporary stick-built houses, where there are a variety of ways to enclose the structure, the cordwood system is constant. Short logs are embedded in mortar, insulation is filled in between, and the build up begins over and over again. In a short time, the construction progresses more quickly towards a complete wall, simultaneously finishing the inside and outside, weatherizing and insulating, at the same time.

There is one additional choice that offers an exciting arrangement of cordwood designs of endless styles and patterns that other construction can only offer repetitive building process. Cordwood arrangement can be a personal mural, a puzzle, a flowering background, a giant pattern system awaiting to be discovered every time you look at it; even after you've been looking at the cordwall everyday for many years. All this poetic wall and it can still hold up the roof too.

Cordwood construction is manageable, both physically and financially. Instead of lifting heavy loads of solid logs, the largest piece of cordwood rarely exceeds 10 pounds. Imagine, no more cranes, no more come-alongs. You can build an average sized house with less then 10 cords of firewood. You can build a completely enclosed unit - a living space - for less than $20 per square foot! Depending on how fancy you want to be with the interior finishing aside from the cost of the walls, at $ 20 per square foot is quite low.

A cynical person may say that if cordwood construction were so easy and inexpensive, everyone would do it. Or there must be something wrong with such mode of building. My

answer is STOP thinking like a consumer led down the path of "good, better, best" marketing ploy, which keeps you from investigating alternative systems of construction. The marketing ploy of promising high quality and low cost of engineering material does not reflect the current high cost of housing. This is a heady issue. Are you a free-spirited owner/builder or are you caught up in the industry's "energy-efficiency" reports, of homes with foam packed, laminated, cooked and machined-to-death materials which one day you and yours will live with and call home?

Granted, commercialization is not always all bad. After all, there are many handcrafters and custom builders of alternative construction who turn out beautiful green homes who would not have a market without commercially promoting their work and their talents.

Put yourself in a special place. For in addition to building yourself a home for you and your family, you will confront issues of the environment, community living, vested interests, bureaucracy, politics, consumerism, money value, time value and more. Building with indigenous materials puts you closer to these issues that affect your family and neighbours and away from the herd mentality and rampant consumerism. This is a healthy, fascinating and worthwhile place to be and it's a good fight to be in.

If you lose the good fight against obscure building codes that will not permit you to build your cordwood home, you can always try across the country, state or province. Find a place where there are less strict building codes, fewer banks and mortgage companies and fewer building inspectors, where it will not arouse the local building department to cite obstructive building codes.

This is not a crusade and does not have to become your life work. The idea of building with cordwood can be promoted by your own alternative construction methods – you are the one who will reap the rewards of low-cost using indigenous materials for cordwood construction. If more owner/builders demonstrate that this alternative system is environmentally friendly and more manageable, it will become more acceptable.

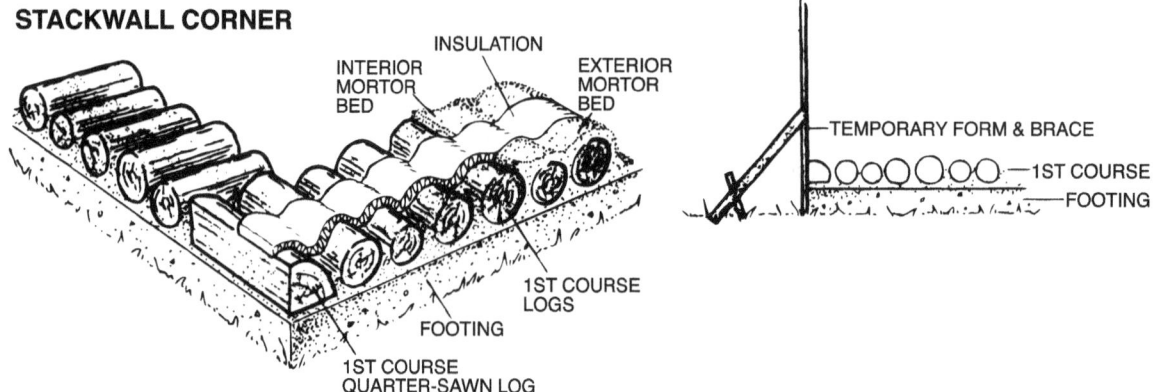

STACKWALL CORNER

Cordwood and Mortar Mix

Different species of wood react to stress, heat and moisture at different rates. You can see this when two different materials - mortar mix and cordwood - react. A homogeneous reaction between them is like finding a common ground which accommodates their qualitative differences.

For instance, by using dry cordwood and adding sawdust to your mortal mix, you can harmonize their reaction and make it more stable. There will still be a reaction between these two materials, but if you are careful, such reaction can be manageable.

Look around you, for you may find old and completely dried wood and timber from a variety of sources including unused barns, hydro posts and old-timber supply dealers. This selection of log-timber of equal in diameter, or even a wide variety of diameters (all split in sections) may give you an appearance you like best.

When you begin collecting dry cordwood make sure that the bark is off, and some wood may have end-grain checking or gaps and cracks that are open all across the radial growth rings. Some cracks may or may not be skin deep; which may provide less resistance to rot and insect damage. You may want to choose cedar cordwood in order to increase the cordwood-wall's thermal efficiency. Simply put, cedar wood radiates the heat more efficiently.

I am not going to insist that you follow my *one and only cordwood-masonry* mix because there is not one. I found this to be true of mixtures used by other cordwood builders. Most open-minded cordwood builders discover improvements in their recipes when they mix their next mixture. All have an aim to reduce or eliminate time-consuming caulking and oakum packing around shrunken joints between cordwood and masonry. Adding fine sawdust and hydrated lime add mass, without increasing the need for more mortar. The hydrated lime acts to preserve the cordwood, and whitens the mix, making it esthetically compatible with the wall's wood tones.

Fine powdered dry sawdust increases the mortar mix bulk and absorbs excess moisture, acting as an air pocket when sawdust moisture is completed.

Here is my mix that I think will best serve you:

10 parts Portland cement; 6 parts hydrated lime (or Mortarmate); 6 parts dry sand; 10 parts sawdust, enough water to make a wet mix. Of course, other more experience cordwood builders will offer you other options. Some prefer to make small quantities of mud and add small amounts of water or sawdust as needed. In all cases, the final consistency must be stiff enough to support the logs and keep the cordwood clean.

Cordwood Wall Construction

Concrete footings for a cordwood wall need not be any different than basic reinforced concrete at least 16" wide and 6" deep. A 1/2" steel rod held at mid slab of footing will secure extra load capacity. In cold areas you must follow building regulations governing foundations constructed in extreme climates.

Whether you include a full basement, crawl space or concrete slab on ground, the rough interior floor should be at level with the upper part of the foundation wall. Assuming you are using 16" cordwood for your wall, dictating 8" for the thickness of the foundation wall, with a 2" overhang, the remaining 6" will rest on the interior floor base. **Do not place vapour barrier under the first layer of cordwood on the wooden floor.**

Start building your cordwood wall by placing 2" of mortar to accommodate the first layer of wood. While it is relatively easy to build up 2' high wall, it would be wise to stop at this point and continue the next day. Continue around the house perimeter one layer at a time to allow the beginning to settle before you place the next layer and so on.

It is advisable to mortar in 4-inch-wide at both edges of the cordwood, thus leaving 8" of insulated air space. Remember that the initial mortar bed must be full bodied and uniform to give the first layer of wood the extra strength it needs. Make sure that you leave at least 2" of mortar between each piece of cordwood. As for the insulation to be placed in the middle air space, Vermiculite or other loose (granulate) fill insulation is the first choice, followed by fiberglass, packing it down into the insulating cavity.

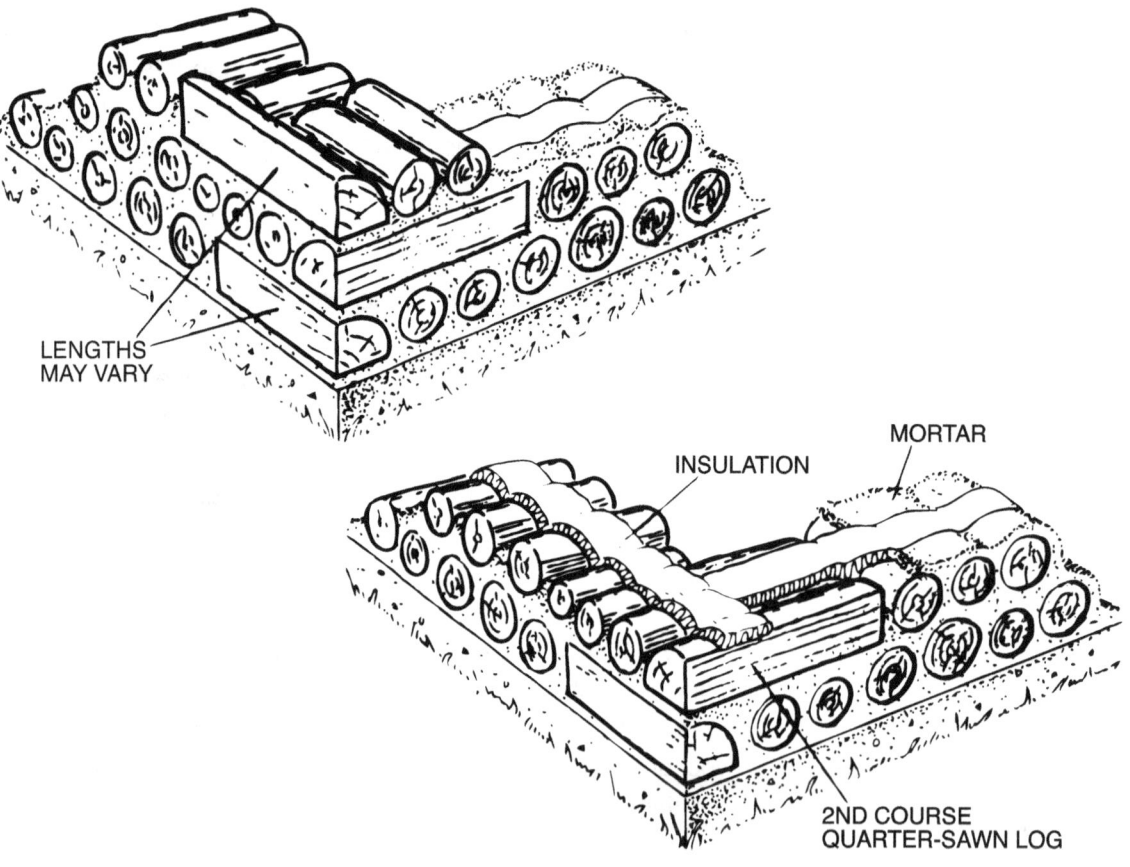

Door and Window Openings

It is wise to prepare both your window and door frames ahead of time. In cordwood construction these frames must be made of a minimum 4 to 6 inches thick wood, glued and bolted together running at least 8" into the cordwood, with protruding nailheads on the cordwood-mortar side on both sides and heading, plus long screws driven from inside of the openings.

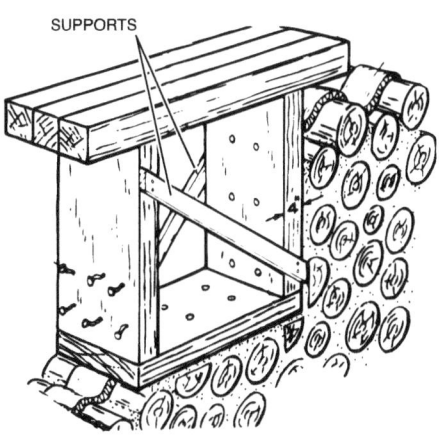

If you plan to use a timber frame, filled with cordwood-masonry, you can plan for lots of doors and windows. Otherwise be sensible with the amount of openings you have.

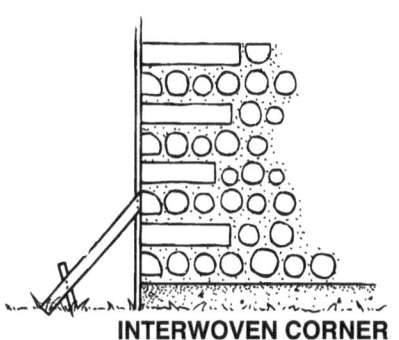

Stacked Timber Corners

In stacked timber corners, timbers are laid in overlapping and with an alternating system: one layer of timber with the length lined-up along one of the walls, the following layer of timber with the length forming a 90 degrees to the first.

Build a small section of each corner to the height of 2' to 3' as a guide, then the wall is filled in between. Repeat this process straight up to the height of the cordwood wall. It's advisable to use squared timber on your corners for easy level and imbed them with nailheads protruding on the mortar side.

CHAPTER NINE: Additional Outdoor Projects

Plastering Cordwood on External and Interior Walls

Plastering cordwood walls is a question of preference: whether you choose to plaster all the walls or only some of them for contrast. This is a good choice if you find cordwood walls a bit busy and need a much more homogeneous surface of alternative pigments pre-mixed with the mortar. Like log-homes, cordwood walls tend to be somewhat darker for some folks, therefore, plastering (white or other tints) makes good sense.

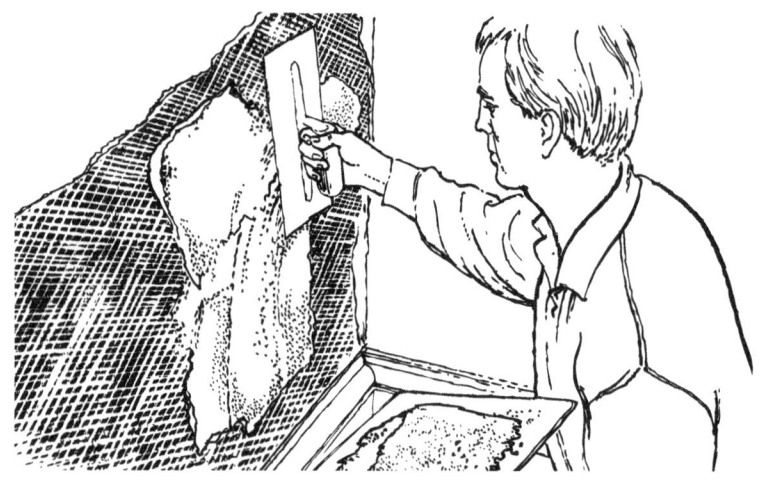

The first, floating coat is applied with a firm, sweeping movement.

A casual survey of any group of buildings in southern Europe and North Africa will reveal an array of plaster covering walls. Some walls protected by coats of lime wash, a pigment made of diluted lime putty. A lime/sand mixed with an added pigment that can be brushed onto wall plaster can create colour a lighter interior environment and add a level of protection and avoid dust stuck on the cordwood wall. A periodic maintenance lime-wash coat for a lime plaster with a pigment will make cordwood walls water-resistant.

Begin by preparing the cordwood wall before applying external plastering or stucco. Cover the desired wall to be plastered with metal mesh (or chicken-wire) purchased at the local farmers co-op. Secure mesh with roofing nails on the exposed cordwood making sure that the mesh is snug against the wall.

The surface must be scratched or keyed to help adhesion of the next coat.

Go to your local library or talk to an experience person with plaster and its decorative application. Find out as much as you can about plaster walls with or without the use of Portland cement. Although, it is beyond the scope of this book, I hope that I have provided you with enough information for you to make a wise choice.

Green Roof

Nowhere are the effects of the environment more relevant than on the roof; the sun's rays, the wind's tugging and the rain's pelting becomes part of the yearly life of the roof. The constant daily cycles of the sun- responsible for the change of temperature between day-time and nighttime freezing temperatures in cold climates and freeze/thaw cycles can eventually cause a lot of damage to the roof. Thus, roof surfaces need constant care or be replaced if the damaged threatens the building below.

Compared to conventional roof surfaces, green roofs required a much stronger support roof structure. A green-roof acts much like natural terrain, for it absorbs water and become the green-space lost by the building-base which is now transferred to the roof.

Compared to the toxic effects of the asphalt roof-tiles on the environment, the plants of the green roof are giving off oxygen rather than radiating the sun's heat to the air.

For more information on this topic, visit your local library or the Internet.

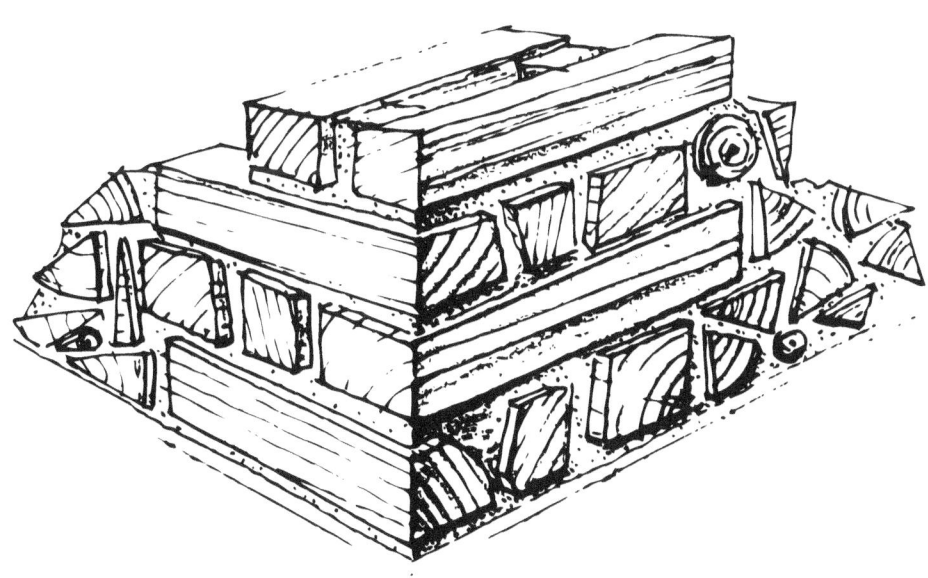

Guest Cabin or Granny's Flat

If you are living in an area where building laws permit you to build a second residential unit, you may wish to adopt this layout to your requirements. If by-laws do not permit a second permanent unit, you can to adopt this small cabin and place it on an above ground base to make this structure 'temporary'. Check with your local township planner or the building inspector.

The drawing to the right shows a simple log cabin design that can be easily modified. The roof can be asphalt shingles or green roof with a wood stove for both cooking and heating.

Designed for an ideal location, this log cabin is built on a side hill, the front deck facing to the south, supported by piers and post. This makes the structure 'temporary'. Notice that the north-facing windows are smaller than the south-facing windows.

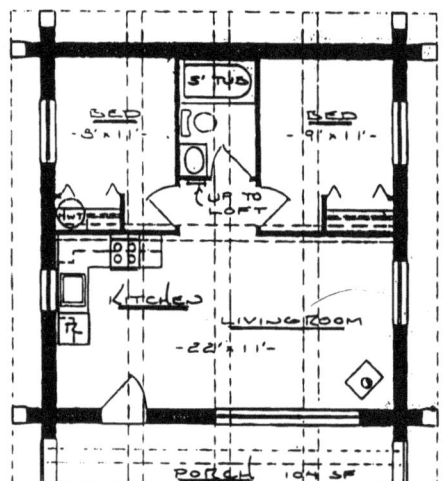

You can build this cabin with logs or cordwood. A porch is optional.

216   PART THREE: OUTDOOR PROJECTS

On Wood and Wood Stoves

I have already briefly touched on the subject of heating with wood. Here I will give you a much better understanding of how to get full heat value from a piece of wood.

Firewood must be allowed to air-dry, preferably for more than a year, before burning. Green wood looses much of its moisture very quickly. After the first two months the seasoning process is half-complete. The heat-produced value is 80 percent at this stage.

When thoroughly dried, wood produces much less smoke and fewer sparks. Wood does not require any additional processes to air dry in order to increase its heat value. Of course, there are always methods to speed up the drying process. This has to do with no cost ways of stacking the wood properly.

After you cut down a tree, you should cut the trunk to lengths that will easily fit into your heating stove, then split your firewood as soon as possible. Splitting green wood is much easier than dry. For quicker results you may want to use a hydraulic wood splitter. Tree branches under 6" in diameter can be cut to size without being split. Larger logs should be split to avoid decay. This speeds up the drying process by increasing the surface area of the log. Splitting also reduces the size to be burned and allows wood stoves to burn cleaner and more efficiently.

When you're storing your firewood indoors to dry (ie: basement), you must contend with dirt and insects. An indoor area gives you easy access to the wood, but moisture from the wood evaporates into the enclosure. This is particularly problematic if the enclosure is your house.

Tree bark is designed to protect the tree and keep moisture in; therefore, removing the bark allows the wood to dry faster. In time, bark will be shed off when the weather gets hot. In my area, by October you must cover the top of the woodpile with a non-porous material (clear plastic) to protect it from the worst of the fall weather. Don't let the plastic sheet cover the woodpile all the way to the ground. Air must pass through the split logs. Moisture evaporates as air passes over the split wood.

Storing Firewood

For best results, firewood must dry for one year in the open air and another year in a storage shed. If you are seriously thinking about using a wood stove as your primary source of heat you should think about constructing a permanent woodshed. For the best location for a woodshed, choose a spot close to the house with the maximum exposure to air and sun.

If you can, build the woodshed built facing south or southwest and with protection from northern winds.

Wood Measurements and Heat Value

The normal unit for measuring firewood is the standard cord. A standard cord is stacked wood that is 8' long by 4' high by 4' wide, or 128 cubic feet. This measurement can be somewhat misleading as it refers to stacked firewood with no air spaces.

Of course, firewood should not be stacked without air spaces. Therefore about 40 of the 128 cubic feet is air space not wood, which you pay for if you choose not to cut your own wood. To save money, buy solid round logs that give you about 90 to 100 cubic feet when stacked. You can split them later with a rented hydraulic wood splitter. Two people working with a wood splitter can split 25 cords of wood over a weekend.

A cord of dried ready-split hardwood weighs about 3,500 pounds per cord. How much wood do you need to get through the winter? How much will the firewood cost compared to other sources of heating material? The easiest way to figure it out is as follows:

- 1 kilowatt-hour of electricity equals 0.60 lbs. of wood.
- 1 gallon (American) of heating oil equals 22 lbs. of wood.
- 100 cubic feet of natural gas equals 14.2 lbs. of wood.
- 20 lbs. of propane (a barbecue tank) equals 67.7 lbs. of wood.

By calling the appropriate suppliers, you can discover how many of the above units of conventional sources of heat an average household in your area uses per year. Compare this yearly number to how many pounds of dry wood you'll need. To be on the safe side, it is wise to double this amount for next year's supply of firewood. For example, if the heating oil company says the average house uses 500 gallons per year then you need 500 x 22 = 11,000 lbs. of firewood or 3.14 standard cords of dry wood. Double that to allow for a margin of error and you will need 6.28 cords of wood.

Remember that green wood weighs almost double that of dry wood. To test whether your wood is dry, take two split pieces and hit them together. If the thud is dull, your wood is dry.

Related Heat Values: Natural Wood vs. Other Fuels

Multiply the current cost of fuel – oil (per gallon), natural gas (therms) or electricity (kilowatt hour) by the corresponding number on the chart. Then compare against the price of a cord of wood.

Type of Firewood	BTUs per Cord*	Fuel Oil per gallon**	Natural Gas***	Electricity****
Apple, Hickory, Ironwood, Locust, Black Oak	24 million	245	300	7030
Dogwood, Elm, White Oak	23 million	235	287	6740
Birch, Yellow Maple, Red Oak	21 million	214	263	6155
Ash, White Eucalyptus, Black Walnut	20 million	204	250	5862
Birch, White Cherry, Black Fir, Douglas Maple, Tamarack	19 million	194	238	5569
Ash, green Pine, Sycamore, American	18 million	184	225	5275
Ash, black Elm, American, Maple	17 million	173	212	4982
Alder, Cedar, Hemlock, Spruce	14 million	143	175	4103
Basswood, Fir, Balsam, Pine, Ponderosa Pine, Sugar Pine, Redwood	12 million	122	150	3517

* Dry wood at low moisture content, burned is 60 percent efficient stove.
** Burned in 70 percent efficient furnace, 98,000 available BTUs per gallon
*** Burned in 80 percent efficient furnace, 80,000 available BTUs per therm (1 therm = 100 cubic feet)
**** Electric heater at 100 percent efficiency, 293 kilowatt hours = 1 million BTUs

Hydro Layout for Posts

Metering: S-base X 10
Wiring Diagram:
CSS Field OrderType: Run Service
Sic Code: Single Family Dwelling
Rate Class Note: Residential-Normal Density

O.H. 50'C4 TP (75)
44-PTP & d/arm corner
3ph-d/arm corner N on 1pt.
Lower N
Install vert 1ph. tap & SW
Pole is inaccessible by truck.

BTC O/H

44kv LT & 4800V 3ph.

15784

+/- 65M

Will require additional men and OPP support for traffic control to string conductor across Hwy.

Hwy 10

776320
776322

776318

J281596

Cust. 40'C6 TP (on knoll)

Rd. x-ing pole by Cust on Cust property to avoid MTO permit $

+/- 70M

Cust. 40'C6 TP

Primary conductor to be #2 ACSR

+/- 70M

ex. trailer

Cust 40'C5 TP pole Vert 1ph. D/E

Cust U/G as per service size

M

Log home under construction

Due to distance away from road - Customer required to construct Primary Service as shown.

ALL WORK TO BE DONE TO ELECTRICAL SAFETY CODE STANDARDS

CHAPTER NINE: Additional Outdoor Projects

Chapter Ten
Groundwork for Financing and Final Thoughts

Preparing the Groundwork For Financing Your Log House

Former President Clinton once said that, "The higher is your dream, the larger is your pain." I can attest to this. Sacrificing - a form of pain - is a primary tool you can use to your own advantage. It's a useful tool because it helps you to overcome obstacles while creating something from very little. Allow me to indulge for a moment, and go back to where it all started.

Nothing had prepared me ahead of time for the obstacles I was about to face when I began dreaming of building my own log home. The obstacles I had to overcome were mainly economic in nature. Why? Because construction expenses are like a river flows; for a time everything flows smoothly and then it increases suddenly.

I remember when I started building my log-wall during the months of April to October. The basic work entailed stacking one log on top the other; logs that were already available to me by cutting them ahead of time. During these months my building expenses were insulation, spikes, gas and oil for both the chainsaw and tractor. These expenses were relatively small - a smooth flow - and were covered by money earned from selling cedar posts and renting my tractor to work for others.

Then one day the construction of my log wall was completed. The river flow suddenly increased, and upcoming high-end expenses had to be met. The steel beam, its delivery and fitting in the proper place; roof insulation and plywood, nails and tar-paper, vapour-barrier, roofing shingles, the concrete base for the main posts, the hiring of the lifting crane for the house post and beams, and the sub-contracting of the roofing. All were expenses that needed to be met at once if I wanted to have a covered structure by the end of the building season.

Here I was faced with two possible choices of sacrificing: embracing the hardship of strict savings and personal and family expenses reduced to the minimum, or the near life long endurance needed when one enters the nasty world of Mort(death?)-gage. Whether you choose one or the other form of sacrifice, it is up to you! I chose the first.

Simultaneously with saving and reducing expenses, one must increase income and thus give a boost to one's savings. I call this the *macaroni and cheese* stage.

Construction work, in general, is a physical activity that 'blue-collar' (tradesmen) workers are accustomed to perform and endure on a daily basis, under all kinds of weather conditions.

Unlike others, those of us who are inclined to physical work are much better prepared physically and emotionally to take a large task, like building a log home.

While experience has its advantages, it is not a prerequisite to log home building and interior construction. This is because construction in general is a 'low-tech' science easily learned by those whose learning capacity is normal. For such low-tech tasks, there is nothing in the building process of a log house that you and I cannot learn (experience) within a few hours of work.

Construction is made of many parts: studwall, drywall, plastering, painting etc. You can learn each part as you go along. Again, stacking logs, nailing, lifting and sawing are easily learned and not a prerequisite skill to successfully complete a physical task of this kind.

On the other hand, planning your project ahead requires some practice and a structured mind that will 'see' the next step that lies ahead and what problems needed to be solved before others. For example, while I was working on my roof, I was also planning to have all my interior material ready ahead of time. Lumber for studs had to be milled and miscellaneous items had to be purchased. Allocating small amounts of money each time the portable sawmill was called, produced enough lumber needed for the whole building season. In other words, once you have your own raw-material drying, you need not spend more then a few hundred dollars at a time (as money is coming in) to cover the cost of the sawmill. Since you are in control - when and how much you want to spend - you can cover your expenses smoothly. Because you are planning ahead of time, you are also in control of your expenses.

The sudden rise or smooth flow of construction expenses is a management problem and a norm during the whole period of construction. Luckily, I was able to see the upcoming sudden large expenses ahead of time. This however, did not alleviate the burden of acquiring the money to cover the cost. It simply made it easier to prepare myself and overcome future challenges. I am grateful to Cecilia's college income which gave us a chance to meet the economic challenge when the sudden expenses appeared. We had the money we needed to meet our large expenses.

It is said that you cannot solve money problems with money. This is true. You can however, solve them by adopting a different lifestyle. You must choose to reduce your personal and family expenses to the minimum; simultaneously, you must find a way to increase your income, and thus your savings. You must do this during the period when all your other expenses run smoothly like a river flow. And this was what Cecilia and I did! We adopted a style of life necessary to solve our money problem. Our effort was based on hope that one day, we would overcome all obstacles in order to build a better future! Is it not hope, a universal wish, that is shared by people everywhere?

* * *

Although I am not a big fan of watching TV, at times, I do indulge with an interesting program. In one show an economist stated that 70% of all Americans are living from paycheque to paycheque. He emphasized that millions of Americans are not living the American dream but are drowning in personal debt. **A large part of this debt is mortgage debt.** Remember that money lending is probably the oldest occupation in human history, and lenders have many centuries of experience in perfecting their skill.

My point is, the easily available credit -- especially private mortgages -- will tempt you as the state of your construction increases your home equity. **Don't do it!** Such credit comes at a high price; about 30% in the first year alone, when you include the broker's fee, lawyer's fee -for both lender and borrower- and the exorbitant interest that you must pay. Remember, you always have a choice to either slow down your construction expenses--there are many things you can still do without spending money for a while-- or try to move into your half-finished house, thus saving money from renting. This way you'll have all the time in the world to continue with the interior finishing at an easier pace.

Though human circumstances can drastically change; when you have to use credit (if you must), plan ahead by trying to get credit with your local construction supplier - paying monthly - rather them entering into a long and painful mortgage debt. This will protect you from any unwanted legal hold over your property. Again, if you are facing an up-coming high cost item - sub-contracting for a new well-drilling for example - plan ahead by preserving your current cash-flow while taking advantage of the short time credit-line with your local supplier.

Your current cash-flow and savings can then be used 100% to pay for the sudden high cost item; especially if the sub-contractor demands full payment at the end of the job. However, do not enter into any future high-cost obligations until you have paid off a large part of your credit-line with your local supplier. And you must replenish a part of your previous saved amount in the bank.

In short, exploring with a cool head, a possible credit line outside of banks, mortgage companies and private lenders, may serve you well for a short run. **Do not make this a habit, and turn mere necessity into a convenience.**

Planning ahead means just that! Plan ahead before you buy your woodlot. Ask yourself what you are intending to build, and how much time you (and your family) are willing to invest in the project.

Are you a self-starter? Then, perhaps, you should settle for a simple but esthetically fine log home. If so, ask your architect to design your blue print for possible future expansion as your family grows.

Do you need logs for your log-shell? Do the math! How much lumber will you need? Remember there is no such thing as having too much lumber milled; if you run short, how will you get what you need? On the other hand, if you milled too many planks, so what, you can always sell them to your neighbours.

Make a simple business plan regarding the material you'll need in the first six months of construction or next year's material needs. Your business plan must include a schedule of when and how you will acquire the necessary raw material for your log shell, roof construction and interior finishing.

How long is the building season in your area? Can you schedule your workload and focus your business plan accordingly?

Can you substitute store bought material - plywood or drywall - for material harvested from your land? Will a milled 1"x6" or 1"x8" plank substitute for store-bought plywood? For example, instead of covering your floor joist with plywood can you install a solid 2" solid planks for both strength and visual effect? This is what I did with my floor; I used different width full 2" white pine planks, which allowed for both strength and a 'barn floor' look for my dining and living room.

Visiting farmers and auction markets is an effective way to meet people who may have wood lots and are willing to sell you hardwood trees for your kitchen and bathroom vanities. By networking with others you may have something that they may need in exchange for what you may need now or in the future. In short, don't be a typical consumer; there many things you can do without buying on credit or cash exchange. Think for yourself, think *outside the box*, in order to preserve your most important stock: **your money.**

Also, many of your tools and equipment can be found in farmers home auctions; check with your local newspaper or local auction houses. You'll be glad you did!

* * *

Most tradesmen are honest and hard working people. However, among them are the occasional bad apples with incompetence that can cost you money. **Never, never, never** give any sub-contractor more them 20% of the agreed price in advance or only on the day the work begins - and only then if he has to buy material. Protect your cash! Since you cannot judge the honesty of a tradesman by looks or rumors, find some way to protect your down payment in relation to the quality of the tradesman's work. I will spare you most of the silly stories about bad apples. However, one story of incompetence stands out that will drive the point at home.

Richard was introduced to me as a very good and honest carpenter. It was the time when I urgently needed to build my cupola in order to protect the interior of the house from rain. I explain to Richard what I wanted him to do and noted that because the diameter of the rafters by the cupola were all different, he should construct the cupola base as I was suggesting. At $25 per hour I thought I was dealing with a professional.

Some four hours later, I had still to hear the sound of Richard's work - cutting or hammering. But I did see him drawing a template design on plywood. I assumed he was making a jig of the cupola's base. At the end of 8 hours, Richard had managed to cut-up a second sheet of plywood, but still I had no cupola base. It was time for him to go home.

By the time Richard returned the next morning, I was already up on the roof, building my cupola base. He was very surprised when I told him that I could not pay him for yesterday's unproductive labour-time, but he could have the cut-up plywood on his way off of my property. Six hours later, I had the main cupola structure built and covered with plastic sheeting for weather protection.

On the other hand, when Lynn MacKenzie came to my property with his portable sawmill, it was the first time we both met in person. He asked me if I had the money to cover his labour-time and I said yes! He asked for $200 in advance before he began to mill my logs. I pulled the money out of my pocket and said no! What I was willing to do instead was to pay him on the hour and every hour until the job was done. As time went by, I used Lynn's portable a number of times and a mutual trust was built between us. To this day I have a great respect for Lynn and his work ethic. The moral of both stories is: protect your most important resource; your money!

Sources to Finance Your Log Home

Financing your construction project outside the banking and lending institutions is only one of the challenges you must be ready to meet head on. Some of the following money generating suggestions may or may not apply to your personal situation; you may also wish to adopt some and/or modify others accordingly.

When you finally click into various cash generating sources, the rewards - like a big bowl of ice cream in a hot day - make it all worthwhile.

Now let's look at 16 ways you can generate a cash flow first assuming the following:

a) You are ready and committed to building and completing your log home for the next three years.
b) By the end of the three years you'll want to have a log home mortgage free and with a built-in equity of $300,000 to $ 400,000 (that's $100,000 per year!).
c) For the next three years the building of your log home is your life's priority above all else.
d) You'll do whatever is legal and necessary to achieve your goal!
e) You have a large woodlot with mixed softwood and hardwood ready to be harvested.

1) Open Air Storage Space: If you have a flat and easy accessible area renting open air storage space for boats, cars, equipment and trailers, by the week, month or season can be quite profitable with little overhead expenses. You can also talk to road construction companies for overnight storage. A simple legal size sign in front of your property will drive the message home.

2) Day Time Camping: City people with tents or small trailers can day-camp in your property in a designated area. Supply campers with portable toilets, rent them a barbecue and sell them large jugs of water in refills. A good quality used barbecue will pay more then its cost to you. If you have hydro, talk to Coke and/or Pepsi reps about installing coin

operated dispensers and ask for a good percentage. A "Day Camping" sign set prominently in front of your property is a must.

3) Cut Your Own X-mas Trees: A good source of seasonal income is selling 'Cut your own Christmas Trees'. If you have white pine growing on your lot, this can bring you a good seasonal income at no cost to you. You may have to plow the paths leading to the trees. Your set up cost is minimal.

4) Small Decorative Trees: In early spring or mid fall you may want to hire students (on weekends) to dig-up small 4' to 6' cedar, pine or maple trees. Many garden centers need them. Pay students per tree; cover roots in soil-burlap style. Talk to the garden centers ahead of time and set-up delivery orders based on "cash on delivery". **Note:** there are people from the city that come to dig-up thousands of decorative trees. They pay rock bottom prices and it is very difficult to control the quantity they take-out.

5) Decorative Garden Stones: Small, medium and large 'antique looking' decorative stones are always in demand by garden centers, landscapers and landscape architects. If you have a solid contact with a garden center, supply them stones by delivering them yourself. If someone else does it for you he will only pay you $5 per ton. In slow seasons a local truck driver with a tractor-trailer and a crane may give you a break on delivery cost.

6) Post and Decking: As a money making project, turn your spare 8' cedar logs into 2" X 6" decking. Keep some logs for yourself and turn the rest into planks. Do not sell logs to others; instead mill them into lumber and sell them for more money. Talk to your local portable sawmill operator and make a deal with him for the use of his sawmill off-season for less cost to you. In my area winter is the slow season for most of these operators.

Sell 6" posts to the public, 3" to garden centers and 1½" to grape growers. Talk to people who may need what you can supply and get paid "cash on delivery." Remember to use the whole tree in sections of 8' for decking and keep the long ones for your log home. You need an investment of a tractor, chains and chainsaw.

7) **Cedar Shingles:** Leftover log pieces of 18" long cedar can be used to produce shingles. Look for a used cedar shingles sawmill or better yet, have someone to build one for you. It would cost less in the long run. A creative welder can do this for you. Since your raw material is available for free you may want to consider this idea and have an operator partner to take care the production end leaving the sales to you. People will pay $1.50 per square foot of shingles which will bring you a hefty income. Beware of those who want to clean up your bush for free; they will take away these short logs and leave the rest behind.

8) **Jams & Shims:** Shims are always needed by installers of windows and doors. These pieces are leftovers of broken shingles but still good enough for leveling doors and windows. At $3 to $5 per bundle it may not sound much, but money is money. The total cost of setting-up a portable **cedar shingle sawmill** is about $3,000 to $5,000. Talk to local log home companies, for they always need to turn their leftover short pieces into shingles for their own use.

9) **Sale of Personal Items:** You may want to sell any your personal items and equipment you can do without for the next 3 years, like your current expensive car, thus eliminating payments. Replace your car with a small utility truck, and sell your second car, motorbike and ATV etc. The idea is to generate more cash; you can always buy them back at another time.

10) **Family Income:** Your partner's income from a steady job, or from a student loan -with no interest- will be a solid backing when you'll need it most.

11) **Extended Family:** Parents, grandparents, brothers and sisters, uncles and aunts and those who owe you a favour are all a source of 'gift-giving' cash that will help their favoured person advance in life. Your role is to ferret it out and use it for a good cause.

12) Snowplowing Driveways: convert your big tractor into a snowplow for the winter months. This will help your neighbours and earn you $100 per hour or $25 per short driveway.

13) Open Air Retreat: Religious and spiritual groups all are looking for a unique landscape for their use. You may want to advertise in their own publications or email them at their website. I once had a Canadian Native Pow Wow ceremony for 3 days. Be a good sales person when you call on groups.

14) Group Home For Youth: Talk to various agencies or churches about a day excursion and/or day camping. It is worth while to invest time to seek results. Talk to group homes that cannot afford expensive camping facilities. For shower facilities these groups can use the local YMCA. Supply them with rental barbecues and outdoor camping stoves, portable toilets etc.

15) Operating Your Own Portable Sawmill: Go on the Internet and check for a good quality used portable sawmill that can also be stationary. If you have a large woodlot, and if you are planning a large project, then you may want to consider milling your own lumber. Learning how to operate a small sawmill is not difficult. The right time to buy a sawmill is as soon as you purchase the woodlot. Start milling your logs for lumber within days of logging, so as to allow the lumber plenty of time to dry before using it for the construction. When you are finished with your project, you may wish to sell the sawmill and recoup your initial investment.

16) Milling Lumber For Others: Another source of money generating is milling lumber for others. Have customers bring their own logs to you and pick-up their milled lumber. At $40 to $50 per hour it could give you a good source of income. You may want to consider hiring an operator for a percentage to mill lumber for customers, thus relieving you from working both in the construction and the sawmill. Remember that you must not give credit to anyone since you'll need cash to pay for your own expenses. I think it is worth looking at this proposition, for it will save you a lot of money by milling your own lumber, and make you cash money that you can use for the big expenses. In the long run, it will bring you income security. It will reduce to minimum the cost for your own lumber. By selling it when you finish with it, you can get your money back, as I did with my tractor and my generator.

Some of the above suggestions can be implemented as soon as you are in possession of the land: choose one or more that will cost you little or the minimum at start. If you can, eliminate before hand any outstanding debts that may impede your general planning of money allocation. In short, this is how you can finance the construction of your own log home.

Land Purchase

The purchase of the land is an exception to the rule for avoiding mortgage. Of course, you can minimize your mortgage and at the same time protect yourself. I'll explain this further.

To begin with, once you decide on the kind of land you'll want, put the minimum down payment possible in order to preserve your cash to implement one of the above income generating suggestions or to be used for the construction of your log home. The point is to build your log home mortgage free, not to get the land free of mortgage that will drain you of all or most of your cash. Unless you have the money for an outright purchase of the land. Here are some suggestions about land purchasing, assuming the following:

a) You will choose **a landlord's buy-back mortgage**, rather than a bank or private lender.

b) In order to build your own log home, **you will purchase a woodlot instead of bare land.**

c) Because you do not have a lot of money, **you will have alternative plans to deal with this issue.**

Look for the right kind land:

1) **Location, location, location** is a must. But, you must be careful because while we all want to have a waterfront property or a private island, this may only be possible in the near future. For the time, look for a location that you can afford to develop. To achieve this you must have certain conditions working in your favour: one is a landlord's buy-back mortgage.

2) **Where and how to look for land:** It makes little sense to look for acres of land in the most expensive newspaper advertisements. Nor does it make sense to look at real estate broker's website promotions. They prefer to promote high-end properties that will yield higher commissions. However, real estate brokers do print a monthly book called MLS which lists every property listed in a given geographical area. Get a hold of an MLS book and go through it carefully. Choose land(s) that look like an opportunity. Do some travelling in the general area of the land you think may be of interest. Ask locals what is the main attraction in this area (within a 40 km radius): a cultural event that takes place every year, a spectacular landscape, a sports event, or a combination of them all. What is the main source of people's income in this area? How accessible is this area from the nearest big city? What is the potential growth of this area in the next 5 years?

Aside from the MLS book, do some actual driving from one country road to another (following a map) and note all properties that carry a private *for sale* sign or a broker's sign that attract your attention. This process is time consuming, and while it must be done carefully, do not forget to have some fun. Also, by talking to local people you may find out if someone in the area is willing to subdivide a large parcel of land. Be respectful to locals, you never know if they will become your future neighbours.

3) **The Right kind of land:** Once you find a potential land you might be interested in, try to deal with the owner himself. Nothing can replace personal contact and personal give and take. Let the owner walk you through his land and have him/her explain anything of interest such as the availability and

CHAPTER TEN: Groundwork for Financing   237

size of trees, any unique land features, the location of a pond, creek or river, and how dry is the land. You do not want to purchase a wetland; building on it can be costly, difficult and it's full of insects.

Check the general health of the trees and the variety of species. Take with you a hand-held counter and count roughly the number of trees that are appropriate for building your log home. Are there more trees then you may need? Is the area in a snow belt? How often does the county or municipality plow the front of the property? Is the front road paved or gravel-dirt? Most important: does the hydro pass in front of the property? If not, how far is the nearest hydro post from the land and how many posts must you install before bringing hydro power to this property? At what cost? Can you afford the cost?

If things look positive - but before you start your negotiations with the land lord - choose one or two building sites and ask the owner to share with you the cost of digging two test holes to determine the water-level of the proposed building site. Leave the hole over 24 hours and by taking a measuring stick you can check the water level in the 5' test hole. If the water level is more than a few inches choose another building site or abandon the land because you will have a wet basement.

4) Negotiating with the Landlord; negotiation is a tricky subject and I don't have a fixed formula that you can adopt and succeed. I have however a number of proven suggestions that you may wish to consider.

i)   Negotiate directly with the landowner or make it very difficult for the broker to refuse your request to deal with the landlord.
ii) Find out how long the property has been on the market. The longer the better - the owner may be keen to sell. In your previous conversations with the landowner, did you sense that he might need the money or is he simply tired of paying taxes on his property? If the landowner needs the money you may be in a difficult position since you cannot satisfy his economic needs. If he is simply tired of having a "white elephant", you have a good chance to succeed!

iii) Try to present yourself as someone who is reliable, honest and hardworking. Do not assume that the other person is an idiot because his speech and body language is different from yours.

iv) Try to pay attention to the owner's concerns and diffuse any doubts he may have about you or about him holding a buy-back mortgage.

v) Negotiations succeed when both parties are willing to compromise. In the final analysis try to get the land for as small a down payment as possible - always prepare to up the ante - and with a yearly interest just one point above a bank's prime. Have the landowner hold the mortgage himself - emphasize the interest rate that he receives annually. Make sure that the mortgage is automatically renewed every two years and set the interest rate at 1% above the prime rate of a bank of your choice.

Take your time with all of the above and look at the positive points against the negatives. Can you leave with the positives against the negatives? Also, be prepared to walk a way from any proposal that you cannot afford to make. There are all kinds of other opportunities waiting for you!

How Much Will It Cost?

Before we put numbers into paper, let me make few things clear; my log home is presented in this book as a finished family residence, a building-code approved structure, built 90% by myself and 10% by hired sub-contractors and casual labour. In other words, this residence was issued a Residence Permit by the local authorities - through the building inspector. This is why someone with a family is occupying the house.

Let me now tell you what my log house is not. It's not a "sort of finished" building that was constructed in the middle of nowhere, far from the sharp-eyes of the building inspector. The pictures that you see in this book were not staged for the readers' benefit, nor was the log house built in order to use the pictures and write a book about it! These pictures were taken spontaneously by visitors who happened to have a camera with them at the time.

Why am I saying this? Because I know of a number of published books on log homes where the instructions leave much to reader's imagination. For example, I know of a fancy book whose authors' 15' x 15' one room structure was 'staged ' in some back-woods open-air 'studio'. Surrounded by professional photographers, art illustrators, graphic designers, horticultural experts, a permaculture/ecological design consultant to advise the reader about 'natural building', environmentally-friendly structures' or green-homes', a 'concrete-paver decorator to help with beautifying the structure. These authors could not have done it without the hoards of helpers. They built a structure and called it 'green'; yet it's builders had the gall to use pre-fabricated support units and still call it a 'green-building'. And, all this in order to produced a fancy six-hundred page book with little useful or practical information.

The 1,250 pictures contained in such a book shows little of essence other then different styles of buildings - using native material - from around the world. Yet, the authors have spent a considerable time and effort trying to convince their readers to choose store-bought 'engineered' material over natural ones. For them, it is okay to use 'engineered' building material so long as you cover-over these with natural wood. Furthermore, they claim that one can only calculate the true cost of construction when one uses new store-bought material for the entire project. In short, the authors appear to underestimate their reader's intelligence.

How much my log home cost is not a difficult thing to determine because most of the material used came from the land itself, and most of the labour was done by me over three years time. Store-bought material and accessories and the cost of sub-contractors and casual labour needs to be estimated. Let me side-track for a moment to make a point.

In our market driven economy the concept of 'time-is-money', is a widely used and a favoured slogan. It was repeated to me many a times by real estate and mortgage brokers, trying to convince me that in the balance-sheet, spending time to build my log house is uneconomical because the cost is near-equal to the price of an independent contractor-built house. Well, let us see if these 'experts' were correct.

So time is money! The 4,000 hours that I personally spent building my log house - including the cutting down of the trees - at $18 per hour (a modest wage) is equal to $ 72,000 spread over three years (or $ 24.000 per year). What shall we call this amount; an earned wage or saved amount? If, for the sake of argument, we called it earned wages, is this a gross or net income? If I was working for someone else, what would it have cost me to earn this income in taxes, travel etc.? If, on the other hand, such yearly income was net earned, would you have saved $24,000 per year in the bank. I don't know many people in my income bracket who could save such an amount per year for three consecutive years.

I called it a net-income-induced-value because it cost me nothing is real terms! A net-income-induced labour-value that triples its 'market-value' or equity, as the construction increases by the hour!

Thinking outside of the box, 'time-is-money' applies only if you are selling it expensively to someone else (while you create reduced equity for the buyer). Just like the contractor would have done to you.

Since we are on the subject of time is money, let us look how this is related to the subject of mortgages. How will you calculate the 25 years of mortgage on your house? Do your payments on your mortgage create a net-income-induced-value on your house? I strongly believe they do not because the equity on your house may or may not increase. This will depend on the housing market fluctuations and is not directly related to your mortgage payment. In fact, by the time you pay off your 25 year mortgage, the latter would have cost you three times more them the original amount you borrowed. Let's assume that in 25 years the price of housing increases to 3 times the original purchase price, then you can only hope to break even. Remember, you need a selling price increase of 300% for you to break even. Time is money for the mortgage company who were able to sell you 25 years of time for your money! How much is your freedom worth? That is, freedom from debt?

What about the contractor's 'time-is-money' (as an equity for me). Do you really believe that the contractor would build my log home for a mere $ 72,000 for 4,000 hours? How then my personal *time is money* balance sheet can be near equal to the price set by an independent contractor? Where is the balance between my *time is money* and that of the contractor's?

What about my own *time is money* investment? I can only add that this has cost me not a single dollar nor has it cost me more then the required time to complete the project.

The cost of my construction; therefore, should be calculated by the real dollars spent to complete the project. This includes all store-bought material, sub-contracting for the septic system, hydro, drilling of the well, constructing the long driveway, roofing, steel-work, widow-glass, custom-made kitchen and bathroom vanities and interior and exterior custom made doors and accessories. In my forthcoming cost estimate, labour refers to casual and professional hired help included with the sub-contractors. My own labour time is not included in the overall construction cost, simply because I was not paid for my labour and therefore it cost me nothing to work for me. Just like the old pioneers!

CONSTRUCTION COST OF MY SIX-SIDED LOG HOME OUTSIDE WORK AND LANDSCAPE

All numbers are rounded to the nearest zero.

Expenses For	Store Bought Material	Hired Labour	Total	Cost by an Independent Contractor
Building Permits	--	--	$2,700	--
Land Clearing, Footing, Wall Foundation	$2,660	$1,500	$4,150	$12,000
Log wall and roof rafters, insulation, steel beam, spikes	$2,500	$500	$3,000	$120,000
Roof	$5,000	$2,800	$7,800	$24,000
Floor, concrete base and slab	$2,500	$1,500	$4,000	$9,000
Rough inside construction	$3,000	$3,000	$6,000	$28,000
Electrical & Plumbing	$4,500	$250	$4,750	$14,000
Kitchen & Bathroom Vanities	--	$5,000	$5,000	$30,000
Custom doors & frames, windows & frames, glass and accessories	$2,000	$2,800	$4,800	$9,000
Interior Finishing	$3,000	$3,000	$6,000	$25,000
Septic System	$3,000	$1,500	$4,500	$7,500
Well Drilling, Sump pump and accessories	$1,500	$5,500	$7,000	$18,000
Hydro post & accessories	$500	$3,500	$4,000	$7,000
Driveway and accessories	--	$5,500	$5,500	$12,000
Misc. material and labour	$5,000	$5,000	$10,000	-
Total	**$35,150**	**$41,350**	**$76,500***	**$315,500****

* $34.77/square foot
** $143.40/square foot

Note: If I include my own labour cost of **4,000 hours** at **$18 per hour** plus **$10,000** for miscellaneous hired labour equals **$82,000**.

The grand total for both mine and hired labour equals $37.27 per square foot. Therefore for both material and labour: **$37.27 + $34.77 = $72.04** per square foot.

The cost by an independent contractor for both labour and material equals **$143.40** per square foot.

CHAPTER TEN: Groundwork for Financing

On the Living Angels

This by no means is an easy subject to tackle, because it is not a theme that I feel qualified to fully explain. How can I explain something which origin and cause are a mystery to me? Should I give the cause of the Living Angels appearance a religious overtone? How can I claim this, when I simply don't know? Should I merely believe - a term which excludes all investigative reasoning - and offer a childlike answer to a question that deserves a thoughtful response? If the following narrative does not measure up to the reader's standards then you can criticize me accordingly.

One thing I am sure of: from its humble beginning, the project had all the makings of a successful drama story. The uniqueness of the land, the designing style of the log home, the unadulterated material used, and above all, the story contained, an infusion of an unfolding drama of the underdog: myself!

Was it a combination of the above that attracted the Living Angels around the hive of the unfolding drama? This, of course, was not the case where all of them appeared simultaneously, waiting in line for their turn to do a good deed. No, each appeared at a specific time and space when their individual qualifications complimented a problem to be solved. It is their orderly and timely appearance which is most difficult for me to comprehend!

As I got to know them, I concluded that; they came for my salvation but they also came for their own salvation and a burning desire to ensure the success of the underdog!

Was this then the **'Queen bee nectar'** that attracted the 'Living Angels' to come as I was building it? Did they come to ensure a successful outcome and prevent its failure, a failure that could have reflected upon their own hopes and aspirations? After all, I noted that all; including the Living Angels, the curious and the came-as-you-are, the good the bad and the stupid, all wanted to be part of a successful story.

Was the positive outcome of the project a concrete reinforcement that they too have a chance to become masters of their own destiny? Was this the reason they identified with me? Was it because each carried within themselves the desire to ensure the success of the underdog? Was it because they too, in their own way, saw themselves as the underdog in this world?

In the early stage of logging, the curious and the come-as-your-are began to appear, and express their disbelieve that I had lifted, with no mechanical help, over 300 hundred wet 12' cedar logs off the ground onto a stacked pile to air-dry! As it turned out, I had become a subject of conversation that introduced the upcoming project and myself to their families and friends. Most of them kept returning to see if I was still there and, in time, they behaved as 'old hands' around my project.

Old-man Frank was the first who with glitter in his eyes and in his own words congratulated me for planning to take such a large project "all on your own." He became more serious and forthcoming with his advice, as the project was developing ahead.

My good friend Jon - from Jonsteel Welding - first repaired my tractor in the bush, and gave me a $40 work-credit. One day, much later, Jon saw me working on top of a not-too-sturdy homemade wooden-horse and expressed his surprise of how far the construction advanced with the minimum of tools and equipment. The following year Jon -- when he saw a steel-scaffolding instead of the same old wooden-horses—jokingly said that I went "high-tech". By giving me a significant break in his cost, he too contributed to the successful outcome of the project.

Who would have thought that Ray - who had very little faith in humans - would claim his own spot within the scope of my project - and in the process revealed his own humanity!! Of course, he never missed a chance to express his lost of faith in humans, right after he finished helping me with a task at hand. I suspected that he expected a betrayal of friendship. The betrayal never came and this made it harder for him to depart when the time came! I hope that I have helped to restore part of his lost faith to humanity, for his own peace of mind!

The moral value of the Living Angels need not be measured by the degree of their work related performance. It is not based on how much they could do or have done; rather, it is the positive influence they asserted with their presence and the impact they had on the surroundings, that made it memorable. In other words, the moral value of a Living Angel has to be prescriptive rather then descriptive in character.

Was I also a Living Angel to those who came while I was building my own log home? Maybe! One thing I am sure of. My project became the focal point where a small entity of Living Angels came to be and while they gave, unintentionally they too received a moral support and a justification for their own past and present hopes and aspirations. Case in point: Ray who always wanted to build his own log home became so inspired by my construction that he too built one not far from where I was. Another friend dismantled an old log cabin in the bush and transplanted to a new location. Others came and spent time watching the portable sawmill transforming simple logs into equity-value lumber. Who can tell what they were contemplating! Of course, I never missed an opportunity to emphasize to them how much better economically - and with peace of mind – it would be for them to spend three short years of constructing, rather them 20 to 25 long years of mortgage-slavery for the same project. Those who were not afraid of physical work, they fully agreed with me! What about you?

EPILOGUE

It is said that a man with ideas and a high level of conviction makes people close to him unhappy! It is also said that a man, in order to achieve his purpose or goal, must have conviction, passion, focus and endurance, overcoming conditions and obstacles that lie ahead of him.

How then can one reconcile both; for a man to achieve his purpose/goal and at the same time keep people that he cares around him happy?

One possible answer lies within the level and scope of the notion of expectancy. A level and scope of expectancy is evident within those persons whose goal is to achieve a better standard of living than the present one. Set a realistic goal based on what we expect of ourselves to achieve and the level of endurance we are prepared to endure in order to achieve our goal.

A higher level of expectancy with an uneven level of endurance will negate the former when conditions and obstacles are beyond a given strength of endurance.

Imagine for a moment a typical family of pioneers in the opening of the prairies in Canada, in the American west, in the Australia plains or in the Brazilian frontiers. A pioneer father's expectancy about what he wants out of life for himself and his family could be as such: to purchase an open land, build a house, cultivate his land in order to prosper one day and thus to provide a good life for himself and his family! For a time, frugality becomes the daily norm and, as such, life is one-sided -- in favour of saving and sparse mode of living. The level of expectancy remains in par with the results derived by the 'fruits of labour' and the gradual increase of the family's standard of living.

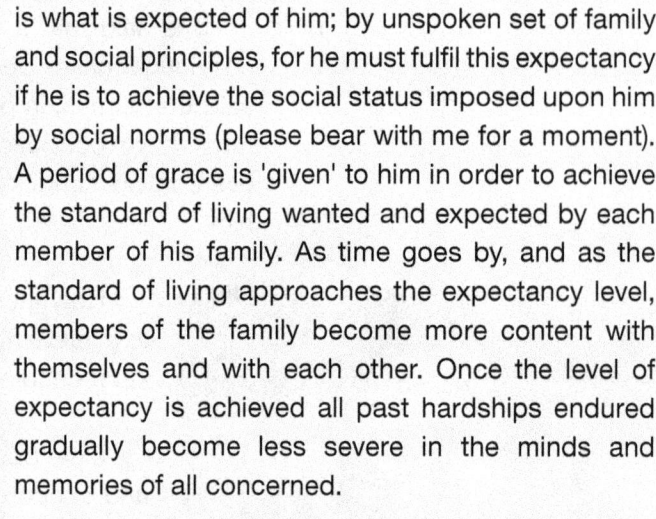

By physical peculiarity and by a set of social conditions the father will adopt a leading role, a protective role as provider to his family and as a teacher to his children. This is what is expected of him; by unspoken set of family and social principles, for he must fulfil this expectancy if he is to achieve the social status imposed upon him by social norms (please bear with me for a moment). A period of grace is 'given' to him in order to achieve the standard of living wanted and expected by each member of his family. As time goes by, and as the standard of living approaches the expectancy level, members of the family become more content with themselves and with each other. Once the level of expectancy is achieved all past hardships endured gradually become less severe in the minds and memories of all concerned.

They can now laugh and joke about the 'good old days' when life was rough but when they were all still so happy! How is the notion and level of expectancy is set in the minds of the husband, his wife and his children?

The short answer to this question is that the level of expectancy is derived and set by the surrounding standard of economic and social expectations set by society as a whole in a given time. A pioneer - in the middle of the plains - sees his immediate neighbours' standard of living that is no better them his own, and he sets his own expectancy in accordance to the rest of society's economic condition. With a variety of degree this applies to the rest of the family members.

What will happen in the case where the immediate economic and social conditions were much higher then his own? Here lies a high possibility that the level of expectancy may be set at different level by each individual member of the same family.

These differences in the level of expectancy would have a negative effect in the level of endurance (grace-of-time) set to achieve a goal, and this, in turn, would cause a friction among members of a family. Outside social pressure to 'have more' - in the shortest possible time – will eventually have a detrimental effect on such members of the same family whose level of endurance is much less than the father's.

The lower the level of personal endurance, the higher is the level of expectancy demanded from those who want to 'solve' all possible economic problems within a grace period of time set conveniently by those whose level of endurance is at lower standard. The higher the level of family pressure placed on the provider; now it sets a new standard of 'all things that is expected of him'.

Yet no one should demand a level of endurance from another that equals yours. We are all different from one to another.

Endurance – the capacity to put up with hardship and inconvenience -- is strengthened by personal peculiarities, personal physical condition, a particular set of beliefs and ideas, and the natural conditions which you are ' ought' to overcome.

Stamina, focus, discipline, mental capacity and physiological conditions make-up the solid base for personal endurance. This endurance can become a personal obsession -- and can cause unhappiness -- **if you do not recognize that others are not like you.** Obsession sets the bar too high for those who are close to you, and yet cannot or are not willing to go through a set of conditions beyond their own level of endurance. And thus, they become unhappy, and while you are blind by your own obsession, you are also drifting apart from those who love you.

When I realized my family was drifting, I was in the awkward position of being in the middle of the construction, pressured by the short construction season and by my passion to finish building my log home under any circumstances!

Should I have spent more time with my family? Should I have taken some of the savings allocated for the construction to provide better living conditions for my family and give the little extras that tend to make life much easier?

One way or another I had to make a decision! I knew that I could not do both! The gap between myself and my family became broader every day! **Sensitivity is not one of my best qualities** - so I turned towards my construction and covered myself with a blanket of wishful thinking; that things would turn all right once the log home was completed. I was no longer able to talk to my family in a sensible manner or to provide them with even the rudimental comfort of living expected by all sensible human beings (all except me).

I was expecting for them to continue giving me their unconditional support - but their level of endurance had diminished a while back! While for myself the construction and completion of the log house was and still is a personal achievement - a desire which gave me a personal endurance-- it was no longer shared by the rest of my family.

My personal life style - before I meet Cecilia - was one of continuous adventure which led me into hot spots around the world and in a most unpleasant circumstances. Self reliance was a survival skill and it had become a seal against life's obstacles; and it was this style of life that had convinced me never to lower my personal standards to accommodate others. Those 'others' now included members of my own family!

Had I been willing to lower my personal standards to include a simple style of log house - one that could easily be constructed within a short period of time - a small rectangle two bedroom log home, I would have had my family in my log home with me.

My personal desire to achieve an overwhelming task, rather than to take into consideration of my family's needs, put my level of expectancy above theirs. Never given a second thought on such a notion - it turned a great achievement into a personal defect - one with enormous consequences.

The moral of this story as written in this book is that I am still a strong believer of setting a personal high standards of expectancy, so long as while you are achieving your goal, you are doing it alone!

I am not the best to tell you how to be sensitive towards the people who are close to you! But I believe that I am the best man to tell you that it is okay to lower your own standards to meet the level of endurance of your loved ones!

Finally, of all the Living Angels who came while I was building my log house, I have sensed a mood of sadness in them for losing my family! They are still wondering about the causes; whether it was the enormity of the task itself, bad luck or something else. These dead-end questions continued to leave a bitter taste in their mouth! You see, they cannot comprehend the fact that this beautiful log home was never occupied by Constantine's family!

As for myself... I am still working on my sensitivity part! Any day now I'll be off to the Highlands and the Jungles of South America, gathering information about my next book on Pictorial Tapestries.

HASTA LA PROXIMA VEZ! HASTA LUEGO!

Constantine Issighos

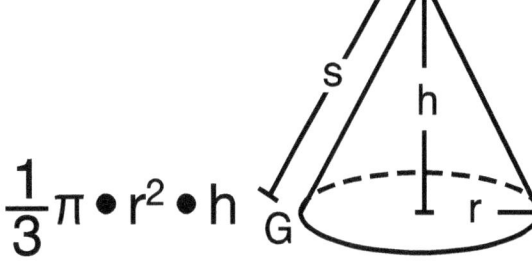

$\frac{1}{3}\pi \cdot r^2 \cdot h$

· a · d

$\left[\frac{3}{2}(a+b) - \sqrt{ab}\right.$

Reference and Index

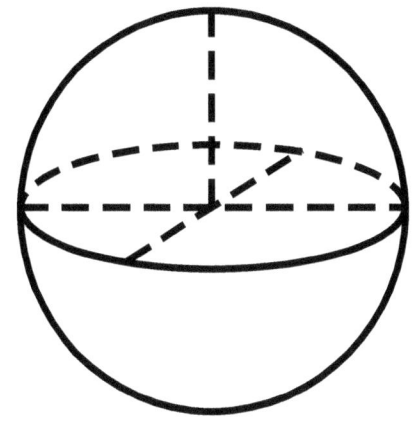

Measurement Conversions

When the time comes, you will find this chart helpful whether you are building your own log home, smokehouse, cooking, travelling, designing, measuring yarn or weighing wool.

Abbreviations
cm = centimeter
m = meter
in = inch
ft = feet
yd = yard
oz = ounce
lb = pound
g = gram
l = liter
ml = milliliter
tsp = teaspoon
T = tablespoon
c = cup
pt = pint
fl oz = fluid ounce
qt = quart
gal = gallon
°C = Celsius
°F = Fahrenheit
sq-inch = square inch
sq ft = square foot
ha = hectare

Weight
1 oz = 28.4 g
1 lb = 454 g
1 g = 0.035 oz
50 g = 1.75 oz = .11 lb
100 g = 3.5 oz = .22 lb
500 g = 17.6 oz = 1.1 lb
1000 g = 2.2 oz = 1 kg
1 ton = 2,240 lb = 1016 kg
1 mt. ton = 2,204.62 lb = 1000 kg

Linear
1 inch = 2.54 cm
1 ft = 30.5 cm
1 yard = .91 m
1 mile = 1609 m
10 cm = 4 inches
1 m = 39 in = 1.09 yd
10 ml = 1 cm
100 cm = 1m
1 km = 0.621 mile
1 mile = 1,609 m

Inches/millimeters
2x8 = 50x150mm
3x6 = 75x150mm
4x6 = 100x150mm
6x6 = 150x150mm
2x8 = 50x200mm
3x8 = 75x200mm
4x8 = 100x200mm
6x8 = 150x200mm
8x8 = 200x200mm
2x10 = 50x250mm
3x10 = 75x250mm
4x10 = 100x250mm
6x10 = 150x250mm
8x10 = 200x250mm
2x12 = 150x300mm
3x12 = 75x300mm
4x12 = 100x300mm
6x12 = 150x300mm
8x12 = 200x300mm

Area
1 ft = 144 inches
1 sq yd = 9 sq ft
1 m^2 = 1.196 sq yd
1 acre = 0.4047 ha
1 sq mile = 640 acres
1 sq mile = 259 acres
1 sq ha = 2.471 acres
1 km^2 = 247.105 acres

Liquid
1 ml = 1 cc = 1/5 tsp
5 ml = 1 tsp
15 ml = 1 T
100 ml = 6 T + 2 tsp
1000 ml = 1 l
1 tsp = 1/3 T = 5 ml
1 T = 3 tsp = 1/2 fl oz = 15 ml
1 c = 16 T = 8 fl oz = 237 ml
1 pt = 2 c = 16 fl oz = 473 ml
1 qt = 2 pt = 32 fl oz = 946 ml
1 gl = 4 qt = 128 fl oz = 3.81 l
1 l = 1.759 pt
10 l = 2.2 gal

Multiplication and Division of Metric Conversion Chart

To convert from imperial measure you must multiply to determine the metric equivalent. To convert from metric to imperial measure you must divide.

Imperial Measure	Multiply By	Metric Equivalent
1 inch	25.4	millimeter
1 foot	0.3048	meter
1 yard	0.9144	meter
1 mile	1.609344	kilometer
1 square inch	645.16	square millimeter
1 square foot	0.09290304	square meter
1 mile	1.609344	kilometer
1 acre	0.40469	hectare
1 ounce	0.02834952	kilogram
1 pound	0.45359237	kilogram
1 ton	0.9071847	tonne
1 fluid ounce	29.57353	milliliter
1 gallon	3.7854412	liter
1 cubic inch	16.387064	cubic millimeter
1 cubic foot	0.02831685	cubic meter
1 cubic yard	0.7645549	cubic meter

Temperature Conversion

Degrees Fahrenheit **Formula** **Degrees Celsius**
minus 32, multiply by 5, divide by 9

Quick Reference Temperature Conversion

°C	=	°F	°C	=	°F	°C	=	°F
-40	=	-40	-14	=	+7	+11	=	+52
-35	=	-31	-13	=	+9	+12	=	+54
-30	=	-22	-12	=	+9	+13	=	+55
-29	=	-20	-11	=	+12	+14	=	+57
-28	=	-18	-10	=	+14	+15	=	+59
-27	=	-16	-9	=	+16	+16	=	+61
-26	=	-14	-8	=	+18	+17	=	+63
-25	=	-13	-7	=	+19	+18	=	+64
-24	=	-11	-6	=	+21	+19	=	+66
-23	=	-9	-5	=	+25	+20	=	+68
-22	=	-7	-4	=	+27	+21	=	+70
-21	=	-5	-3	=	+27	+22	=	+72
-20	=	-4	-2	=	+28	+23	=	+73
-19	=	-2	-1	=	+30	+24	=	+75
-18	**=**	**0**	**0**	**=**	**+32**	+25	=	+77
-17	=	0	+1	=	+34	+26	=	+79
-16	=	+3	+2	=	+36	+27	=	+81
-15	=	+5	+3	=	+37	+28	=	+82
			+4	=	+39	+29	=	+84
			+5	=	+41	+30	=	+86
			+6	=	+43	+35	=	+95
			+7	=	+45			
			+8	=	+46			
			+9	=	+48			
			+10	=	+50			

Perimeter and Area

SQUARE

$S = a^2$

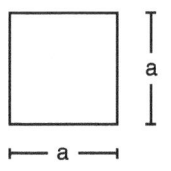

CIRCLE

$S = \dfrac{\pi \cdot d^2}{4}$

$P = \pi \cdot d^2$

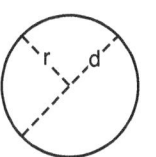

TRAPEZOID

$S = h \cdot \dfrac{a+b}{2}$

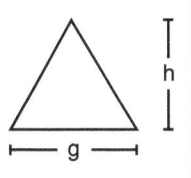

RADIUS

$S = \pi \cdot a \cdot d$

$P = \pi \left[\dfrac{3}{2}(a+b) - \sqrt{ab} \right]$

TRAPEZOID

$S = \dfrac{g \cdot h}{2}$

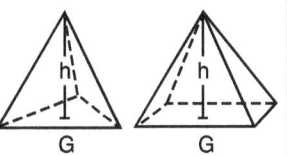

Area and Volume

CUBE

$V = a^3$

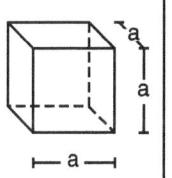

CONE

$V = \dfrac{1}{3} G \cdot h = \dfrac{1}{3} \pi \cdot r^2 \cdot h$

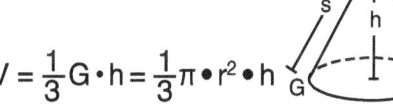

CYLINDER

$V = \dfrac{\pi \cdot d^2}{4} \cdot h \quad \pi \cdot r^2 \cdot h$

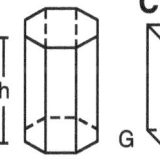

POLYGON HEXAGON   **CUBIC**

$V = G \cdot h$

PYRAMID

$V = \dfrac{G \cdot h}{3}$

SPHERE

$V = \dfrac{4}{3} \cdot \pi \cdot r^3$

$O = 4 \cdot \pi \cdot r^3$

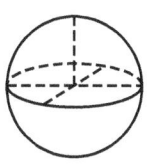

Log Wall and Timber Glossary

Anchor Fastener: A bolt, bar, or spike protruding from the foundation, used to anchor the sill.

Axe Pattern: Shape and slope of the axe head for special applications: e.g., swamping, hewing, battle, and camping.

Backcut: The final felling cut in felling a tree.

Backfilling: Replacing the excavated soil around a foundation wall.

Baluster (also Banister): An upright support for the handrail on a staircase.

Bar (also Blade): The part of the chainsaw on which the cutting chain travels.

Bay: A uniform division of a building, such as the spaces between a series of four posts.

Beam: A principal horizontal support member in the buildings floor or roof frame.

Bearing Partition: A wall that carries second story or roof loads.

Bent (Framework): A framework of vertical posts and horizontal beams.

Bevel: Angled or sloped cut applied to the edge of trim or other material.

Bight: A loop or bend in a line or rope.

Birdsmount: A V-shaped joint resembling a birds open beak, used to join a rafter to the top plate.

Bow (of a log): The direction of the bend or belly of a log.

Blockwork: A method of horizontal notched corner log and timber construction.

Brace: A diagonal support member used to stiffen unstable walls or frames.

Bucking: To saw a felled tree into log lengths.

Butt: The large end of a log or tree sawn from the stump.

Butt Joint: Any joint made by fastening two members together without overlapping.

Camber: An upward arch given to a beam or girder to prevent its becoming concave due to its own weight or the weight of the load it must carry.

Cap Log: The log that will cover (or cap) the ends of the floor joints, often the last log on the wall.

Cantilever (Beam): A projecting beam that supports a structure, such as a balcony or overhang.

Carrier: Water, oil, or a solvent used to disperse a preservative or finish on a wood surface.

Chainsaw Mill: Chainsaw attachment intended to guide the saw to produce lumber.

Caulk: To make tight against wind and water using a sealing material.

Chamfer: A decorative slope or beveled edge on a piece of timber. Also used for tenon joints for easier insertion into a mortise.

Check: A longitudinal crack in a log or timber cause by too rapid seasoning.

Chinking: The process or materials used to fill gaps between horizontal wall logs or half timbers.

Chipper Chain: The cutting teeth of a chainsaw chain whose round backs allow for planning and curved cuts.

Chisel Chain: The cutting teeth on a chainsaw whose straight-edged backs prevent planning or curved cuts and allow only straight cuts.

Collar-tie: A horizontal member connected at the midpoint between two rafters to reduce spreading or sagging of the rafters.

Come-along: A hand operated winch.

Common Rafter: One of a series of support members extending from the top of an exterior wall to the ridge of a roof.

Compression: A pressing or crushing type of force.

Conduction: Movement of heat through a material.

Corbels: Short supporting logs.

Cord: The principal top or bottom member of a truss.

Cordwood: Round pieces of wood 12" – 16" (300-400mm) long and 1"- 6" (25-150mm) in diameter, used in stacks for stackwall construction.

Countersink: Burying the head of a pin, screw, or bolt into an enlarged hole, which is then usually plugged.

Course: A continuous horizontal row of material: brick, shingles, shakes, stones, etc.

Cove: A concave groove cut lengthways in a log.

Crawlspace: A shallow space between the lowest floor of a house and the ground beneath.

Cross Grain: Grains that run perpendicular to the straight grain of the wood. In wood joinery it is more difficult to work the cross grain.

Cross-cut Saw: A saw designed to cut across the wood grain.

Crush (Tab): A short length of wood intended to collapse under weight.

Cull: A tree or log considered unmarketable because of defects.

Cut (of the roof): The metric measure of the angle of incline of a roof.

Dado: A rectangular groove in the wood that runs perpendicular to the grain, usually cut with a dado plane or router.

Drawknife: Heavy two-handed knife used to peel or shape wood.

Darby: A plasterer's float made of a narrow piece of wood or metal with two handles, used to smooth a stucco surface.

Diagonals: Used in the squaring procedure for establishing right-angle accuracy when laying out a foundation or testing frame accuracy.

Dovetail: A tenon and mortise shaped like a doves fantail; a locking joint.

Drip Break: Groove cut under a bottom log to prevent water intrusion. Also flashing or molding placed to prevent rainwater from entering the building. Both methods serve the same purpose.

Eave: The part of the roof that projects beyond the face of the wall.

Em Seal: An efficient commercial product used to seal logs.

Expansion Joint: A joint in concrete or plumbing designed to permit expansion without damage to the structure.

Fascia: A board placed around the edge of the roof to cover lower ends of rafters.

Flashing: Sheet metal or other material used to shed water away from the building.

Flush-cut: An even cut which is level with an adjacent surface.

Frame: A structure comprised of vertical and horizontal members.

Framework: The braced frame timber construction method.

Froe: Tool used to hand split cedar shakes.

Furring: Wood nailing strips laid on a roof of the application of wood-cedar shakes and on walls to support finishing material.

Gable: The triangular portion of the end wall of a building formed by the roof.

Gabel Roof: An A-shaped roof with two equal slopes meeting at the ridge.

Gasket Seal: A commercial product used to seal joints between logs.

Girt: A short beam that joins two bents which are frames that go across a building.

Grade Beam: Foundation beam above ground supported by piers or piling.

Gray Water: Sink, bath, or laundry water drained into the septic system.

Girder: A principal beam used to support loads.

Groove: A rectangular slot running parallel to the wood grain.

Gusset: A wood or metal plate attached to one or both sides of a joint to increase its holding power.

Half-lap: A joint in which half of the opposing wood of each member is removed and the connection lapped.

Half-log: A log split in two.

Half-Timber: A log whose sides have a flat-surface while the top and bottom are left round.

Hammer-beam: A component of a truss.

Hang-up: A log that is held up unintentionally by another tree.

Header: The horizontal wood member above a window or door.

Hew: To square a timber or half-timber by hand using a scoring axe and broad axe.

Housing: A mortise or cavity cut to receive the end of a beam, for example a floor joist.

Infill (Pannel): The material – such as a log, half-timber, or cordwood wall – which is placed between the bays of a post and beam frame.

Jamb: The side member of a door way or window lining.

Jig: A commercial or homemade divide used to hold work during the manufacture of an assembly, such as a panel or truss.

J-Bolt: Anchor bolt used in concrete foundations to secure the wall's plate.

Joinery: The craft of joining posts and beams or round logs to form a structure with the use of various joints.

Joist: The horizontal planks used to construct and support a floor or ceiling.

King Post: Upright central component of a truss.

Kick Back: A jerk of the chainsaw bar that is a frequent cause of cuts.

Keyway: Groove in the log ends.

Knee Brace: A timber or round log placed diagonally between a post and a beam, used to secure a frame.

Lap-notch: Two timbers fitted end to end.

Layout: The process of drawing a joint's dimensions in preparation for cutting.

Lofting: A graphic layout representation, as of the roof truss, drawn to full scale.

Log Dogs: Device used to keep logs in place.

Main Stack (also Main Vent): The main vent pipe of a house's plumbing system.

Mallet: A hardwood hammer used to drive a chisel.

Mortise: Recessed hole cut into wood, usually rectangular, designed to receive another part, such as a tenon.

Notch: The groove in a log or timber to receive another log or timber.

On Center: The marking along the center line. It identifies the center of a timber or log, and is the point used to measure from when laying out spacing for rafters, floor and roof joists, etc.

Outrigger: Log placed outside the wall line as a plate log.

Overhang: Extension of the roof beyond the wall.

Overscribing: Scribing a groove larger than the gap in anticipation of wood shrinkage.

Partition: An interior wall which separates rooms.

Parbuckle: The action of rolling a log with a line.

Parging: Covering masonry with mortar or grout to produce a smooth surface.

Peavey: Tool used to roll logs.

Peeling Spud: Heavy tool used to peel bark off logs.

Pitch: A roof's angle identified by standard measurements.

Plate Log: Last log on a wall from which the roof line will originate.

Plumb: Vertical. Also, to test for a vertical plane.

Post and Beam: Construction method with a framework of horizontal and upright beams.

Purling: A horizontal beam supporting rafters or roof boards.

Queen Post: An upright component of a truss.

Rabbet: A groove cut along the edge of a timber or log to receive the edge or tongue of another piece, such as a window or door.

Recurve: A line that curves under or backwards.

Rafter: A sloping support structure of the roof frame which extends from the right to the left side ridge.

Rip Saw: A saw designed to cut parallel to the log grain.

Rough-in: Enclosing the plumbing or electrical lines in the floor, wall or ceiling.

Rough Opening: An opening framed to receive a window or door.

Run: The horizontal distance from the building's outside wall to the ridge line.

Sash: The framework that holds both sides of the glass in a window.

Scarf: Shallow mitter on a log or timber.

Scarf Board: Template for scarf layout.

Scribe: The process of duplicating the shape and dimensions of one surface onto another for shaping a joinery.

Settling: A estimated amount of shrinkage of horizontal laid green wood; calculated at ½" per vertical 12".

Shakes (also Wind Shakes): A defect in the trunk showing a separation between the wood's growth rings.

Sheething (also Ice Sheething): A covering of plywood boards on the exterior of a building.

Shim: A thin cedar shingle used to level a window or door.

Sill Log: Bottom log on house.

Sod Roof (also Green Roof): An environmental friendly roof covering made to two layers of grass turf.

Soffit: The underside of the rafters, outside the wall (the overhang).

Span: The horizontal distance between a building's side walls, beams, rafters or joists.

Stackwall: A wall constructed by using cordwood embedded in mortar with an insulated middle cavity.

Stucco: A concrete-like material used as an exterior/interior wall covering, similar to plaster.

Tenon: A projecting piece of wood made to fit into a mortise on another piece of work.

Tie-Beam: A beam of wood or steel spanning between the two side walls of a building and locking them in place to prevent wall-spanning.

Tongue and Groove: A method of joining woodwall to the post, where the infill pieces are fitted with tongues which fit into a groove in the post.

Top Plate: The top horizontal log in the building's wall which serves to tie the walls together and provides support to the roof.

Truss: A structural frame designed to form the house roof and to withstand external loading.

Undercourse: Strip of tarred paper placed under the roof's shakes.

Undercut: A wedge piece cut-off from the base of a tree to cause it to fall.

V-Groove: A groove in the log made with two cuts in the shape of a "V".

Vapour Barrier: Plastic material used to prevent the passage of moisture.

Wall Channel: A vertical groove in a log wall that allows connection with a slip joint and a partition.

Wracking: Leaning and twisting.

Plumbing Glossary

ABS (acrylonitrile butadene styene): A rigid, black plastic pipe used to drain waste and vent system; it has its own cement-glue, and it should not be mixed with PVS.

Aerator: A device that snaps onto the faucet spout and creates bubbles in flowing water to prevent splashing.

Auger: A tool used to clear drains or toilets; turning a crank on the auger causes a coiled wire to spin and auger or 'drill' through solid waste.

Ballcock: A valve inside the toilet tank that automatically fills the tank to a preset level every time the toilet is flushed.

Ball-type Faucet: A type of faucet that uses a rotating ball to control water flow and temperature.

Cartridge Faucet: A type of a faucet that uses replaceable cartridge to control the flow and temperature of water; easily identified since the cartridge moves up and down with the handle.

Clean-out: A fitting with a removable plug that provides access to obstructions with a snake or auger.

Closet Flange: A fitting that attaches to the floor and accepts the toilet. The slots in the flange hold the flange bolts, which pass up through the base of the toilet to hold it in place.

Compression Faucet: A fitting used in situations where the connection may need to be taken apart later. A nut forms a seal by forcing a compression ring against a pipe.

Coupling: A fitting that is used to connect two lengths of copper pipe in a straight run.

CPVC (chlorinated polyvinyl chloride): A kind of plastic pipe that is approved for both hot and cold water distribution.

Disk Faucet: A type of faucet that uses a disk assembly to control the flow and temperature of water; as the handle is turned on, the disk assembly rises and falls and breaks contact with a spring-loaded seat.

DWV (drain waste vent): The system that carries away liquid and solid waste; allows sewer gas to escape safely and prevents water from siphoning out of traps.

Elbow: A fitting that connects one pipe to another at an angle. The angle may be 45o or 90o and can have two female ends or one female and one male.

Flare Fitting: A fitting most often used with flexible copper pipe for LP gas lines when the connection may need to be taken apart.

Gate Valve: Uses a regulating mechanism similar to the gate in old irrigation systems; the gate is raised to allow water, typically used as the main water shutoff in older homes.

Glove Valve: Uses a stem and waster setup similar to a compression faucet to regulate the flow of water more reliable than a gate valve, and easily repaired.

Hose Bib: A valve with an externally threaded outlet to accept a hose fitting; found outdoors for hoses and in laundry rooms for connection to a washer.

Main Shutoff Valve: A valve located between the water service coming into the house and the interior distribution system that is used to turn off water to the house.

Main Vent Stack: The principal artery in the drain-waste–vent system that all branch lines connect to.

Pipe-joint Compound: A sealant with the texture of toothpaste that is applied to female threads of pipes to create a watertight joint.

Plumbing Code: Regulations adopted by the provincial, state or local community to control any plumbing work done in the community.

Plumber's Putty: A dough-like sealant used prevent gravity leaks; typically used on drains, under faucets and under sinks to prevent water seeping in.

P-Trap (also U-Trap): A curved drainpipe that attaches to a fixture, such as a sink or bathtub, that traps water to create a seal to prevent sewer gas from passing into the house.

PVC (polyvinyl chloride): A rigid plastic pipe designed for cold water use.

Reducer: A fitting that allows connection of pipes of different diameters.

Soldering: A method of using heat and usually lead to join together copper pipes and fittings.

Supply line: Any piping that is used to distribute either cold or hot water within a house.

Teflon Tape: A thin tape that is wrapped around male pipe threads to create a watertight joint.

Trap: A U-curved device that allows water and waste to pass through while blocking the flow of air and gas from the opposite direction.

Valve: A device that controls the flow of water through a pipe.

Vent: A pipe that allows air to flow into, and gas out of the DWV system. It prevents water from siphoning out of traps.

Wax Ring: A donut-shaped ring of wax that fits between the base of the toilet and the closet flange to create a watertight seal.

Log Home and Cordwood Building Schools

Acacia School of Log Building
P.O. 384, Larkspur, CO, U.S.A. 80118
phone: *303-995-8000*
email: *info@logbuild.org*
website: *www.logbuild.org*

Arbor Vitae Log Craft, Industry Training and Consulting
Robert Savignac
217 Mabel Lake Road, Lumby, BC, Canada V0E 2G5
phone: *250-547-8750*
email: *logbob@telus.net*
website: *www.arborvitaelogcraft.com*

Blockhausbau Porrenga GmbH
Roger Porrenga
Gewerbestrasse 3 Hombrechtikon 8634
phone: *00141 55 244 16 06* fax: *00141 55 244 16 86*
email: *postmaster@blockhausbau.ch*
website: *www.blockhausbau.ch*

College of the Rockies
Mike Flowers
555 McKenzie St., Kimberley, B.C. Canada V1A 2C1
phone: *250-427-7116* fax: *250-427-3034*
email: *kimberley@cotr.bc.ca*
website: *www.cotr.bc.ca/timberframing/*

Construction EN Bois Rond Amishk Inc.
Robert Vacchino
2174 Du Vacchino, St. Jérôme, QC, Canada J5L 2M2
phone: *450-512-1966* fax: *450-438-9027*
email: *info@amishklog.com*
website: *www.amishklog.com*

Del Radomske's Okanagan School of Log Building International
Del Radomske
1231 Philpott Rd., Kelowna, BC, Canada V1P 1J7
phone: *250-765-5166* fax: *250-765-5167*
email: *info@okslb.ca*
website: *www.okslb.ca*

Earthwood Building School
366 Murtagh Hill Road, West Chazy, NY, U.S.A. 12992
phone: *518-493-7744*
website: *www.cordwoodmasonry.com*

Great Lakes School of Log Building
Ron Brodigan
1350 Snowshoe Trail, Isabella, MN, U.S.A. 55607
phone: *218-365-2126* fax: *218-365-7106*
email: *courses@schooloflogbuilding.com*
website: *www.schooloflogbuilding.com*

Heritage Home Learning Seminars
119 West Dumplin Valley Road, Sevierville, TN, U.S.A. 37764
phone: *1-800-456-4663*
email: *info@heritagelog.com*
website: *www.heritagelog.com*

Island School of Building Arts
James Mitchell
3199 Coast Road, Gabriola Island, BC, Canada V0R 1X7
phone: *250-247-8922* fax: *250-247-8978*
email: *info@logandtimberschool.com*
website: *www.logandtimberschool.com*

Lasko School of Log Building
8125 Whiteland Road, Martinsville, IN, U.S.A. 46151
phone: *317-690-2325*

Log Home Builders Association of North America
14241 NE Woodinville-Duvall Road, Suite 343
Woodinville, WA, U.S.A. 98072-8564
phone: *360-794-4469*
email: *info@loghomebuilders.org*
website: *www.loghomebuilders.org*

Montana School of Log Building
1227 U.S. Hwy 287, Three Parks, MT, U.S.A. 59752
email: *info@logcabinliving.com*
website: *www.logcabinliving.com*

Moose Mountain Log Homes Inc.
Lloyd Beckedorf
P.O. Box 26, Bragg Creek, AB, Canada T0L 0K0
phone: *403-932-3992* fax: *403-932-9299*
email: *info@moosemountain.com*
website: *www.moosemountain.com*

Pat Wolfe Log Building School
Pat Wolfe
RR #2, Lanark, ON, Canada K0G 1K0
phone: *613-256-0631* fax: *613-256-8413*
email: *pwolfe@istar.ca*
website: *www.logbuildingschool.net*

Rocky Mountain Workshops
505 N. Grant Ave., Fort Collins, CO, U.S.A. 80521
phone: *970-482-1366*
email: *peter@rockymountainworkshops.com*
website: *www.rockymountainworkshops.com*

William M. Lasko School of Log Building, Inc.
William & Amy Lasko
8125 Whiteland Road, Martinsville, IN, U.S.A. 46151
voice-mail: *1-800-292-8043*
email: *LogSmithy@aol.com*
website: *www.laskochooloflogbuilding.com*

Yukon Alaska Log Homes
Raymond Mikkelsen
207 Tlinget Street, Whitehorse, YK, Canada Y1A 2Z1
phone: *867-668-2206* fax: *867-393-3498*
email: *mikkelsen@yt.sympatico.ca*
website: *www.ykakloghomes.com*

INDEX

A

Alternative Energy: 149,150

B

Barbecue: 200,201
Bathroom: 25,156,157
Batter Boards: 58,60
Beam: 90,92,95
Building Code: 57,61,65,90,107,124
Building Site: 45,47,48,57

C

Caulking: 86,93
Capola: 93,106,109,114
Ceiling: 26
Concrete:
    Footing: 60,62,91
    Forming: 61
    Blocks: 63,64,79,80
    Ready-Mix: 64,65,124,125
    Slab: 66,123,124,127,132
Cordwood: 29,206,215
Corners: 87,107,129
Cost: 240,241
Credit: 15,17

D

Decking: 105,106,107,124
Design: 48,49
Distribution Box: 173,179
Door: 25,79,84,129,131,159
    Frame: 77,131
Drainage: 45,57
Driveway: 45,47,179,180,181
Drying: 44,90

E

Eave Detail: 113
Electrical:
    Post: 46,47
    Wiring: 83,146,147,148
Equity: 26
Events and Wisdom: 32,52,68,96,118, 134,168
Excavation: 68
    Trench: 60
Exterior: 78

F

Fencing: 189,190,202
Financing: 13,26,27,225-232,233-236
    Mortgage: 14,18,42
Foundation Wall: 44,57,58,64,65,111,124
Frost Level: 57,58

G

Gutter System: 111,112

H

Heating System: 149,217-220

I

Inside Construction: (see interior finishing)
Insulation: 79,81,108,124,126,132
Interior Finishing: 25,66,83,131

J

J-Bolts: 65,78,79,80
Joist: 77,123,126,127,132

K

Kitchen Cabinetry: 25,58,60,78,154,155, 199

L

Labour: 26,27
Land: 13,14,237-239
Landscaping: 189,190
Living Angels: 6,11,18,19,42
Log Homes: 14,23,25,27,42,45,48,66,79, 84,88
    Model: 14,16
    Square: 75,76,87
    Kits: 12,23,24
    Shell: 24,26,27,76
    Stacking: 14,75,82
    Wall: 44,65,83,84,85,87,111
Loggers: 28
Logging: 43
Lumber: 27,28,44,76,78
    Milled: 27,28,77,78,87,90

M

Material: 26,27,43,108,127,130
Melissa: 30,31
Mezzanine: 25

P

Pioneers: 13
Planning: 75
Plumbing: 128,141,142,143,144
    Rough-in: 124,125,126,132
Plywood: 93,108,109,124,127
Posts: 28,90,91,92
Projects (outdoor): 195-198
Purlings: 77, 88,107,108,109,110,127

R

R-Value: 108,161
Rafters: 26,75,76,83,88,89,90,82,93,106, 108
Real Estate: 12,15
Roof: 24,76,81,88,90,103,105,106,108,109, 215

S

Septic System: 173
Shingles: 110
Smoke House: 203-204
Spikes: 80,81,82,92,93,126
Stoves: 151,152
Studs: 128,129,130,132
Sump-Pump: 145

T

Tools: 50,51
Trees:
    Cherry: 25
    Cedar: 25,41,43,46
    Pine: 25
Trusses: 86,88,89

U

Utility Room: 158,180

V

Venting: 144

W

Water Well: 182-189
Windows: 77,79,84,85,129,159,161
Wood Stove: 217

GIVE A LIFE TIME GIFT TO YOUR FRIENDS AND COLLEAGUES

How I Built MY SIX-SIDED LOG HOME from scratch MORTGAGE FREE!!!

FULL COLOUR ILLUSTRATIONS!!

Like yourself, the author to had a dream to build his own lot home from scratch. This book, with its real-life pictures, diagrams and actual copies of blueprints is the proof because the author has done it himself. Be prepared to think outside the box, when it comes to an unconventional method of financing your construction. When you, the reader, finish reading this book, you will no longer need to go before a lender with cap in hand to ask for a mortgage.

With over 300 full colour pictures, illustrations, and real-life events. This is an inspirational book of self-reliance and personal achievement.

(272 pages)

IN HARD COVER

NOW IN PAPERBACK!!

This book is one of its kind, because it is written about an equally one of a kind log home; a six-sided log home. This is a smart book – informal, unconventional in its approach. It helps the reader to understand that you do not need a mortgage hanging over your head in order to build this or any other style of log home. The author will guide you through beginning stage of getting started, how to purchase the right kind if building lot, planning and designing your project, to the final phase of construction.

A 272 page (in black tone) with over 300 real-life pictures and actual copies of this house, this inspirational book will take the reader through an easy to follow step-by-step guide.

BUILD IT MORTGAGE FREE!!

BUILD IT MORTGAGE FREE!!

BUILD YOUR LOG HOME MORTGAGE FREE!!

This is a working copy for every day use. This book is a condensed version, which contains all the essential construction information – with easy to follow step-by-step instructions and illustrations. This book contains:

- A copy of the actual blueprints of the six-sided log home.
- Design for a two – story round log home and of a small cabin.
- A glossary of construction, plumbing, and logging tools and terms.
- An inspirational narrative of actual events and wisdom.

A paperback edition.

YOUR SITE COPY

CD-ROM
How I Built MY SIX-SIDED LOG HOME from scratch

PC/MAC

Contains the entire text of "My Six-Sided Log Home" with all its easy to follow step by step guide and over 300 colour illustrations.

(PDF Format)

To purchase these books: www.awaqkunabooks.com

www.ingramcontent.com/pod-product-compliance
Lightning Source LLC
Chambersburg PA
CBHW081936170426
43202CB00018B/2933